Elizabeth Stride
and Jack the Ripper

Elizabeth Stride and Jack the Ripper

The Life and Death of the Reputed Third Victim

DAVE YOST

McFarland & Company, Inc., Publishers
Jefferson, North Carolina, and London

ALSO OF INTEREST

The News from Whitechapel:
Jack the Ripper in The Daily Telegraph (McFarland, 2002),
by Alexander Chisholm, Christopher-Michael DiGrazia
and Dave Yost

LIBRARY OF CONGRESS CATALOGUING-IN-PUBLICATION DATA

Yost, Dave, 1962–
    Elizabeth Stride and Jack the Ripper : the life and death of the
reputed third victim / Dave Yost.
        p.   cm.
    Includes bibliographical references and index.

    ISBN 978-0-7864-3318-6
    softcover : 50# alkaline paper ∞

    1. Jack, the Ripper.   2. Stride, Elizabeth, d. 1888.
3. Murder victims — England — London — History —19th century.
4. Serial murders — England — London — History — 19th century.
5. Whitechapel (London, England) — History — Sources.   I. Title.
HV6535.G6Y67   2008
364.152'3092 — dc22   2008020053

British Library cataloguing data are available

On the cover: Mortuary photograph (detail) of Elizabeth Stride;
Berner Street in 1909 (both courtesy Evans/Skinner Crime Archive)

Manufactured in the United States of America

McFarland & Company, Inc., Publishers
    Box 611, Jefferson, North Carolina 28640
    www.mcfarlandpub.com

In memory of
Adrian M. Phypers

Acknowledgments

I nvariably, every student of this "subject of mutual interest" has in common at least one person who stands behind him. For me, there have been several such people over the years. These individuals silently mentored me or debated the various issues; pointed out missteps or assisted with a pet project; tolerated what seemed like an unforgiving hobby, moments of insistence, and the time I spent hacking away on the computer. Or said straight out, "You can do it."

To all of the people I have met, worked with, spoken to, and learned from during my study of this subject, I owe my gratitude. But a special thank you goes out to those in particular who have assisted with this work: Adrian M. Phypers for his invaluable geographical assistance; Allan Jones for his genealogical research on many people associated with Jack the Ripper; Alexander Chisholm for his *Daily Telegraph* transcriptions and permission to use various sketches; The Casebook Press Project for making available transcripts of hundreds of contemporary newspaper reports and articles; Chris George and Paul Begg who thought of me regarding *Ripperology: The Best of Ripperologist Magazine*; Christopher-Michael DiGrazia who sparked my interest in the Stride case; Ebbe Appleros (Church of Torslanda) for permission to use a photo of the church; Daniel Olsson for his invaluable genealogical research on Elizabeth Stride; Jon Brillman for his correspondence on various medical aspects; Sam Flynn for his additional information on lunar conditions; Serge Zavyalov for his transcription of Inspector Swanson's report; Stephen P. Ryder of casebook for permission to use various photos and sketches; Stewart P. Evans for permission to use various photos and sketches; Tom Wescott for his updated information on various IWEC members; and Wikipedia for its publicly available sketch of the *Princess Alice* disaster.

An extra special thank you to Stewart Evans for his time and review of this manuscript and for his kindly advice. Finally, to my wife, Sandra, *thank you*.

Table of Contents

Introduction

For 115 years, the Whitechapel Murders have remained an enduring riddle: a murder mystery that has intrigued many people on various levels, which is why some refer to it as a "subject of mutual interest." While some look to identify the man known by the notorious sobriquet, Jack the Ripper, others delve into the history. Some prefer the quiet review of genealogical records while others investigate the deaths themselves. This book is about one murder, in particular. It is an attempt to bring to light in a single volume as much information as possible about a specific victim — her life, death, and the aftermath, while exploring the mysteries that surround her existence and her demise.

There is no doubt that Elizabeth Stride, or Long Liz as she was called, will always be viewed as the third canonical victim of Jack the Ripper. And yet her inclusion originates from a double event. Two murder victims were discovered in the early hours on the last day of September in 1888 — Elizabeth and Catherine Eddowes. (A list of names and a glossary are found in the Appendix.) Eddowes died nearly a half mile due west from Elizabeth. With two victims already attributed to the same hand, Mary Ann Nichols and Annie Chapman, few if any doubted that the killer racked up two more prizes to his tally, and the press readily gave credit to the lone killer as early as October 1. But it should be noted that other murders did occur in or around the London area, apart from the canonical five, between the end of August and early November 1888. Contemporarily, however, none of them were attributed to Jack the Ripper.

The idea of a double-event is not wholly without merit, yet Elizabeth's acceptance as an actual victim is not without its controversy, either. It is what we in the trade call a grey area. For at times, there seems to be as much speculation as there are facts, and the Elizabeth Stride case does indeed have its ups and downs for the modern researcher to ponder. The murder can be viewed separately, but it can also be viewed as part of a series. And each aspect, individual murder or serial killing, has its own unique set of problems to overcome. Providing some comfort for the present-day investigator is the fact that it was just as frustrating for the contemporary police, if not exceedingly more so.

Regardless of the reason for taking up this subject, what stands out the most is the mystery. The mystery of the killer, the mystical and romantic era of Victorian England, the at times mysterious witnesses, and the mystery of the victims themselves. For me, the mystery lies with the events, or in a broad sense, the victims — the Berner Street case in particular because of the double-event. And from across the distance, the victim, her inquest and the witness interviews bit-by-bit tell a story. However, the story is never complete without the background — the history through which the victim traveled, giving a better view of what she and the general population experienced, read, heard, and discussed. To that end, I take pen in hand and put to paper my thoughts on the victim case of the Berner Street murder — Elizabeth Stride.

∾1∾

The Good Ol' Days

It was four weeks till Christmas, and November 27, 1843, was just another wintry Monday in Sweden. Except this chilly day saw a new arrival. After four years of marriage, a thirty-two-year-old farmer called Gustaf Ericsson and his thirty-three-year-old wife, Beata Carlsdotter, increased the size of their family with the birth of another baby girl. She was born on the family farm in the village of Stora Tumlehed, a small place compared to some and comfortably situated within the Torslanda Parish. Before long, the small child took her first of many trips to the local church, and there, on December 5, the proud parents baptized their second daughter, Elizabeth Gustafsdotter. Over the years, she grew up within the island community of Hisingen near Gothenburg. She had a fairly happy childhood working on the farm with her family, amidst the stone fences, the voice of the North Sea and the usual sibling rivalry with her older sister, Anna Christina, and two younger brothers, Carl-Bernhard and Svante. Between walking to school and the typical bumps and bruises, which might have included an injury to her right leg, Elizabeth continued her church education, and on August 14, 1859, before she reached her sixteenth birthday, she was confirmed at Torslanda Kyrka, the Church of Torslanda. This quaint little church, which still exists, has all the appearances of a large cottage, nestled amid a grove of trees with its well-worn pathway and gated entrance. And although it is not ancient, it is one of the oldest churches in Gothenburg, and is part of the Gothenburg diocese of the Evangelical Lutheran Church, the Swedish religion. However, despite being raised with a rural work ethic and a religious upbringing, Elizabeth was not destined to live the quiet life on a small country farm.[1]

Two months before Elizabeth turned seventeen, she left the farm and her family. She knew where she had to be, and it was only about a half-day's walk to the east across the Göta River. Following in her sister's footsteps, Elizabeth traveled to the neighboring city of Gothenburg. Anna left home three years earlier, at the age of seventeen, to make a life for herself in the big city,

3

where she eventually settled down with a husband and raised a family. Once there, Elizabeth applied for a certificate of altered residence, which was approved on October 25, 1860. It was said she had a good behavior and an extensive religious knowledge, which was in itself a good thing, considering biblical education was expected and even tested. Elizabeth had already spent four months in the 100,000-person town when she became employed as a maid by a månadskarl, a workman who contracted his laboring talents to various employers for a month at a time. This man of sufficient means was thirty-two-year-old Lars-Fredrik Olofsson. He was married to Johanna Carlsdotter Nilsson, a thirty-two-year-old domestic servant. The couple lived in the Karl Johans Parish of Gothenburg in the Majorna district with their two children, four-year-old Carl-Otto and three-year-old Johan Fredrik. Sadly, Lars and Johanna lost their firstborn, Johanna Elisabeth, to pneumonia the year before they took on Elizabeth. Including their departed eldest, the Olofssons would go on to have six children in all by the end of 1867.

Despite the decency of this particular job for a new maid, it would only last three years. Without reason, Elizabeth left the Olofsson family on February 2, 1864. Even though the Olofssons had another servant, Lena Carlsson, Johanna probably could have used the extra help that was afforded by Elizabeth's presence within the household. The year before, Johanna gave birth to another son, Anders Gustaf. With one child not readily walking and the other two boys being seven and six, the Olofsson family was full of life. Yet the young Elizabeth departed in apparent haste — a runaway. But she did not run far, moving to the Domkyrko, or Cathedral Parish, in the central part of Gothenburg. Once there, she still claimed to be a domestic servant. But even a change of scenery seemed to be unsatisfactory, and Elizabeth's life began to take a turn for the worse. Six months later on August 25, Elizabeth lost her fifty-four-year-old mother to "chest disease." Life continued spiraling downward and by March 1865, Elizabeth was "registered" by the Gothenburg police. She was only 21. Traditionally, this has been accepted as her being "registered as a prostitute," but there is no certainty, because this particular police document does not state why she was registered. One tragic event followed another that spring, and after only seven months of pregnancy, Elizabeth gave birth to a stillborn girl on April 21. Due to the parochial attitude of the time, her daughter was not baptized, because the child was illegitimate. Even though the father was "unknown," according to the church book, Elizabeth gave her baby the last name of Gustafsson.[2]

Those two years, 1864 and 1865, were terrible years for the young Elizabeth. Between the ages of twenty and twenty-two, she experienced more grief and suffering than most twenty-somethings typically see during the course of their entire young existence. Elizabeth left her job, her mother died, she turned to prostitution for her livelihood, and she lost her only child. This picture of destitution did not subside while she walked the streets trying to earn what money she could. But adding injury to insult, she was hospitalized several times for venereal disease in Kurhuset (later renamed Holtermanska). Her first visit was on April 4, and by May 13 she was described as healthy. Yet this did not sway her from prostituting herself. Three and a half months later, she was readmitted to Kurhuset on August 30 for a venereal ulcer, the main stage of syphilis. She was finally discharged on September 23 as cured. (Contemporary medicine may seem very primitive, at times, but it was fairly capable for its day. Venereal disease, that is to say syphilis, was as treatable in the mid–1800s as it is today. If left untreated, however, the disease would cause madness after about fifteen to twenty years.)[3]

Despite these medical problems, Elizabeth maintained her profession and had a certain amount of comfort in knowing that she would not be arrested for selling herself. For the authorities, at least, accepted prostitution and took measures to ensure a healthy sex-seller and sex-buyer. But this is not as tame as it sounds. Starting in 1700, most continental European countries began to change their views on prostitution from suppressing it to implementing a system of registration, licensing, and medical inspections. These governmental requirements for exams and enrollment have been described as a "never-ending cycle" and as "sexual slavery." And Elizabeth was no exception. On October 17 she was entered into the police records when they sent her to Kurhuset for her third visit, which is the first known instance of the police officially recognizing her as a hooker. Elizabeth had to be treated for a chancre and would remain hospitalized for fifteen days, until she was finally discharged as healthy. As a result, she had to pay regular visits to the police, giving evidence that she was still healthy, which she did on November 3, 7, and 10. Four days later, during her final visit, and still showing that she was healthy, Elizabeth was finally removed from the prostitutes' register, but not because she was "healthy." There were only two ways to be removed from this list of ill repute: employment or marriage. Either could prove to be extremely difficult because of the disgrace and distrust associated with being a harlot. At around this time, Elizabeth informed the police that she lived in Pilgatan Street, Östra Haga, the eastern part of Cathedral Parish. The police probably accepted this without much thought, since Pilgatan is known for its prostitutes, but there is no record showing that she actually lived there. Elizabeth also informed the police that she was confirmed at the age of seventeen. It is curious that she would have given the wrong year, since being confirmed is a major event in a religious community, but this is the first recorded instance of Elizabeth altering a truth.[4]

After struggling for those two horrendous years, Elizabeth finally found good fortune. By her third mandatory visit to the police on November 10, she had secured a legitimate job as a domestic. "The servant-maid Elizabeth Gustafsson was engaged in my service on the 10 of November, and I am responsible for her good conduct as long as she stays in my service. Gothenburg the 13 of November 1865 Mrs Maria Wijsner Husargatan House No 42"

Whether from a good, kindly Christian act, a basic belief in helping one's fellow man, or a rising domestic need, Maria of Husargatan and her husband, a theater musician, took Elizabeth into their household.

According to Daniel Olsson's research, Maria was born Inga Maria Hansdotter. At the time of the 1865 census, she lived at 27-29 Husargatan Street with her husband, Carl Wenzel Wiesners, a thirty-nine-year-old German musician, working for the Grand Theater in Gothenburg. Maria and Carl would eventually have another maid by 1869. On the surface, these could appear to be different individuals, but it is such a striking, if not an extremely remarkable, coincidence — similarly named employers hiring a similarly named maid at around the same time, and living in the same street. The only conclusion is that these are the same people; apparently, Elizabeth had assumed the surname she gave her stillborn child. While Elizabeth's employment has been commonly viewed with some misgiving, it was a legitimate maid's position.

It must have been interesting for the twenty-two-year-old Elizabeth to have a mistress who was two years younger, especially after a month or two into her employment, when the youthful Maria would have learned that she was expecting her first child. This had to have been at least somewhat painful for Elizabeth, working so near to what was probably an everyday reminder of her tragic loss. While the couple reveled in the happy thought of their future family, Elizabeth's personal wealth would increase, as would her desire to leave again.[5]

Sometimes a personal tragedy can turn into good luck, and Elizabeth experienced this first hand. Because of her mother's death, Elizabeth received an inheritance of sixty-five Swedish crowns. This might seem to be a pittance by today's standards, but it was a treasure and best of all it was hers. And with her very own money in hand, Elizabeth set out for freedom by submitting a new certificate of altered residence. While this has been typically viewed with suspicion, Elizabeth rightfully stated on the application that she was living in Cathedral Parish and working as a domestic servant, based on her employment with Maria and Carl. But Elizabeth was not looking at another area of Gothenburg, nor was she even considering any part of Sweden. This time, she set her sights across the North Sea to the island nation — the Swedish parish in London. And a month or two after receiving her inheritance, on what assuredly must have been an exciting Friday, Elizabeth's application was approved. Five days later on February 7, 1866, she said her good-byes and set sail for England. Elisabeth the domestic servant, became Elizabeth the immigrant. Yet it would be five more months before she registered at London's Swedish Church, located in St. George's-in-the-East, at Prince's Square. (The present-day Swedish Church of London has two locations: the Parish Church, Harcourt Street, Old Marylebone Street, and the Seaman's Church, Lower Road, next to Southwark Park. The Seaman's Church was not established until 1899.)

When Elizabeth finally registered on July 10, she said she was single, and while she did not know it then, this contemporary house of worship would figure prominently in her later years, as a source of sustenance, if not solace. Now the church did not require Elizabeth or any of its members to register. According to Sven Olsson, the clerk at the Swedish Church, all church members were registered if they entered England "bringing a certificate and desiring to be registered." So apparently Elizabeth had no desire nor felt a need to do so until July. At the inquest on her death, Elizabeth's boyfriend Michael Kidney stated that she said she came to England to see the country, and expressed doubts about that explanation. Understandably so. Not only would a change in permanent residence not be required for a tourist, but eventually Elizabeth would tell him that she "came to England in a situation with a family." That is to say, she arrived as an employed domestic servant.[6]

However, the newly landed Elizabeth would learn soon enough that London was far more dangerous than at first it might have seemed. The Irish terrorist group known as Fenians was fairly active, if not persistent. They derived their name from the second and third century Irish warriors known as "Fianna." The Fenian Brotherhood was originally founded as the American branch of the Irish Republican Brotherhood about 1858, but the term Fenian would eventually be used to represent all factions. Eighteen months after Elizabeth's arrival, several Fenian members miserably failed to detonate a barrel of explosives in broad daylight due to a damp fuse, but they were more determined than daunted. The next day, on December 13, 1867, in full public view, including the view of at least one policeman, the second attempt succeeded. About 60 yards of the Clerkenwell prison wall was destroyed, including several nearby houses, and the percussion of the terrific explosion shattered windows over a large area. Six people were killed instantly. A total of 120 passersby, mostly women and children, were injured, and six other people died later from their injuries.[7]

Despite the terrorist activities that loomed over the city and which occupied considerable police manpower, especially the Secret Department, later renamed the Special Branch, the youthful Elizabeth lived fairly quietly for her first three years in London, until the day she met a local artisan, John Thomas Stride. He was a carpenter by trade, and it was no wonder that John entered into such an occupation, for his father, William Stride, was a shipwright. William and his wife, Eleanor Elizabeth Monk, had been married four years when John came into their lives on February 8, 1821. John was born in Sheerness, Kent. Like Elizabeth, he also had the voice of the North Sea for companionship while he grew up, and he had also lost his mother when she was in her fifties. Sheerness was a port city on the Isle of Sheppey, with the North Sea on one side and the Medway estuary to the northwest. Access to the mainland was possible by traveling across The Swale, which arced west to southeast between the two waterways, making up the southern boundary of the island. But while Elizabeth had to travel by ship to reach London, John merely had a two-day westerly journey by foot.

But John was not the only man who dated Elizabeth, for apparently a policeman, who possibly lived near Hyde Park, also courted her at the same time. But the friendship between John and Elizabeth eventually blossomed into romance, and she made her choice between the two suitors. Despite their age difference, or perhaps because of it (John was twenty-three years her senior) he should have been able to provide for her with an established and much-needed trade. And marrying a carpenter, surely a desirable profession, would constitute a safe and secure family life. Interestingly enough their age difference was similar to that of Elizabeth's last Swedish employer, Maria and Carl. When they decided to tie the knot, John and Elizabeth resided in the Westminster area of London, living only about a half-mile apart from each other. The forty-eight-year-old John and the twenty-five-year-old Elizabeth exchanged vows on March 7, 1869. The small ceremony took place at the St. Giles in the Fields Church, situated at 60 St. Giles High Street, part of the diocese of London in the Church of England.

Being married at this particular church might have been apropos, or an omen to future happenings. Queen Matilda, wife of Henry I, originally founded St. Giles as a leper hospital and chapel, which was named after St. Giles, the patron saint of outcasts. Even though John Marjoribanks Nisbet, canon residentiary of Norwich, was St. Giles' presiding rector at the time of John and Elizabeth's wedding, it was the Reverend Will Powell who performed the service. (This might be Reverend William Powell, who was rector for Newick, Sussex in 1868.) Whether they were friends of the happy couple or simply asked to observe the proprieties, Daniel H. Wyatt and N. Taylor witnessed the nuptials. Elizabeth's conversion to the Anglican Church as a result of the marriage can only be speculated. Either way, any religious mixture within the new family did not cause too much discord for the Swedish Church, which made an undated entry about the marriage. On the marriage certificate itself, Elizabeth's maiden name is listed as "Gustifson." But it should be noted that Elizabeth's maiden name in the Swedish Church register is "Gustafsdotter," which was, no doubt, taken from her altered residence certificate.[8]

Yet a stranger in a strange land naturally tends to migrate to where his fellow countrymen are. "Little Italy" and "Chinatown" are good examples, and this can be affirmed, to a degree, for the average Swede who moved to London. By 1933 at least, if not sooner, a number of Danes and Swedes populated St. George's-in-the-East. They primarily delved into the timber trade. More importantly for the Swedes, the parish was also the location of the Swedish Protestant Church, or simply the Swedish Church. But at the time of her marriage, Elizabeth was living more than three and a half miles to the northwest from the Swedish Church. The address she gave was 67 Gower Street, where the inhabitants consisted of the middle class and those who earned a comfortable living. (Present-day 67 Gower Street sits several blocks north of the British Museum.) This is a pretty good indication that Elizabeth continued with her domestic service duties after her arrival in London. Several blocks north of Gower Street on the other side of Euston Road, John resided at 21 Munster Street, Hampstead Road. Despite being on the western side of London, this area stood in stark contrast to Elizabeth's neighborhood. The Hampstead folk were quite a collage of economic backgrounds, ranging from middle class, to merely comfortable, to those considered poor, and to many who existed below the poverty line.[9]

Soon after their wedding, John and Elizabeth moved to East India Dock Road, Poplar, where they might have set up a coffee shop in Chrisp Street. This is a somewhat interesting way for newlyweds to start out — changing professions from carpenter to coffee shop keeper. And, relocating the entire household from Hampstead Road, St. Marylebone, to more than five and a half miles overland to Chrisp Street, Poplar — literally from one side of the London to the other. But it could have been a worthwhile gamble, considering their new home and business were in the vicinity of the Poplar Workhouse, a goods depot, the India Docks, and the London and Blackwall Railway. Yet, though it might have appeared to be a good location for starting their new enterprise, Chrisp Street did not work out too well. Before the fall of 1870, John relocated his bride and their coffee shop to Upper North Street. This move was not as extensive as their first one. To the west, East India Dock Road's junction with Upper North Street was less than half a mile from the corner of Chrisp Street. The Stride coffee shop was now situated on the western side of Upper North Street, somewhere between Grundy Street and Trinity Chapel.[10]

But the fates were not kind, and a settled domestic lifestyle was not in the cards for John and Elizabeth. Having been married for about a year and a half, the newlyweds were once again on the move. Sometime between the fall of 1870 and the spring of 1871, they resituated the coffee shop closer to the docks. John and Elizabeth now held lodgings at 178 Poplar High Street. Their new abode sat on the southern side of High Street, as it was also known, between Simpsons Road and Harrow Lane. More importantly, however, their business occupied a spot that was closer to the goods depot. Before long they probably met their new next door neighbors, even though they most likely did not have much in common with them. On one side, at No.180, lived an elderly watchmaker, Charles Porter, who received visits from his sister Hannah and her daughter, Annie. Another elderly person, Mary Ramsey, occupied lodgings on the other side, at No.176, along with her daughter, Emily. Both of them were described as "annuitant," a beneficiary of an annuity. Apparently John did not boast nor brag about being an entrepreneur. Either that or he had to maintain two jobs, carpentry and the coffee shop, in order to make ends meet. On the night of April 2, 1871, a census taker arrived at their residence, and John informed the man that his occupation was carpenter. More than likely, the couple needed the money, and this type of two-income household is not unknown. With John hammering, nailing, and sawing the hours away, Elizabeth no doubt ran the coffee shop. (Similarly, contemporaries like Joe Barnett ultimately resorted to maintaining two jobs: laborer and fruit porter, and Emily Marsh looked after her father's leather trade shop in his absence.) On the night of the census, the Stride family shared their company with several people: a fifteen-year-old boy named Charles Thew, born in Portsmouth, Hampshire, and a woman in her early thirties, Mary A. Ronis. It is unknown if they were friends, relatives, or merely overnight guests, for the census records simply list them as "visitor" with respect to the head of the household, John.[11]

The first two years as man and wife were obviously bumpy for John and Elizabeth, and after an apparently slow start at making a go at business, it seemed things were picking up, finally. Over the next three years, they managed to maintain their small business in Poplar High Street. Arguably, this was a more successful location than the original choices, especially since they now had their supply closer to what railroad workers and dock laborers could demand. But what prosperity they might have achieved was short lived. On September 6, 1873, John's father, William Stride, died at his hometown of

Sheerness, and by 1874, John Dale had taken over the coffee shop. That event saw the beginning of the end for John and Elizabeth's marriage, after only five years. Yet they would remain together, trying to scratch out a living in the parish of Poplar. Living fairly quiet lives, Elizabeth went about her daily activities, while John most likely continued with his carpentry trade as best as he could. But this, it seems, had more downs than ups. At the time, the clerk of Swedish Church took notice that Elizabeth was "very poor," and in March of 1877 she was briefly admitted as an inmate of the Poplar Workhouse.

The Poplar Workhouse was established in 1735, and within twelve years it had been relocated to the south side of Poplar High Street, just east of Wade Street. Even though such a drastic relief was sought in the most dire of circumstances, it was fortunate that the workhouse was relatively nearby for it allowed Elizabeth to avoid a long, drawn-out walk to get there. Between 1871 and 1882, the local Government Board conducted an "experiment" whereby the Poplar Workhouse would only accept "able-bodied paupers" who were subject to a "labour test," which was intended as a deterrent. Fortunately for Elizabeth, her stay was not very long. For life in a workhouse was intentionally harsh in order to keep out the able-bodied poor who could find work, and these institutions had decades if not more than a century of practice; the first records of a workhouse go back as far as 1631. The residents, referred to as "inmates," were often treated no better than prisoners, making many inhabitants wonder why they were being punished for being poor. Discipline was at the hands of the workhouse master, and punishment could range from reducing what meager rations someone received to beatings for the men. Husbands and wives were segregated, and a couple could readily forfeit custody of their children. It was said that a workhouse could make a married man with children into a bachelor. It is no wonder that it was Elizabeth who entered the Poplar Union, while John continued to ply his trade. But despite the treatment the workhouse mustered against Elizabeth and others like her, it would almost pale in comparison to what was to come. For a year and a half later, tragedy struck.[12]

Over 600 people died on the evening of September 3, 1878, when the passenger steamer *Princess Alice*, carrying approximately 700 passengers, collided with the steam collier *Bywell Castle*. The *Princess Alice*, used for Thames excursion routes, was making a "moonlight trip" to Gravesend and back at 2 shillings per ticket. By 7:40 P.M., on the return leg of the journey, the North Woolwich Pier was in sight, as was the *Bywell Castle*, which was en route to fill her haul with coal. The *Princess Alice* turned toward the north side of the river, and the skipper of the *Bywell Castle*, Captain Harrison, adjusted his course to avoid the passenger ship that was crossing his bow. Seemingly

Contemporary sketch of *Princess Alice–Bywell Castle* collision (courtesy Wikipedia).

confused by this, the commander of the *Princess Alice* adjusted his course and unwittingly steamed for the *Bywell Castle*. Despite attempting to reverse her engines, the *Bywell Castle* struck the *Princess Alice*. Less than 200 people were rescued from the water with hundreds of excursion passengers found piled up at the exits. What was meant to be a typical trip around the Thames and an ordinary pickup of cargo, became a horror to many.[13]

In her latter years, at least, Elizabeth would recount to friends and companions how she lost her husband and two of her nine children, and how she herself received a mouth injury from the colliding ships. After this sad event, the remaining seven children either stayed with her husband's friends or in a school operated by the Swedish Church. Yet John not only survived, he did not die until six years later. As for the children — no record indicates that Elizabeth ever had any beyond the one she lost back in 1865, and the Swedish Church had no school in London at the time. Plus, she and John would not have been able to afford the 8 shillings required for the pleasure cruise. That would have been more than a third of a common week's wage for someone living in poor circumstances, and there's no indication that John and Elizabeth lived better than meagerly at that time.[14]

Even though Elizabeth was not involved with the disaster of the *Princess Alice*, tragedy did strike her family the following year. In 1879, her widowed father Gustaf died. From what is known of Gustaf and Beata's children at this time, Elizabeth's sister Anna had settled down with a husband, Bernhard Olsson, and by the year of Gustaf's death, the couple had a decently sized family of four children. If Anna had managed to get word to Elizabeth, there was no going back for the younger sister. As might have been the situation with her mother years earlier, Elizabeth could only privately take her leave of her father. But there is no certainty, since Elizabeth and John lived like semi-nomads in an industrial society. Within the next two years the distressed couple moved again. This time, they headed north, about a mile and a half from Poplar High Street, and on the night of April 3, 1881, they had a visit from another census taker. They resided at 69 Usher Road, Bow. Usher Road ran north to south from Old Ford Road and Tredegar Road, crossing Roman Road. It was a relatively decent area situated south of Victoria Park and west of Parnell Road, supporting a mixture of the poor and the comfortable. Presumably, John and Elizabeth were amongst the poorer inhabitants, since they shared their residence with two other families: a married Irishwoman called Burpin, her daughter Grace, and the Levitt family — John, Mary, and their three young children. (It is presently unknown if 69 Usher Road was a multi-family tenement or a single residence with three families.) John had maintained his carpentry trade, and he might have relocated his family there in an attempt to improve their financial situation, possibly thinking that the Mile End/Bow area of London had better opportunities for a carpenter. That hope was soon dashed. Whether from marital strain, the closeness of their new neighbors, financial pressures, or the previous failure at business, 1881 saw the final collapse of John and Elizabeth's marriage after twelve years.[15]

Toward the end of '81, Elizabeth and John's marriage completely broke down, and she left him, moving to Brick Lane. Brick Lane was a fairly lengthy avenue starting from Columbia Road at its northernmost point and stretching south to the junction of Wentworth Street and Old Montague Street. Being east of and almost paralleling Commercial Street, its inhabitants consisted of those who earned a comfortable living, and those who existed either at or below the poverty level. After Christmas, on December 28, 1881, Elizabeth was admitted to the Whitechapel Infirmary with bronchitis. A week later, on January 4, she was well enough to transfer to the workhouse. The first Whitechapel Workhouse was established in 1724, with the Whitechapel Poor Law Union being formed on February 16, 1837. Unlike some workhouses that consisted of a large single building, the Whitechapel & Spitalfields Union had several structures in an attempt to improve conditions with accommo-

Photograph of Whitechapel Union Workhouse (courtesy Stephen Ryder/Casebook).

dations that could handle nearly 700 people. This included the Casual Wards at 35 Thomas Street (present-day Lomas Street) and the Infirmary that sat on the western side of Baker's Row (present-day Vallance Road) opposite the workhouse facility, which sprawled northward across several acres with its southeast corner at the junction of Baker's Row and Thomas Street. The workhouse location was also known as South Grove.

Elizabeth might have returned to street walking at this point. Resorting to prostitution in a pinch is not necessarily uncommon. But there is no certainty, and it is just as possible that John might have given her some subsistence upon separating, similar to the "maintenance" William Nichols paid Mary Ann Nichols at their separation. What is certain is that she really did not have the money to keep herself in Brick Lane. At some point after her departure from the South Grove facility, Elizabeth started living off and on at a common lodging house, 32 Flower and Dean Street. Flowery Dean Street as it was also called ran west from Brick Lane to Commercial Street, lying between Fashion Street and Thrawl Street. While Flower and Dean Street consisted mostly of those who lived by very poor means, most likely dossers, there was a mixture of poor, the comfortable, and the middle class, who owned or ran businesses near the main thoroughfare, Commercial Street.[16]

But as tough as life was becoming again for Elizabeth, surely a déjà vu of her two horrific years in Gothenburg, it was already tough on London, and especially for the British government. Six months after her separation from the workhouse, a Fenian faction called the Invincibles assassinated Lord Frederick Charles Cavendish and Thomas Henry Burke in Phoenix Park, Dublin. Cavendish, the British chief secretary for Ireland, was not the primary target, though. That was Burke, the undersecretary. As misfortunate had it, Cavendish took a walk with Burke, and at 5:30 P.M. on May 6, 1882, they were both assassinated. The killings later became known as the Phoenix Park murders. Their deaths resulted out of protest over the Coercion Act of 1881, which gave the lord lieutenant of Ireland the power to arrest anyone suspected of treason, intimidation, etc. It was bad enough for Her Majesty's government that both men were high officials, but the death of Cavendish was also a personal tragedy because he was the nephew of Prime Minister Gladstone.

While Elizabeth did what she could to live, the Fenians planned for a more direct hit. In 1883, they coordinated a bombing attack on London. This time, several public buildings were dynamited. Many innocent people were hurt and killed. The Rising Sun pub also got caught in the middle when it was damaged by the explosion at Scotland Yard that had targeted the Special Irish Branch. (Despite the damage, Scotland Yard did not relocate until 1890, when it became known as New Scotland Yard.) While the authorities fought against the terrorists, Elizabeth eked out an existence, and at some point after their separation, it seems John moved back to Poplar. It would not be long before Elizabeth was alone in England with no family. On October 24, 1884, she was widowed when her estranged husband John Thomas Stride died of heart failure at the Sick Asylum, Bromley (the building still functions today as St. Andrews Hospital). Completed by 1871, the Sick Asylum was almost one mile due north from the junction of Chrisp Street and East India Dock Road; the same area where John and Elizabeth tried to have a go at a coffee shop when they were first married. At the time of his death, John was said to have been living at the Poplar Union Workhouse, where Elizabeth got her first real taste of institutionalized poverty. Whatever feelings Elizabeth had for her dead husband, they were probably buried along with him.[17]

2

A Prelude to Murder

Whether from habit, remorse, or lack of a steady occupation, Elizabeth was cited for being drunk and disorderly and for soliciting on November 13, 1884. Two months later on January 25, the Fenians once again practiced their own brand of disorderly conduct when they bombed more public locations in London. This time, the explosions targeted the London Bridge, Tower of London, and the House of Commons. The Irish Brotherhood wanted separation while Elizabeth wanted, or needed, someone to look after her. After all, she was looked after for most of her life: by her family on the farm; her employers; and her husband, who seemed to have tried everything he could to make a decent life for himself and his young wife. And at the same time, she apparently had a continued desire for freedom — the proverbial have your cake and eat it too; or perhaps in Elizabeth's case, the grass is always greener. But even in the best of times, some people never really appreciate what it means to be married. Despite years of togetherness, or possibly in spite of them, some spouses act and live as if they are single. They just happen to have a roommate. And so it seems to have been for Elizabeth. Her outward attitude for wanting to escape into some unknown, but presumably better life would not diminish, but become more solidified as the years rolled on. Inwardly, she wanted a man she could leave and who would still take her back afterwards — and she found him. Less than a year after her estranged husband's death, Elizabeth hooked up with a man who was nine years younger, a waterside laborer and former army reservist by the name of Michael Kidney. Before long, she moved in with her new boyfriend at 33 Dorset Street, which was on the northern side near the middle part of the road. And unfortunately, the Blue Coat Boy pub was next door on the right at No. 32.[1]

Between her departure from the workhouse in early January 1882 and her moving in with Michael by 1885, Elizabeth remained off the radar, and pretty much kept to her herself for the most part, which was apparently fairly easy to do, until she was taken in for drunkenness. She might have been performing domestic service duties, "at work among the Jews," sewing or cleaning as she later claimed to the Swedish Church clerk and Elizabeth Tanner, widow and lodging house deputy at 32 Flower and Dean Street. More likely than not, such work was probably part-time, yet very possibly in demand. By 1881, the estimated Jewish population of London had risen to over 60,000 with continued immigration from Russia and Poland. But it is equally possible that she went back to prostitution, at least now and again, considering that the 1884 citation included soliciting. However, this new living arrangement with Michael came with its own set of problems, and Elizabeth was no better off financially with the waterside laborer than she had been with the carpenter during the latter years of her marriage. Their neighborhood, Dorset Street, has been described as part of the "Wicked Quarter Mile." It was a short road, which ran west from Commercial Street to Crispin Street, lying between Brushfield Street and White's Row. It held several lodging houses, consisting of nearly 700 beds, at least one pub and several chandler shops, which are small grocery stores or cook shops. The result was a very poor street, as compared to some of the relatively decent neighborhoods in which she and John lived earlier.[2]

However, Elizabeth and Michael were not the only ones trying to scratch out a living. The population of London continued to increase dramatically. In fact, its migrant population, native British and foreigners tripled between 1850 and 1888. In the West End, builders could not keep pace with the demand, but the East End conditions worsened, and what attempts were made to improve the situation could be classified as paved with good intentions. This was by no means a matter of design, but the common workman planned to show that he had had enough. On the February 8, 1886, what started out as a protest march from Trafalgar Square to Hyde Park soon became a riot. By the time the crowd reached the park, it split into two factions. One of the mobs was said to have an estimated four hundred to one thousand men. The rioting, mostly looting and smashing of windows, continued until one inspector and fifteen constables confronted them. After a brief scuffle, the crowd dispersed. Despite their overwhelming numbers, the disgruntled unemployed obviously had no stomach for confronting the authorities, but in the end they succeeded in causing about £50,000 in damage. Later, this riot was viewed as "preventable" and led to the downfall of Colonel Sir Edmund Henderson, the Metropolitan Police commissioner. His replacement was a very capable military man, Sir Charles Warren. This workman protest was merely the start, for 1886 has been described as a terrible year for labor with wage reductions and an increase in unemployment. So it is not surprising that Elizabeth asked for and received financial assistance on May 20 and then again on May 23 from the Swedish Church, giving an address of Devonshire Street, Commercial Road, although she and Michael were still living in Dorset Street at that time. Even though both areas, Dorset Street and Devonshire Street, were made up of similar economically challenged people, Elizabeth possibly said Devonshire when she sought financial aid, because Devonshire is nearer to the Swedish Church.[3]

Over the next year, the household finances would not improve much, and Elizabeth re-entered the Poplar Workhouse on March 21, 1887. The time that she and Michael would be together has been described as stormy — and small wonder. Elizabeth was convicted eight times for drunkenness at the Thames Magistrate Court between 1887 and 1888. Yet any lack of harmony between the live-in lovers did not stop or start with her drinking, sometimes described as "habitual drunkenness." The couple lived within poor means, at best, and such circumstances tend to foster rocky relationships. But no matter how tenuous the couple's livelihood, they managed to move to 36 Devonshire Street around April 1887. Elizabeth's admittance to the workhouse was possibly a coordinated effort with Michael to relocate what belongings they had to their new lodgings. Devonshire Street sat just west of Watney Street and ran north from Tarling Road to Commercial Road, sometimes called Commercial Road East. It was less than half a mile to the northeast from the Swedish Church and consisted of very poor residents and the lowest class. And there in this downtrodden neighborhood, their unsteady relationship gave way. On April 6, Elizabeth turned Michael over to Police Constable 357H. Charge: assault. Yet the case was dropped, because she did not appear in court against him. Elizabeth's absence is not surprising, assuming there was any foundation to the charge, for it is fairly common for a complaining spouse not to show up at a hearing. One modern-day example comes from Ontario Canada, where spouses have dropped assault complaints enough times that the police are now empowered to file the charges without their consent.[4]

But the approaching summer promised better times ahead, at least for some. On June 20–21, Queen Victoria celebrated her Golden Jubilee. After a quiet breakfast Her Majesty traveled by train from Windsor to Paddington. That evening, across the parks at Buckingham Palace, she had a "large family dinner" with fifty foreign kings and princes. The following day, the beloved and respected monarch had a procession through London, traveling to Westminster Abbey with an Indian cavalry escort. Six cream-colored horses drew the open royal landau. The miles of onlookers and well wishers were probably not surprised to see that she wore a bonnet and a long dress instead of her crown. But the Fenians had planned for a more spectacular display. In what was surely reminiscent of Guy Fawkes, they attempted to detonate a bomb at Westminster Abbey, but the chief conspirator had been scared back to America. The plot was foiled.

Yet the terrorists were not the only ones causing civil unrest. Despite the happiness afforded to Her Majesty, the unemployed remained discontent and the Socialists had no problem in using the jobless to their advantage. On November 13, 1887, they held another mass demonstration. Several members of the Social Democratic Federation led approximately 10,000 people marching from different directions and converged on Trafalgar Square. This location was most likely chosen because of the ban that had been placed on the square restricting its use on certain days, which was a direct result of the many squatters who lived there and the complaints of the middle class shop owners. Of the 5,000 constables on duty that day, Sir Charles Warren, head of the Metropolitan Police, positioned 2,000 constables around the square with support from 300 mounted police, 300 grenadiers and 300 life guards. (The number of people involved in this clash varies in different sources. The marchers have been estimated at 20,000 and at 40,000–50,000. The number of police has also been estimated at 4,000 with 7,000 constables in reserve, while the number of troops has also been estimated at 200.) To call the huge number of disgruntled civilians coming into contact with such a large reactive police force an accident waiting to happen would be the understatement of the year. By the end of the day, the police were successful in clearing the square, but the ensuing clash resulted in over 275 injuries to protestors and police, incurring about 300 arrests with some convictions. Two marchers ultimately died from their injuries. Sir Charles Warren was publicly praised for his actions by the middle class and the mainstream press, and he received a Knight Commandership of the Bath from Queen Victoria. The radicals, however, viewed the events differently and never forgot let alone forgave the incident. They were quick to denounce the police as "oppressors of the poor" and readily labeled the incident "Bloody Sunday."[5]

The arrival of 1888 saw more determination from the anti-establishment. This time, the Fenians were determined to conduct an assassination campaign, and they decided to centralize control of the operation in France. Their primary target was the new chief secretary for Ireland, Arthur James Balfour. His heavy-handedness in suppressing the "disturbances" that took place the previous September earned him the nickname "Bloody Balfour." But the fates were not on the brotherhood's side; neither was their conviction or courage. After being confronted by Scotland Yard, who made their presence known to the "French connection," the plot was the only thing to die, and some of the conspirators never even entered England.[6]

Whatever relationship issues Elizabeth and Michael had, her drinking did not help to improve matters. Several months later, on June 10, she caused a disturbance at the Ten Bells public house, a popular Commercial Street pub for many and only about a block north from Elizabeth's home away from home, the lodging house in Flower and Dean Street. She was taken into custody that Sunday morning and brought to the Thames Police Court for being drunk and disorderly. This time she might have used the name Annie Fitzgerald. (Elizabeth's use of Annie Fitzgerald as an alias has not been firmly established, but this particular arrest is curtly referenced during the inquest.) A month later, it seems Michael had resigned himself to his fate. Disturbed about work, low income, or his relationship with Elizabeth, he became drunk and disorderly, using obscenity. He was sent down for three days. Elizabeth also had had enough and walked out. Many couples who argue and temporarily separate return to each other after their impassioned moment subsides. And so it was for Elizabeth and Michael. They were on-again, off-again, which he admitted at the inquest. They lived together "nearly all" the time for "three years." "She would occasionally go away ... about five months altogether." Michael blamed it on Elizabeth's drinking, and commented, "I treated her the same as I would a wife... She always came back again." Whether Elizabeth's "drunkenness" corresponded with the times she left Michael, no one knows for sure. But five months apart out of the nearly three years of being together is not too shabby for a couple living within that kind of relationship. Assuming that her known bouts of drunkenness did indeed correspond with the times that she left Michael, then of her nine or so absences, she was only gone for an average of two weeks at a time. The house deputy of 32 Flower and Dean Street would paint a similar picture during the lengthy inquest. She "lodged in our house, on and off, for the last six years."[7]

But the days continued on, and August 7, 1888, started out like a fairly normal Tuesday. London woke from its cool slumber after celebrating a bank holiday to be greeted by a cloudy morning. Spots of rain fell upon the East End, as the temperature rose to a warm 78°. All was as it should be. Nothing was out of the ordinary. And like many others, John Saunders Reeves, an unemployed waterside laborer, arose that morning to look for work. He lived in the George Yard Buildings, an old weaving factory converted to a tenement. This sat to the back of Toynbee Hall at the northwest corner of George Yard, a narrow alley which supported the very poor and lowest class and ran south from Wentworth Street to Whitechapel High Street. As he passed the first floor landing of his apartment building, John Reeves's day became anything but ordinary. Lying on her back in a pool of blood was Martha Tabram. Sometimes going by Martha or Emma Turner, she died, before the canonical victims, due to blood loss from multiple stab wounds.[8]

Because Coroner Baxter was on vacation in Scandinavia at the time, the duties fell to Mr. George Collier, deputy coroner for the Southeastern Division of Middlesex. Two days after the body's discovery, Mr. Collier opened the Tabram inquest on Thursday, August 9, 1888, at the Working Lad's Institute. This seat for the Whitechapel Coroner's authority was located on the north side of Whitechapel Road, approximately one block west of Brady Street and opposite London Hospital. Five people testified that day, and after Dr. Timothy Robert Killeen, the presiding doctor for the case, completed his description of Tabram's injuries, Mr. Collier adjourned the inquest until August 23. Chances are Elizabeth and Michael had little sympathy for the murdered woman. They had their own issues. Most of London's general population probably gave little reaction

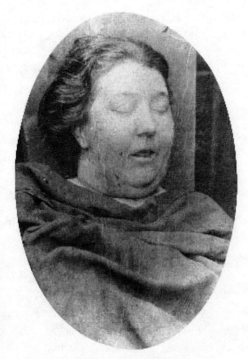

Mortuary photograph of Martha Tabram (courtesy Evans/Skinner Crime Archive).

to the tragic death. This basic lack of concern was not because no one cared or no one discussed the brutal murder. It was due to the minimal media coverage, especially compared to that which would be provided for future murder victims. Few London newspapers reported the inquest, while some gave the murder only a blurb, and others did not mention Tabram's death until two days to about a week after the inquest opened. Often mentioned are the cries of "another 'orrible murder" ringing out from the boys selling their papers. No doubt this happened, especially as the eventual circulation war developed. And yet a curious aspect is that the newspapers did not necessarily make the murders front page news. They might have bannered the topic as a leading story, but even the *Daily Telegraph*, for example, never gave the mounting deaths anything better than page two and more often than not they reported it on page three or page five. In contrast, however, the *Star* and the *Illustrated Police News* seemed to readily report these tragic events on page one. One reason why some papers might not have reported the death until much later is that it seemed to be a common practice for many of the smaller or ad-hoc newspapers to merely reprint or offer a summary of what the larger London daily papers reported. An ironic footnote in the history of the news coverage is that the *Daily Telegraph*, carrying the largest readership, did not even report the first day of the inquest. But they were not the only one.[9]

A fortnight later Mr. Collier resumed the Tabram inquest at two in the afternoon, which was a fairly common practice. The date was August 23, and only five people testified that Thursday, including Tabram's husband, Henry Samuel Tabram, and her live-in boyfriend of nine years, William Turner. With insufficient cause to adjourn the inquest any further, Mr. Collier summed up the evidence this way: "The crime was one of the most brutal that had occurred for some years. For a poor defenceless woman to be outraged and stabbed in the manner which this woman had been was almost beyond belief." The jury agreed, and for the cruel act, they returned a verdict of "wilful murder against some person or persons unknown."[10]

A week after the conclusion of Tabram's inquest, several fires broke out in London on the night of August 30. The one at the Shadwell Dry Docks burned until late the following morning. Fueled by 800 tons of coal, a "great glow in the sky" could be seen even as far away as Whitechapel. Some people even went to watch despite the chilly air, and such a sight can only be imagined, a luminescence that would have been noticed by even the most casual observer walking in the streets. Yet Londoners are resilient, and their lives continued on through the brisk night and wee hours of the morning. Ships came and went from other docks; markets prepared to open by five o'clock; shops hoped for a good day of selling their wares; and the unemployed sought work. The wheels and cogs of industrial society kept turning. Everything was fine until, in the early hours of that Friday morning, a cart driver, or carman, Charles Andrew Cross of Doveton St., Cambridge Heath Road headed for work, walking westerly through Buck's Row (present-day Durward Street). This was a stretch of road, lying several blocks north of Whitechapel Road, which ran from Brady Street to Baker's Row. As he neared the overpass at the western end of the road, he saw what he first thought was an old tarp. By coincidence, another carman happened to be walking through Buck's Row behind Cross. He was Robert Paul, a resident of 30 Forster Street, and he too was on his way to work. Cross pointed out to Paul the object lying at the side of the road, near the gateway of the stable yard. But it was not a tarp. It was the body of Mary Ann Nichols. To her friends, she was known as Polly. Nicholls, as the press so often misspelled her name, is viewed as the first canonical victim. She died from blood loss due to a slit throat, with other stabs and incisions being post-mortem.[11]

Nichols's death invited more media coverage, and they would not miss a beat in order to get the scoop on this latest excitement. Most, if not all, did not forego this opening kickoff. Interestingly enough, some citizens stood up to be counted from the onset. That same day, L.P. Walter of 11–13 Church Street, Spitalfields, wrote the Home Office, suggesting that a reward should be offered for the capture of the murderer. (This is a good example of how fast news could travel. Not only were some papers, like the *Daily Telegraph*, on the streets by 10 A.M., but there were also several mail pick-ups during the day.) While this might have seemed like a good idea, E. Leigh Pemberton, who worked in the Home Office under the direction of the secretary of state, Henry Matthews, ultimately denied the request, as a practice discontinued by the government since 1884. Despite some contemporary theorists who viewed this as

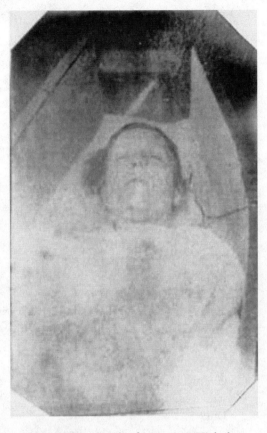

Mortuary photograph of Mary Ann Nichols (courtesy Evans/Skinner Crime Archive).

a class issue, the justification was fear that such a reward would become "blood money."[12]

The very next day, on Saturday, September 1st, Wynne Edwin Baxter, coroner for East London and Tower Hamlets, opened the Nichols inquest at the Working Lad's Institute. Members of the Criminal Investigation Department (CID) attended the proceedings, but only three people gave testimony. After Dr. Reese Ralph Llewellyn, medical officer to East and East Central Districts and City Mission, presented his evidence about Nichols's injuries, the inquest was adjourned until Monday. Unlike his deputy, Corner Baxter had a habit of conducting lengthy inquests, adjourning and resuming numerous times, which could span an entire month. This was not typical, as most coroner inquests lasted two days at most, because their only purpose was to determine the cause of death, such as heart attack or murder. But Coroner Baxter has been described as flamboyant, notably dressy, and garrulous. This combined with his seeming tendency for deductions and apparent arrogance leads some to conclude that Coroner Baxter intentionally extended his inquests in order to play sleuth. If it was not possible to determine or establish the victim's identity, then that person would be listed as "woman (or man) unknown," as was the situation for the Whitehall Torso or Pinchin Street Torso cases.[13]

Monday, September 3 saw the second session of the Nichols inquest. Seven people testified including Nichols's estranged husband, William Nichols. The last to testify was Mary Ann Monk, a former inmate of the Lambeth Workhouse, who helped to identify the body. After she gave evidence concerning the last time that she saw the deceased, the inquest was adjourned for a fortnight. Sadly, enough areas in the world have their share of murders, and the Old City was no different. Fortunately, the number of unsolved killings in London was virtually non existent. Despite some contemporary news accounts lambasting the authorities as bunglers, the police were in fact reliable and professional. With competent police and a persistent coroner, East Enders could relax with the thought that the killer would not only be caught, but that such brutality would not happen again. Some suspected who the assailant was. On September 5, the *Star* published an article about a man named "Leather Apron," calling him the "noiseless midnight terror" and claiming that he was the only person associated with the three Whitechapel victims Emma Elizabeth Smith, Martha Tabram, and Mary Ann Nichols. The "Universal Fear Among the Women" began.[14]

Fear or not, Nichols's funeral took place during the following afternoon. Her body was transported in a polished elm coffin to Mr. Henry Smith, an undertaker in Hanbury Street. There the cortège consisted of the hearse and two mourning coaches, which carried Nichols's father, Edward Walker, her estranged husband, William Nichols, and their eldest child, Edward John Nichols. The procession went to the City of London Cemetery, Ilford, sometimes called "Little Ilford," at Manor Park Cemetery, Sebert Road, Forest Gate. She was interred at grave 210752. The mournful relatives — her father, husband, and son — paid for the funeral.

Yet in spite of such tragic and sudden loss of life, the world kept turning, and on the morning of September 8 the sun finally rose shortly before 5:30. After a fitful sleep, a carman known as John Davis pulled himself from his bed at his residence, 29 Hanbury Street, a three-story brick building located on the north side of the road between Wilkes Street and Brick Lane. This was a neighborhood where the poor and sufficiently comfortable inhabitants blended together, populating a fairly long stretch of road, for Hanbury

Street curved southeast from Commercial Street to the junction of Baker's Row and Old Montague Street. Having had his cup of tea, Davis proceeded down the stairs from his third story digs, a converted attic which he and his family occupied. He made his way to the outhouse that sat in the back yard. It was a bright and brisk morning. But the chilled air was not the only thing to greet Davis as he opened the back door. Annie Chapman was lying on her back between the fence that separated the yard from No.27 and the back steps. She was disemboweled. Known as Dark Annie, she is the second canonical victim. She died from blood loss due to a slit throat with the other injuries having been carried out post-mortem.[15]

People reacted to the news of this latest death, and reacted en masse. The building's hallway leading from the street to the yard had to be cleared by police. Some spectators paid 1 pence for a peak at the murder scene from nearby windows. By the time Chapman was removed by ambulance, a covered, wheeled stretcher, several hundred people had flocked to the area. With talk of the killings and news accounts of "Leather Apron," apprehension filled the populace. The police did indeed have a sense of urgency — two dead women within a week's time. In light of Chapman's death, the police knew they had a serial murderer on their hands. In two days' time, Coroner Baxter's workload for sensational cases doubled. On Monday morning, September 10, he opened the Chapman inquest at the Working Lad's Institute. Four people provided testimony, including John Evans, the night watchman at Crossingham's lodging house, 35 Dorset Street. Once he finished, the inquest was adjourned for several days. While Coroner Baxter carried out the medical inquiry, another event took place that Monday morning. Sergeant William Thick of H Division arrived at 22 Mulberry Street. His mission: bring in "Leather Apron." John Pizer, a shoemaker, was quickly and easily apprehended

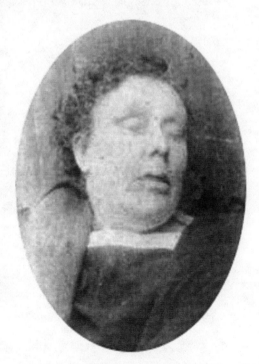

Mortuary photograph of Annie Chapman (courtesy Evans/Skinner Crime Archive).

at his home. Sergeant Thick escorted him to the Leman Street Police Station, which sat on the southeast corner of Buckle Street and Leman Street. There, the hapless Pizer was questioned and placed in a lineup. With a lack of any satisfactory identification and no evidence against him, Pizer was released Tuesday evening.[16]

Wednesday, September 12 saw the second day of the Chapman inquest. Eleven people gave evidence, including Chapman's brother, Fountain Smith. The inquest was adjourned until the next day after Henry John Holland, a box maker, spoke. One of the more interesting people to testify was Pizer himself, and he gladly did so. True, he admitted that his nickname was Leather Apron, but he said he was not the "Leather Apron" described in the *Star*'s article, assuming such a person actually existed. Even the *Manchester Guardian* questioned the reality of "Leather Apron" in its September 10 issue, which is not surprising considering the *Star*'s reporter claimed to have interviewed fifty women in three hours, each giving "almost identical descriptions." Pizer was not the killer sought by the police and he wanted to publicly vindicate his name. Coroner Baxter had no objection to this. Not only had Pizer been released from custody, but he could also prove that he was not associated with Nichols's death or Chapman's. The "Leather Apron Scare" did fade, partially as a result of Pizer's testimony. But another, more horrific nom de querve would eventually fill the void. Some view Pizer's arrest as for public display, to eradicate the "Leather Apron Scare," which was created by the *Star*, rather than as any real attempt to prosecute Pizer. Ironically, the *Star* was one of the biggest antagonists the police had, in addition to the *Pall Mall Gazette*, and yet the *Star* had no issue with fabricating possible frenzy. It was all part and parcel of being a radical newspaper.[17]

The next day, Thursday, September 13, Coroner Baxter resumed the Chapman inquest. Five people presented information during that third session. They included Dr. George Bagster Phillips, H Division police surgeon and medical official called to the scene, who described Chapman's injuries. Coroner Baxter adjourned the inquest again after Mary Elizabeth Simonds, a resident nurse at the Whitechapel Infirmary, testified. No doubt Elizabeth and Michael knew of the terrible events that had gripped the city over the past two weeks. In fact, the three publicized murders occurred no more than three-quarters of a mile away from their humble abode in Devonshire Street. And they, like their contemporary counterparts "were not ignorant closet-cases, isolated from local happenings; they read the papers, and talked about current events with their friends and neighbors." But despite any mounting fear that grew amongst London's East End population, the life of the average citizen continued.[18]

Chapman's funeral was held the following morning. It began at seven, when a hearse supplied by Henry Smith went to the Whitechapel Mortuary. Chapman's body was placed in a black-draped elm coffin and was then driven to Harry Hawes of 19 Hunt Street, a Spitalfields undertaker who arranged the funeral. At 9:00 A.M., the private procession consisting of only a hearse with no mourning coaches made its somber way with Chapman's body. Like Nichols, Chapman was taken to the City of London Cemetery for her final resting place. She was buried at gravesite 78. Chapman's relatives, who paid for the funeral, met the hearse at the cemetery, and, by request, kept the funeral a secret and were the only ones to attend.

Elizabeth and Michael's situation had not subsided with the "Leather Apron" scare nor was it buried along with Chapman. The next day, Saturday, September 15, Elizabeth paid another trip to the Swedish Church. As with previous visits, she asked for and received financial assistance.[19]

By mid–September several groups of people had decided to organize themselves and act on behalf of the public interest. They were called Vigilance Committees, and while some existed prior to the murders for social enforcement or improvement, some sprang up purely as a result of the killings. Their primary aim was to aid public order and act as pressure groups. Two of these committees, the Central Vigilance Society and the Spitalfields Vigilance Committee, dealt with suggestions and urgings in the East End, demanding that the police harass prostitutes or sending congenial requests for improved street lighting. The more notable but still self-created council was the Whitechapel Vigilance Committee. This group stood out for several reasons. They were not run-of-the-mill disgruntled laborers; they were in fact middle-class tradesmen. Their president, George Lusk, was a fairly well to do building contractor living in Mile End. Upon inception, they announced that at least one of the sixteen committee members would be at The Crown pub, where the committee was founded, each morning to receive suggestions or information from the general populace regarding the murders. They also petitioned the Home Office numerous times for a government-sponsored reward. These requests were always denied because rewards had been discontinued.[20]

The third day of the Nichols inquest was conducted several days later, on September 17. Nine people testified, including a second appearance by Dr. Llewellyn. After some banter between Coroner Baxter and the jury foreman over the lack of a government offered reward, the inquest adjourned until Saturday. But Coroner Baxter kept a full plate, and two days later, on Wednesday, he resumed the Chapman inquest. Among the seven people who gave evidence that afternoon was Dr. Phillips, who had been recalled. After William

Stevens, a painter and lodger at 35 Dorset Street, testified, the fourth session concluded, with Coroner Baxter saying, "As far as we know, the case is complete." The jury was willing to hand down a verdict at that time, but it was "agreed to adjourn the inquiry until next Wednesday before deciding upon the terms of the verdict."[21]

During the three years that Elizabeth and Michael had been together, their problems never really diminished, even though they might have been on hiatus from time to time. That Thursday, Elizabeth returned to the Swedish Church. They did not refuse her request for money, but this would be the last time she received alms for the poor.

Yet some people had greater concerns than one person's privation. On the following Saturday, September 22, the Nichols inquest came to a close with its fourth session. Only one person gave evidence, a signalman, Thomas Ede, who was recalled. Coroner Baxter wrapped up the proceedings with a lengthy summation, and "the jury, after a short consultation, returned a verdict of wilful murder against some person or persons unknown. A rider was added expressing the full coincidence of the jury with some remarks made by the coroner as to the need of a mortuary for Whitechapel." The need for an actual Whitechapel mortuary was more than a local gripe — it was a reality. The contemporary facility was essentially a shed at the end of a cul-de-sac, Eagle Place, off Old Montague Street, west of Baker's Row. Two inmates from the Whitechapel Workhouse ran the mortuary.[22]

Less than a week later, Elizabeth left Michael again. She gave their next-door neighbor, Mrs. Smith, her Swedish hymnbook for safekeeping, and according to Michael, they were on friendly terms that Tuesday night when they parted company in Commercial Street. He was on his way home from work and expected to see her there shortly afterwards. He never saw her alive again. Unknown to Michael, Elizabeth would return one more time, using her key. He was unaware that she had a duplicate of their lodging's padlock key. So even though Michael would lock up their residence behind them when they both left, Elizabeth would still let herself in and out. The following day, she entered their Devonshire lodgings when Michael was at work. After picking up some items, she left. While Elizabeth fetched a few things, Coroner Baxter concluded the Chapman inquest. It was Wednesday, September 26, and it had been a long month. After four adjournments, no "further evidence was to be adduced." Coroner Baxter then presented his summation, during which he referenced an American who, "some months ago," allegedly sought organ specimens for distribution with "each copy of a publication on

Opposite: Coroner Baxter (courtesy Evans/Skinner Crime Archive).

which he was then engaged." After Coroner Baxter summed up the evidence and his thoughts, the foreman stated, "We can only find one verdict — that of wilful murder against some person or persons unknown. We were about to add a rider with respect to the condition of the mortuary, but that having been done by a previous jury it is unnecessary."

The last two days of the Chapman inquest demonstrated Coroner Baxter's willingness to leave no stone unturned, especially if it gave him a better opportunity to interject his own hypothesis. The press seemed to have given Coroner Baxter its adulation for raising awareness associated with the dangers of "Burking," which refers to the method used by William Burke and William Hare to kill people in order to sell corpses to medical schools. The method involved suffocation and chest compression, leaving no visible signs of injury. However, the British Medical Journal quickly and decisively refuted Coroner Baxter on his killing-for-body-parts notion. Publicly, at least, the Whitechapel coroner would not repeat his theory.

But such things were probably of no concern to Elizabeth. Errant doctors and organ specimens would have meant little. For she had her moment of freedom and the following day, Thursday, she returned to her usual haunt. It had been three months since she last roomed at 32 Flower and Dean Street, and Elizabeth Tanner, a long-time associate, and Catherine Lane, who had known Elizabeth for six or seven months, first saw her that night after her long absence. It was sometime between ten and eleven o'clock when Lane first saw Elizabeth. According to her compatriots, Elizabeth was living with a man in Fashion Street. Fashion Street, which ran from Commercial Street to Brick Lane, was only one block away to the north of Flower and Dean Street, and its inhabitants were either poor or comfortably situated. Interestingly, however, Michael lived in Devonshire Street, more than three-quarters of a mile overland, to the southeast. Elizabeth told Lane that she came back to the lodging house after she and her man "had a few words." But no matter how long she might have stayed on previous visits to the lodging house, this one would be comparatively short. In two days time, Elizabeth would have a date.[23]

3

Death Becomes Her

The last day of September arrived like many other days that month — it was cloudy. Yet this Saturday was unseasonably fair even though it was the early part of autumn. With the previous night's cool air, the citizens of London were afforded a decent sleep, one where they could relax, feeling comfortable, if not safe, for it had been three weeks since the last murder. Surely the killer had moved on or did himself in over the remorse he had to have felt. Slowly the day brightened, and shortly before six the sun finally greeted the hustle and bustle of the London streets, warming up the day. By the afternoon, Elizabeth was busy cleaning a couple of rooms at the lodging house, instead of her usual chores for the local Jewish residences. For her efforts, her friend and house deputy, Elizabeth Tanner, willingly paid Elizabeth 6 pence. The minutes stretched into hours with little care or hassle, and shortly after dusk, around 6:30, Elizabeth and Tanner went to the one of the favorite haunts for local residents, the Queen Head's pub. It was nearby, at the south corner of Commercial Street and Fashion Street; the public house was only one block up the road from Flower and Dean Street. Whatever good times a drink among friends might have brought, the two companions did not stay long.

Returning to the lodging house by seven o'clock, Tanner went to another part of the building, leaving Elizabeth in the kitchen. There she saw fellow lodger, Charles Preston, a barber, and asked to borrow his brush to tidy up her clothes, but he refused. This did not dampen Elizabeth's spirits any, and within the hour she gave another lodger and apparent friend, Catherine Lane, a married charwoman, a large piece of green velvet to hold. While a piece of velvet might not seem like much, Elizabeth obviously counted it among her prized possessions and wanted to ensure its safeguard. She had no problem letting a friend or entrusted neighbor keep a watchful eye on such items during her anticipated absence, as she had with her hymnbook. (Similarly, Emily Birrel gave Catherine Eddowes, the fourth canonical victim, a pawn ticket to

31

hold.) This relatively minor event said much. Not only did Elizabeth expect to return to the lodging house at some point, but she also planned on going back to Devonshire Street, if for no other reason than to fetch her book from Mrs. Smith. It is curious that she did not merely bring the book with her, unless she did not trust the other lodgers with what was probably more than a religious memento, for it is doubtful that she was a practicing Lutheran, let alone Anglican. Chances are the Swedish hymnal, though given to her by the clerk of the local church, was a personal keepsake — a reminder of her distant homeland. The disposition of the velvet and wanting to borrow a clothes brush indicate that Elizabeth was preparing for a night out. Not a night of drinking, but a rendezvous. For she made no attempt to pay for a night's doss. As she left the lodging house that night, Elizabeth passed by the watchman, Thomas Bates. She looked cheerful and still had the money she earned from Tanner.[1]

By nine o'clock that night, Philips Krantz, who changed his name from Jacob Rombro, went to work. Having arrived in London earlier in the year, the twenty-nine-year-old socialist was now the editor of *Der Arbeter Fraint*, "The Worker's Friend," a weekly Yiddish publication for socialist Jews that was apparently held in some regard far beyond London, and even beyond the British Isles. This was quite an accomplishment, considering the paper's offices consisted of two rooms, one for editing and one for composing. This unimpressive work of stone was located behind the International Workingmen's Educational Club (IWEC). Situated on the western side of the road at 40 Berner Street, the club, which owned the "radical" *Der Arbeter Fraint*, was a three-story brick building. Though typically narrow for the time (the front facade at ground level consisted of only a door and a window), it stretched away from the road, and its height made it one of the more impressive structures on the street, one

Contemporary sketch of Dutfield's Yard (courtesy Alex Chisholm).

that could easily be seen from the junction of Berner and Fairclough Streets, which was only a gateway and three doors to the south. The spacious club could readily handle at least 200 people for performances, discussions, or poetic readings, and some of its members lived there. The main door led out into the street, but a pathway to its rear, or kitchen, entrance was accessible through Dutfield's Yard, next door on the left at the southern side. Named after Arthur Dutfield, the yard had access from the street through a nine-foot-wide gateway, supporting two wooden gates. The gate closest to the club had a man door. This may have seemed like a fairly wide entrance, but each gate was less than five feet long. The yard itself had no light of its own, and "none of the street lamps lit it." In fact what illumination there was came primarily "by the lights through the windows at the side of the club," but that fell more upon the opposite tenement. If any light shone through the tenement windows, which could be seen from within the yard, it offered very little to aid someone passing through the yard. If the kitchen door was open or the printing offices occupied, their light fell further into the yard, leaving Dutfield's essentially dark after sunset. Although "the intervening passage is illuminated by means of a fanlight over the door." But the yard was not unfrequented nor was it merely an empty lot for it provided access to an occupied tenement house, an unused stable, Walter Hindley's workshop for manufacturing sacks, Dutfield's van and cart manufacturer, and the ever important necessity of two outhouses.[2]

Earlier that day, the overcast skies had turned into spots of rain for some parts to the east and south of London. As the weather continued to worsen, the damp day made sales even harder for the small businessman like Matthew Packer. He was a greengrocer, also commonly called a fruiterer, because that was his main stock-in-trade. With his small, one-man barrow of goods, he had set out for the day, hoping to sell what he could. But sometime around 9:30 or so he finally had enough, and he headed for home, as "the night had come on wet," so he could take the place of his wife at their small shop at 44 Berner Street. Living and working out of the two-story brick building, the fifty-eight-year-old Packer and his wife shared their digs with Harry Douglas and Sarah Harrison. They resided on the same side of the street as and just two doors south of the socialist club. To their right was a tenement, or cottage, and on the left, at the northwest corner of Berner and Fairclough Streets, sat their other next door neighbor, The Nelson, a beer house or beer retailer owned by Louis Hagens, which has at times been described as a pub.[3]

While Packer made his way home, Police Constable William Smith came on duty for the shift change. He was assigned the "Berner Street beat," and by 10 P.M., he began patrolling the various neighborhoods with a slow, methodical plod typical of a beat cop. This slow pace was used to ensure that the patrolman did not miss anything, and when he passed by a business, he commonly checked the doors to make sure they were locked. (PC Smith's City of London counterpart was expected to cover a beat at an average pace of two miles per hour.) PC Smith's rounds usually lasted twenty-five to thirty minutes, while he traveled through Commercial Road, Grove Street, Christian Street, Fairclough Street, and Berner Street. Berner Street (present-day Henriques Street), lying west of Cannon Street Road, ran south from Commercial Road to Ellen Street with Fairclough Street crossing near its middle. (Fairclough Street ran west to east from Back Church Lane to Grove Street, intersecting with Berner, Providence, Batty, Brunswick, Christian, and Grove Streets. Its inhabitants were a combination of poor and those who earned a comfortable living, with out liers of very poor people.) Berner Street had a number of side streets and alleyways. Approximately a third of the way south, between Commercial Road and Fairclough Street, Sander Street ran westerly to Back Church Lane. Further south was an alleyway that led into Batty's Gardens and on into Back Church Lane. On the eastern side, another alleyway led to Batty Street. South of Fairclough, Boyd and Everard Streets ran between Berner and Back Church, with another alleyway on the eastern side going from Berner to Providence Street. The residents who occupied Berner Street were mostly poor with a mixture of those who were comfortably situated. But the neighborhood was more than a residential area. It supported two schools: one was just north of the Batty's Gardens and east of Mission Hall with a primary access from Back Church Lane. The other, commonly referred to as the Board School, sat at the northeast corner of Berner and Fairclough. The Board School, stretching north along Berner Street, was "opposite" about seven buildings, including the IWEC and Packer's shop. In addition to Packer's, The Nelson, and the businesses accessed by Dutfield's Yard, there were several other greengrocer shops, one near each end of Berner Street, and a pub at the junction of Boyd Street. Despite some grumbling from the media about the area being poorly lit, the residential neighborhood, had "six lamps within 700 feet." According to the parish plans, there were "four lamps within 350 feet, from Commercial-road to Fairclough-street." Even though there were "no public-house lights in Berner-street," the residential neighborhood was, in fact, as well lit as other side streets, if not more so, since most of them were rather dark.[4]

The minutes ticked away, and soon an hour had passed. Krantz still busied himself with his paper while PC Smith continued patrolling the neighborhoods without incident. Elizabeth had already hooked up with her date, spending some time at 34 Settles Street, a public house. The Bricklayer's

Arms pub sat at the south corner of Settles and Fordham Streets and was about 237 yards from the corner of Berner Street and Commercial Road.

A few minutes before eleven, a couple of laborers, John Gardner of Chapman Street and his friend J. Best from Lower Chapman Street arrived at the public house as Elizabeth and her young man were coming out. It was raining very hard at that time. Waiting for the weather to break, the affectionate pair quietly stood in the doorway, hugging and kissing. The two friends could not help but notice the couple — a respectably dressed man "going on" with a poorly dressed woman. The young man, they observed, stood "about 5 ft. 5 in. in height. He was well dressed in a black morning suit with a morning coat [a cutaway coat]. He had rather weak eyes ... sore eyes without any eyelashes... He had a thick black moustache and no beard. He wore a black billycock hat, [a wide-awake hat], rather tall, and had on a collar," but the color of his tie was not readily noticed. His date was a slight woman with a somewhat prominent nose, wearing a short jacket with dahlias on the right side. The two laborers "chipped" the young man, but without success. When their teasing failed to give even a little entertainment, they changed tactics by trying a softer approach.

"Why don't you bring the woman in and treat her?" they finally asked.

The young man responded to the workmen with silence.

Best was somewhat put out by this. He expected the young man to leave or at least tell him and his mate to mind their own business. Getting nowhere with the man, the two laborers then focused their attentions on Elizabeth.

"That's Leather Apron getting 'round you," came the snide remark.

Elizabeth responded in kind, with silence, but she and her young man decided to leave and "went off like a shot." It was shortly after eleven when they headed south out of Settles Street. Instead of moving straight on into Christian Street, the couple apparently turned right onto Commercial Road.[5]

The rain had already begun to subside by the time Elizabeth and her young man left the pub. Leaving the taunting behind, they made their way along Commercial Road until they reached Back Church Lane, where they decided to venture south. Eventually they came into Berner Street, and as they walked into the residential neighborhood, passing the corner beer house, they might have heard the German discussion or even music emanating from the nearby club. Before long, they came upon Packer's greengrocer shop. It was an "insignificant place," from which he ran his "small business." "With a half window in front" and fruit "exposed for sale" at the "lower part of the window case," Packer watched the couple as they approached. "It was a dark night and the only light was afforded by an oil lamp which Packer had burning inside his window." While the couple stood there, "talking close in front of the window," the shopkeeper obtained a sufficiently clear view" of their faces. The young man was middle aged, perhaps thirty-five years old. He stood about five feet seven inches in height and was stout — squarely built. He wore dark clothes with a wide-awake hat. He seemed to be an educated man, possibly a clerk. For even though his voice was rough, he had a loud, yet quick, sharp way of talking. He had a quick commanding way with him. The woman standing beside him seemed to be middle aged, as well. She wore a dark dress and jacket, which had a white flower pinned to it. After a minute, and possibly with the question, "why don't you ... treat her," ringing in his head, the young man stepped forward.

"I say, old man, how do you sell your grapes?"

"Sixpence a pound the black 'uns, sir, and fourpence a pound the white 'uns," answered Packer.

The young man turned to Elizabeth, asking, "Which will you have, my dear, black or white? You shall have whichever you like best."

"Oh, then I'll have the black 'uns," she said, "'cos they look the nicest."

"Give us half a pound of the black ones, then," ordered the young man.

With that, the elderly shopkeeper placed the grapes in a paper bag and handed it to the man, who in turn handed it to Elizabeth. Packer was glad enough to have sold the grapes, since he had had a slow day with his barrow.[6]

A few sprinkles of rain continued to fall, but instead of taking cover, the couple walked a few doors north in the direction of Commercial Road. There they stood at the gateway of Dutfield's Yard, apparently listening to the music that came from the club. After a minute or two, the couple crossed the street and stood near the Board School, talking. With little else to do, the fruiterer watched the couple in amazement.

"Why, them people must be a couple o' fools to stand out there in the rain eating grapes they bought here, when they might just as well have had shelter!" he exclaimed to his wife.

The elderly shopkeeper, who had spent enough of his day in the rain, could not understand why the couple wanted some privacy instead of enjoying the grapes near his small shop. But the poor weather would not last much longer. By 11:30, what little rain there was had ended, and the couple decided to move on, walking slowly toward Fairclough Street. Packer, wanting his supper, closed up his shop for the night due to the lack of customers. PC Smith's patrol brought him back onto Berner Street, and an indigo, or ink, warehouse laborer named William Marshall went outside and stood in front of his residence at 64 Berner Street. Breathing in the after-rain air, he took in his surroundings, only two doors north of the George VI pub that sat at the northern corner of Berner and Boyd Streets.[7]

Now the club members commonly held Saturday night discussions, which were alternately conducted in German and English. This night was no different, with the talk being "Why Jews Should be Socialists." It was conducted in German and chaired by Morris Eagle, a Russian Jew who traveled and sold jewelry. At some time between 11:30 and a quarter to midnight, the formal discussion came to a close. Eagle left the club through the front door, and walked his girlfriend home. Of the ninety to a hundred people who attended that night, about sixty to eighty retired from the club, leaving through the front door, this being a more convenient exit than cutting through the yard. The remaining twenty to thirty members stayed on and finished the night downstairs or in the upstairs lecture room singing or continuing the evening's discussion with their own take on the topic.[8]

Further south and moving at a lover's pace, Elizabeth and her young man, possibly a different man, strolled down Berner Street. Around a quarter to midnight, Marshall noticed the couple. They were in the street only three doors away, standing "opposite of No. 58." Elizabeth stood on the pavement as she and her young man talked. Even though the laborer had been standing outside for nearly a quarter of an hour, it was the couple's loitering and kissing that finally caught his attention.

"You would say anything but your prayers," overheard Marshall. Elizabeth laughed. The couple had stood there for about ten minutes before they decided to resume their stroll down Berner toward Boyd and Ellen Streets. Elizabeth's young man walked on her right side with his arm around her neck as he looked at her. They passed Marshall, taking no obvious notice of him. With the man's head turned and the nearest gas lamp twenty feet farther away at the corner, Marshall had no opportunity to get a clear view of the man's face, but he saw enough. The young man seemed to be middle-aged. He wore "a round cap, with a small peak. It was something like what a sailor would wear." He stood about five and half feet tall and was rather stout. The man was "decently dressed" in a black cutaway coat and dark trousers. From what he could tell, Marshall was sure the man "was in business, and did nothing like hard work.... He had more the appearance of a clerk." Yet, it was the man's voice that gave Marshall the idea of a clerk, for "he was mild speaking," and seemed to be educated. Because the man never directly faced Marshall, the laborer could not really tell if the man had any whiskers, but he did not think that he had any. The young man wore no gloves, but if the man carried anything in his hands, Marshall was not aware of it. Despite her small stature, the laborer saw the black bonnet worn by Elizabeth, and "she did not then have a flower in her breast." In a matter of seconds, all Marshall saw were their backs as they walked away, and he "did not take much notice whether she was carrying anything in her hands." The couple continued on, probably walking past Boyd Street. Marshall remained outside and by the time the pubs closed, he decided to return indoors.[9]

About ten minutes after PC Smith's patrol took him back through Berner Street, dock laborer James Brown arrived home at 35 Fairclough Street, which was near the intersection of Fairclough and Christian Streets. At around this time, William Wess, the club secretary, left the IWEC by the rear door. As he entered into the yard, he noticed lights in two second-story windows from the tenement. He traveled through Dutfield's Yard to the printing offices of *Der Arberter Fraint*, where he worked as a printer, and stayed only long enough to leave some literature. Retracing his steps back to the club, Wess noticed that the yard gates were open, but they "sometimes remain open," and that nothing unusual was going on. Once inside the club, Wess called for his brother, and they headed for home. Another member, Louis Stanley, quickly joined them. They left the club together through the front door, and upon coming out into Berner Street, where Wess noticed no one about, they headed to Fairclough Street and traveled east to make their way toward Grove Street. Stanley walked with the two brothers as far as James Street. There, Stanley said his farewells and parted from the brothers, who continued on to their home in William Street.[10]

Over the next fifteen minutes, Charles Letchford, a twenty-something Berner Street resident, walked through the neighborhood on his way home. He lived just five doors north from the club, where he grew up, and everything seemed to be "going on as usual." Joseph Lave was also in Berner Street around that time. A Russian who recently emigrated from the United States, Lave dwelt at the club and went out into Dutfield's Yard for some air, because he was "feeling oppressed by the smoke in the large room." After a few minutes, he "strolled into the street, which was very quiet at the time, and returned to the concert room without having encountered anything unusual."[11]

With his girlfriend safely home, Eagle returned to the club. He "came along by the small streets in this district, but noticed nothing unusual. There were a number of men and women about, as there always are about that time; but the streets were not more lively than usual," and he saw nothing suspicious. When he arrived back at the club, he found the front door closed. "It is customary for members of the club to go in by the side door to prevent knocking at the front." So he "passed through the gate on the left-hand side of the house to get in by the side door.... The gates were thrown wide back. In fact it is very seldom that they are closed." As soon as he entered the gateway, he could hear a friend of his singing in the upstairs room. He walked down the path, and accessed the building through the rear door, noticing nothing unusual or anything on the ground. As Eagle went back inside to join his friend in singing songs in Russian, Elizabeth and what seemed to be a younger man returned to the neighborhood.

By this time, between 12:30 and 12:35, PC Smith's patrol brought him back to Berner Street. As he plodded his way down the road, the constable noticed the couple easily enough, because there were "few about in the bye streets." They were standing by the Board School, across from Dutfield's Yard. PC Smith did not take much notice of the man, but believed that he stood about five feet seven inches, and had no whiskers. His cutaway coat was dark, as was the deerstalker he sported. He was of a respectable appearance for someone who was only twenty-eight years old. While the man was not making any overt gestures, he carried something that was readily noticed. Wrapped in a newspaper, the man had a parcel in his hand. This package was about eighteen inches long and six to eight inches broad. PC Smith noticed that Elizabeth "had a flower in her breast," as she stood on the pavement facing her young man. The added boost in height from the sidewalk made it easier for the five-foot-two Elizabeth to see into his face. The couple continued talking, as the constable patrolled past, but he could not overhear their conversation. Since they both seemed sober and were not causing an incident, PC Smith continued on with his patrol. Around this time Brown went back out for a late supper, heading to Henry Norris's, a local chandler shop that sat at the southwest corner of Berner and Fairclough Streets, across the road from The Nelson.[12]

About ten minutes after PC Smith last came into the neighborhood where he saw Elizabeth and her young man, a Hungarian immigrant by the name of Israel Schwartz turned onto Berner Street from Commercial Road. He was heading to his previous residence to see if his wife finished moving to their new lodgings at 22 Ellen Street off Back Church Lane. Not a moment passed when "he noticed some distance in front of him a man walking as if partially intoxicated." The half-tipsy man seemed to be about thirty. He was a broad shouldered chap, rather stoutly built, but only stood five feet five inches tall. Despite his light complexion, he had dark hair underneath a full face, which supported a small brown moustache. He was respectably dressed, wearing a dark jacket and trousers with a black peaked cap on his head. As Schwartz continued walking south down Berner Street, behind the man, he eventually noticed Elizabeth, "standing in the gateway."

Even though they were not walking together, it was a quarter to one when Schwartz and the inebriated man reached Dutfield's Yard. The "half-tipsy man halted and spoke to" Elizabeth. The half-tipsy man tried to pull her into the street, but Elizabeth refused. "Feeling rather timid of getting mixed up in quarrels," Schwartz started to cross over to the other side of the street, walking towards the Board School. The half-tipsy man put his hand on Elizabeth's shoulder and "turned her around," pushing "her back into the passage." Elizabeth fell upon the footway and "screamed three times, but not very loudly," for it did not even alert the neighboring club members or the patrolling PC Smith, all of whom should have been within an earshot of several loud screams. Schwartz "heard the sound of a quarrel, and turned back to learn what was the matter, but just as he stepped from the kerb," he saw another man standing in front of The Nelson, the corner beer house, lighting his clay pipe. This other person who appeared on the scene was taller than the half-tipsy man, perhaps nearly six feet in height, but not as stout. He seemed five years older and had a fresh complexion to go with his light brown hair and red moustache. This second man seemed to be of the same grade of society as the first, and wore a dark overcoat with an old black hard felt hat that had a wide brim. Upon catching the light from the match, the half-tipsy man quickly glanced to his left and saw the other man. Possibly thinking he was Jewish because of the club, the half-tipsy man called out "Lipski," an anti–Semitic insult, apparently to this man who stood only a few doors away. Wanting to leave the situation behind, Schwartz continued walking on, but soon found that this second man was following behind him. Without knowing the man's purpose, Schwartz "ran as far as the railway arch, but the other man did not follow so far."[13]

With her head turned towards the left, Elizabeth must have watched Schwartz and the second man leave the area, as she got up and dusted herself off. But drink had fueled a temper. Swiftly moving past Elizabeth's right side, the man probably grabbed her by the scarf. Pulling tight with his left hand, he promptly took her just inside the entrance behind the open gate. A confused Elizabeth would have been caught off guard. Without thinking of the commotion this might cause but being sufficiently concealed within the darkened confines of the yard, the man would have pivoted behind Elizabeth as he yanked her into him. With a knife brandished in his right hand, the man rashly, yet decidedly sliced her neck. It would have taken seconds. Quickly and quietly, he cut a gash in the left side of Elizabeth's throat. Astonishment would have come upon her as she reached on impulse and clutched the wound with her right hand, in reaction to the pain. Whether because his anger was vented or he was struck by a sudden realization, the man was done with her. While she fell onto her left side, he hurried out of the yard, leaving a dying Elizabeth to her fate. Even if she had wanted to, a severed windpipe kept her from yelling. She could only lie there, facing the wall of the club with her feet towards the street. Elizabeth's only chance for help would have been from the dozen or so members still inside the club. But no one heard a sound. No one stepped into the yard for a breather. Elizabeth curled up and slowly bled to death still clutching the cachous she held in her left hand, pastilles to sweeten the breath.

At the gateway, the killer would have been eager for a quiet exit. But he probably noticed a young couple moving slowly along in Fairclough Street opposite the Board School. Attracting attention was the last thing he wanted. The decision was obvious. He would have turned and headed north. He dared not run for fear of being conspicuous, so with a brisk pace, he made his getaway. He quickly moved along the pavement,

Contemporary impression of Elizabeth Stride meeting her killer (courtesy Evans/Skinner Crime Archive).

no doubt hoping that the neighbors were all bedded down for the night.[14]

Around this time, Brown left the chandler shop with his late-night meal. Being more hungry and tired than observant, he crossed through the intersection. He was in the road by the curb when he noticed the young couple. They were still standing by the Board School, that part which faces Fairclough Street. It was rather dark where they were, so Brown never got a clear look at them, but he could easily see that she had her back against the wall, leaning toward "her sweetheart." The man stood about five feet seven inches in height and faced the young woman with his arm against the wall. His long overcoat, which might have gone down to his heels, did not hide his apparent stoutish build, which might have been an average build. Brown never really noticed if the man wore any kind of hat or cap. Since he wanted to get home with his supper, Brown did not pay much attention to them, until he happened to have overheard something.

"No, not tonight, some other night," said the woman, obviously replying to what her boyfriend had asked.

Brown never heard what the man had said, but when the woman spoke, without any kind of detectable accent, Brown turned around and looked at the couple, but not for very long. He never saw any kind of flower and saw nothing light in color about either of them. They appeared sober, but they were not talking to him. With his curiosity satisfied, Brown continued on home so he could enjoy his supper.[15]

One of the neighboring residents was still awake, however. When the killer passed the house of Mrs. Fanny Mortimer, wife and mother of 36 Berner Street, his footsteps caught her attention. She and her family lived only two doors up from the club, and after hearing a "heavy measured tramp," of what she thought was a patrolling constable, Mortimer went to the door, but instead of "shooting the bolts," she stood in the open doorway. But it was too late. The killer had already managed to duck into a nearby, arched entrance for a covered footpath that stood beckoning barely three doors north of Mortimer, which led into Batty's Gardens. From there it was a quick jaunt into Back Church Lane. He escaped.[16]

~4~

The Aftermath

I t was nearly ten minutes to one, and Mortimer's attention was elsewhere. With a deserted street, Mortimer's eyes were soon drawn to the young couple standing by the Board School. Mortimer casually observed them for about five more minutes, when Leon Goldstein went past, walking "very fast down the street." He came from Commercial Road, having left a coffeehouse in Spectacle Alley a short time before. He might have been on his way home, since he lived at 22 Christian Street. Carrying a black bag filled with empty cigarette boxes, Goldstein looked up at the club as he passed. He soon disappeared onto Fairclough Street, as he rounded the corner by the Board School. Mortimer then returned inside and locked the door, preparing to retire to a bed that was in the front room on the ground floor.[1]

Shortly after, the young couple decided to move on, as a pony and cart pulled onto Berner Street. The small trap rounded the corner from Commercial Road and slowly made its way south. Thankful that the baker's clock near the corner said nearly one, instead of two, which occasionally happened, Louis Diemschütz guided his pony towards the IWEC. The Russian had only been the club steward for the past six months, but it was good arrangement, not only politically and religiously but also economically, since he and his wife lived there. And she herself took on the feminine role of looking after the club as its stewardess. But Diemschütz had other things on his mind — it had been a long day for the Russian and he was glad to see his home looming ever closer. He traveled in cheap jewelry (what today would be considered costume jewelry), and as was his custom, he had spent all day Saturday selling his trinkets and bobbles at the Westow Hill market, near Crystal Palace. It was fortunate he was in a position to have a pony and cart, unlike Packer who walked with his barrow. After the Great Exhibition of 1851, the Crystal Palace was relocated across the Thames to Upper Norwood, which was about five miles overland from Berner Street. Being only a few doors away from the club and still awake, Mortimer heard the club steward drive by and even mentioned it to her husband. Despite the unused stables within Dutfield's Yard near the printing office, Diemschütz maintained his pony in Cable Street, which lay beyond Ellen Street. Since he had no desire to trek back home with an armful of goods, he wanted to drop off his wares before bedding down his pony. The club sat squarely on his right; he was home even though his day was not over. The steward veered his trap toward the entrance of Dutfield's yard. Upon entering the gateway, his pony shied to the left. Diemschütz knew that his companion tended to "shy a little," but something was different this time. The pony "wanted to keep too much to the left side against the wall." Looking to see what was frightening his pony, the club steward bent his head forward and peered down into the yard. He noticed that there was "something unusual about the ground." It was not even. Perhaps it was a dust heap or possibly a mound of mud that had been swept up. He took his whip and with its handle, touched the heap. It was not mud. He got down from his cart and struck a match. "It was rather windy," and even a ha'penny candle would have been better, but he had "sufficient light to see that there was some figure there." From the dress, Louis Diemschütz knew it was the "figure of a woman." Not knowing whether the woman was drunk or dead, he ran inside the club and asked where his wife was. The stewardess had a weak constitution, and her husband "did not want to frighten her," because "anything of that kind shocks her." He did not have to look long, for she was sitting downstairs close to the side entrance in the kitchen which was to the back of the dining room, the front room on the ground floor.[2]

Seeing that his wife was okay, the relieved Diemschütz wanted another club member to go back with him to look at what he found in the yard. Standing nearby was a young Russian from Warsaw, Isaac Kozedbrodski. His comrades called him Isaacs, and he readily went along as the club steward asked. Out of curiosity, Mrs. Diemschütz followed her husband as far as the kitchen door. While they went outside to investigate, another member, Gilleman, who had overheard the news, ran up to the second story.

"There is a woman dead in the yard," he informed the others.

Within a moment, word of the discovery spread through the remaining members who were still at the club. The alarm was raised. Approaching the still body, Diemschütz and Kozebrodski "struck a match and saw blood running from the gate all the way down to the side door of the club." The woman "was lying on her left side two yards from the entrance, with her feet towards the street." The shaken Diemschütz thought the woman to be about twenty-seven or twenty-eight years old, maybe thirty. The now dead woman seemed to have a light complexion, despite the small amount of light in the yard. Her dark clothes appeared to be in perfect order, except for the black crepe bonnet, which had fallen from her head and came to rest nearby. Both hands were clenched. When the two club members saw that "her throat was fearfully cut," Kozebrodski immediately set out for help, going towards Grove Street. By this time, another club member, Jacobs, joined Diemschütz in the yard.[3]

After hearing the dreadful news from Gilleman, Eagle ran downstairs and out the kitchen door. He quickly went over to a panting Kozebrodski, who had already returned without success. The constables on fixed-point duty usually left at 1 A.M. (because of their shift, they are sometimes referred to as "night police"). Kozebrodski was left standing watch over the body. By the time he had reached Kozebrodski, Eagle had seen Diemschütz and Jacobs heading toward Fairclough Street to fetch the police. He had also noticed the body of the woman. She was "lying on the ground ... near the gates. Her feet were towards the gates, about six or seven feet from them. She was lying by the side of and facing the club wall." He struck a match for a better look. The woman was lying in a pool of blood. Upon seeing that much blood, Eagle "got very excited," and without hesitation, he, along with Kozebrodski, ran for the police in the opposite direction, heading toward Commercial Road. By this time, Krantz had learned of the body and also went for help.[4]

The cries of "murder" and "police" rang throughout the streets, catching the attention of nearby residents. Brown had nearly finished his supper when he heard the screams. He opened his window, but he did not see anyone, let alone the people who were yelling. Not far away, however, at the northwest corner of Christian and Fairclough Streets, stood a horse-keeper, Edward Spooner, and his young woman. The couple had previously been at a public house in Commercial Road before finishing off the night at the beer retailer, The Beehive. Spooner saw Diemschütz and Jacobs go running along, calling out. As the two came into view, Brown and Spooner watched them run past, heading towards Grove Street. Without seeing a constable, the two club members turned around and came back. Brown continued watching from his window. Curious as to why these two men had been running, Spooner stopped them.

"What was the matter?" asked the horse-keeper of the exhausted men.

"A woman had been murdered," they gasped out through their panting.

Watching the exchange, Brown thought the two club members were talking with a policeman. With the horrible news of this latest deed, Spooner took off for Berner Street with Jacobs and Diemschütz following right behind him.[5]

Eagle and Kozebrodski had raced up the street for help. Mortimer heard the "commotion outside, and immediately ran out, thinking that there was another row at the Socialists' Club close by." Letchford "heard the commotion when the body was found," and eventually "heard the policemen's whistles," but he "did not take any notice of the matter, as disturbances are very frequent at the club." He "thought it was only another row." Abraham Heahbury, who lived only six doors north of the club at No. 28, eventually "heard a policeman's whistle blown, and came down to see what was the matter." Nearly a block away, even Marshall heard the cries and screams. But Barnett Kentorrich, living right next door to the club, must have been in a very deep sleep, for he heard nothing until hours later.[6]

Mortimer soon arrived after Spooner, Jacobs, and Diemschütz. Only a few men stood inside the gateway, but fifteen people had already collected in the yard, merely standing around the body, for no one dared touch it. She was "informed that another dreadful murder had been committed in the yard adjoining the clubhouse." Upon entering the yard, she "saw the body of a woman lying huddled up just inside the gates with her throat cut from ear to ear." She was "lying slightly on one side, with the legs a little drawn up as if in pain, the clothes being slightly disarranged, so that the legs were partly visible ... and in her hand were found a bunch of grapes and some sweets," or sweetmeats, which were also called cachous. Spooner could see the woman, but he crouched down to see her face, which was turned towards the club wall. Someone lit a match, and Spooner put his hand under her chin, which had no blood on it. It was slightly warm. He did not touch any other part of the body and was sure that he did not alter the position of her head. Blood was still flowing from her throat, and he "noticed that she had a piece of paper doubled up in her right hand, and some red and white flowers pinned on her breast." Because "the onlookers seemed afraid to go near and touch the body," for "as a rule, Jews do not care to touch dead bodies," Spooner kept watch over the dead woman until the police arrived.[7]

Police Constable Henry Lamb was patrolling west down Commercial Road. (Even though part of PC Smith's patrol took him through Commercial Road, it is common to have patrols overlap.) Having recently passed Christian Street, heading toward Batty Street, PC Lamb saw two men running towards him. As the Constable approached them, they must have seen him as well.

"Come on, there has been another murder," called out the two frantic club members.

Reserve Police Constable Albert Collins was ending his fixed-point duty between Grove Street and Christian Street in Commercial Road when Eagle and Kozebrodski told PC Lamb about the murder, and he quickly joined the three men. PC Lamb asked where the body was, and the two club members had the policemen follow them. Whistles were blown to alert the other constables in the area. Upon reaching the corner of Berner Street, the men paused, but only for an instant.

"There," said one of the panting members, pointing down the road.

PC Lamb could already see people moving about in the distance. With whistles blowing, PC Lamb ran down the street and was soon accompanied by another constable, 426H.[8]

When PC Lamb arrived at the gateway, "there were about thirty people in the yard, and others followed" him in. One was Heahbury, and when he viewed the body he saw "a short dark young woman lying on the ground with a gash between four and five inches long in her throat." Quickly noticing that part of the yard which held everyone's attention the constable "observed something dark lying on the ground on the right-hand side." He turned on his light for a better look and "found that the object was a woman, with her throat cut and apparently dead." PC Lamb then sent Constable 426H for the nearest doctor, and Eagle, who was standing nearby, was "dispatched to the police station to inform the inspector what had occurred." Despite being tired, Eagle was probably glad to have the assignment for he did not have to see any more of the blood. While heading back up Berner Street might have seemed a natural course to take, apparently Eagle made straight away for the Lemen Street Police Station by going onto Fairclough Street then up Back Church Lane. "No one was nearer than a yard to the body," when PC Lamb approached it, but as he began to examine the "deceased the crowd gathered round." He "begged them to keep back, otherwise they might have their clothes soiled with blood, and thus get into trouble." PC Lamb put his hand to her face, and it felt slightly warm. Checking her wrist for a pulse, he "could not discern any movement." The dead woman "was lying on her left side, with her left hand on the ground." There was nothing obvious in her hand. Her right arm lay across her breast, and "her face was not more than five or six inches away from the club wall." Her feet extended just to the swing of the gate, so that "the barrier could be closed without disturbing the body." Her clothes were not disturbed and only the soles of her boots were visible. "There were no signs of a struggle." Some of the blood was still in a liquid state, and had "run towards the kitchen door of the club. A little — that nearest to her on the ground — was slightly congealed." He was not able to tell if any blood was still flowing from her throat.[9]

About 176 yards from the scene, at the eastern corner of Commercial Road and Batty Street, Mr. Edward Johnston, the assistant to Drs. Kaye and Blackwell, was abruptly woken by Constable 426H and informed of the murder. As Johnston hurried to dress, the constable then quickly notified the physician and surgeon, Dr. William P. Blackwell, who also lived at 100 Commercial Road. It was ten after one. With Johnston dressed and the doctor getting ready, the assistant and the constable took off for Dutfield's.[10]

Unaware of what had happened, PC Smith came back into Berner Street during the normal course of his patrol. (Based on his patrol route and timing, PC Smith was possibly near the corner of Grove Street and Fairclough Street when PC Lamb learned of the murder. This explains why PC Smith did not hear the whistles or shouts. By coincidence, the course of his patrol apparently had him situated at a street corner that was diagonally opposite from the action.) But it did not take long for the unaware constable to notice a crowd standing outside the gateway. He hurried to the area, noticing no one passing him as he went. Already on the scene were two constables, RPC Collins and another who arrived after PC Lamb examined the body. The "gates at the side of the club were not then closed." Seeing that the woman was dead, he "went to the police-station for the ambulance, leaving the other constables in charge of the body." Mr. Johnston and Constable 426H arrived just as he was leaving.[11]

Spooner and PC Lamb closed the outer gates as Johnston entered the yard. The assistant saw the body of a woman lying on her left side. Her bonnet lay three or four inches from her head on the ground. With the aid of a constable's lantern, he performed a cursory exam. He easily found the incision on the throat and noticed that it had stopped bleeding. He undid the top button of her dress to feel the warmth of the chest. The body was "all warm except the hands, which were quite cold." There was a clotted stream of blood that ran down to the gutter. Because "it had all run away," there was very little blood near the neck. "The left arm was bent, away from the body. The right arm was also bent, and across the body." Only a moment or two behind Johnston, Dr. Blackwell checked his watch, as he was let into the yard. It was 1:16. Mr. Johnston made way for his superior, and with the aide of a constable's lantern, Dr. Blackwell began his examination of the body. Inspector Charles Pinhorn of the Leman Street Police Station soon entered the scene and took charge of the situation. PC Lamb already had a constable posted outside the gateway, to prevent people from entering or leaving. Meanwhile, Dr. Phillips was woken at his home, 2 Spital Square, Spitalfields, and summoned to the Leman Street Police Station, and Inspector Edmund John James Reid, head of the local CID, received a telegram about the discovered body.[12]

During the course of his examination, two of the things Dr. Blackwell had a close look at were Elizabeth's hands. Her "right hand was open and on the chest," and her left hand, which was nearly open held a "packet [that] was lodged between the thumb and the first finger, and was partially hidden from view." His impression was that the left hand "gradually relaxed while the woman was dying, she dying in a fainting condition from the loss of blood." When he removed the packet, some of the cachous spilled on the ground. Some of the onlookers saw something else, however. When Dr. Blackwell opened the hands, Diemschütz "saw that she had been holding grapes in one hand and sweetmeats in the other." Kozebrodski also got a better look. He "noticed that she had some grapes in her right hand and some sweets in her left," and saw a "little bunch of flowers stuck above her right bosom." While the examination continued, Diemschütz and Heahbury struck up a conversation, and the club steward mentioned that "he thought it was his wife at first, but when he found her safe at home he got a candle and found this woman." PC Lamb then proceeded to inspect the hands and clothes of the fifteen to twenty club members, who were inside on the ground floor. Afterwards, he "went over the cottages, the occupants of which were in bed." PC Lamb was "admitted by men, who came down partly dressed; all the other people were undressed. As to the water closets in the yard, one was locked and the other unlocked, but no one was there." He also "examined the store belonging to Messrs. Hindley, sack manufacturers."[13]

While PC Lamb continued his perfunctory investigation, Chief Inspector John West, the acting superintendent for H Division during Superintendent Arnold's absence, had arrived, and Dr. Blackwell finished his examination. Elizabeth was lying on her left side, obliquely across the passage. Her head rested beyond the carriage wheel rut with her neck lying over the rut. Her face was looking towards the right wall, at the club, as viewed from the gateway. Her legs were drawn up, and her feet were close against the wall of the right side of the passage. Her feet were three yards from the gateway. Her dress was unfastened at the neck, which was done by Mr. Johnston. The neck and chest were quite warm, as were her legs. Her face was slightly warm, and her hands were cold. Her right hand was open and lay on her chest and was smeared with blood. Her left hand held some cachous that were wrapped in tissue paper. There were neither rings nor marks of rings on either of her hands. Her face appeared to be quite placid, and her mouth was slightly open. Around her neck, she wore a check silk scarf, the bow of which was turned to her left and had been pulled very tight. Corresponding exactly with the lower border of the scarf, there was a long incision in the neck. The border of the scarf was slightly frayed, not from wear and tear, but as if by a sharp knife. The incision in the neck started on her left side, two inches below the angle of the jaw, and almost in a direct line with it. The wound nearly severed the vessels on that side, cutting the windpipe completely in two. The incision terminated on the opposite side, one inch below the angle of the right jaw, but without severing the vessels on that side. Dr. Blackwell could not ascertain whether or not the bloody hand had been moved. The blood was running down the gutter into the drain in the opposite direction from the feet, but there was about one pound of clotted blood close by the body, and a stream of blood ran all the way from there to the back door of the club. "Taking all the facts into consideration, more especially the absence of any instrument in the hand, it was impossible to have been a suicide."[14]

Having been sent directly to the scene once he arrived at the Leman Street Police Station, Dr. Phillips arrived at Dutfield's sometime between 1:36 and 1:46 that morning. He was beginning his examination when Inspector Reid arrived upon the scene, followed shortly by Superintendent Thomas Arnold, head of H Division. PC Lamb returned from his inspection of the area and saw the divisional surgeon viewing the deceased; details were recorded by Inspector Pinhorn. Elizabeth was lying on her left side with her face turned towards the wall. Her head pointed into the yard and her feet toward the street. The left arm was extended from the elbow. A packet of cachous had been in her left hand with others that Dr. Blackwell had spilt lying in the gutter. The right arm was lying over the body, and the back of her hand and wrist had clotted blood on them. Her legs were drawn up with her feet close to the wall. Her body was still warm, as was her face. Her legs were quite warm, but her hands were cold. The silk neckerchief she wore seemed to be slightly torn, which corresponded to the right angle of the jaw. The throat had a deep gash, which ran from Elizabeth's left to right. It was a clean-cut incision six inches in length, starting two and a half inches in a straight line below the angle of the jaw. The left carotid artery was severed. The wound trailed off about two inches below the right angle of the jaw and the damage to the tissues was more superficial. It was "evident that the haemorrhage which produced death was caused through the partial severance of the left carotid artery." Also, there was an abrasion of the skin under the right clavicle, about an inch and a quarter in diameter.[15]

While Dr. Phillips examined Elizabeth's lifeless body, another grisly discovery was being made. Police Constable Edward Watkins of the City of London Police was on patrol within London proper. During the normal course of his route, he came up Mitre Street and entered Mitre Square. Located just northwest of Aldgate High Street, Mitre Square consisted of businesses and residential housing. It had two main entrances: Mitre Street from the southwest and Duke Street from the northeast by a passageway. Flashing his lantern for a proper look, as he had fifteen minutes earlier, PC Watkins saw nothing unusual. Everything was quiet, until he turned to the right. There in the southwest corner lay Catherine Eddowes — horribly mutilated. She also used the names Kate Conway and Kate Kelly, from her alleged husband and boyfriend of the last seven years, respectively. She is the fourth canonical victim of Jack the Ripper and the second of the double-event. She is also the only canonical victim to die within the actual City of London. She died from blood loss due to a slit throat with the other injuries being post-mortem.[16]

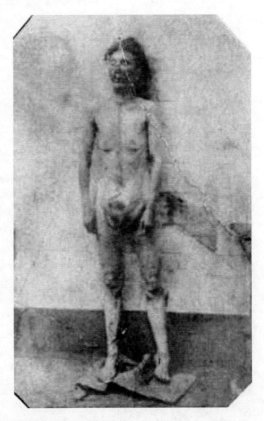

Back in Berner Street, the police were making a thorough search of the yard and houses, "but no trace could be found of any person who might have committed the murder. As soon as the search was over the whole of the persons who had come into the yard and the members of the club were interrogated, their names and addresses taken, their pockets searched by the police, and their clothes and hands examined by the doctors. The people were twenty-eight in number. Each was dealt with separately, and they properly accounted for themselves.

Mortuary photograph of Catharine Eddowes (courtesy Evans/Skinner Crime Archive).

The houses were inspected a second time and the occupants examined and their rooms searched. A loft close by was searched, but no trace could be found of the murderer. A description was taken of the body, and circulated by wire around the stations. Inquiries were made at the different houses in the street, but no person could be found who had heard screams or disturbance during the night." Inspector Reid personally "examined the wall near where the body was found, but could detect no spots of blood." This included a recess by the dustbin. During his previous search, PC Lamb did not recall looking over the wooden partition, but he and Dr. Phillips investigated it together.[17]

Despite the noise and commotion over the past two hours, it was not until three o'clock, when several people were talking loudly outside his door, that Kentorrich woke up. His curiosity got the better of him, and he went outside, to see what was going on. He learned of the murder and went back inside. He was probably not surprised to learn what had happened, considering he did not think the yard had "a very good character at night." Especially since he knew "that the gate is not kept fastened."[18]

"The fact that another murder had been committed soon became known in the neighbourhood, and long before daybreak the usually quiet thoroughfare was the scene of great excitement. Extra police had to be posted right along the street, and even with this precaution, locomotion from an early hour was a matter of extreme difficulty." "Thousands of people of all classes flocked to Berner-street, but they were able to see little to gratify their curiosity. The double doors of the court yard were closed, and the approaches guarded by a dozen constables under the charge of an inspector...." "Luckily there was an outlet at either end of this street, so the pent-up feelings of the jostled and the jostlers had time only for vent in an occasional paliasage at arms before the 'move on' tactics of the police began to take effect. No one could say there were not enough police in the East-end to-day."[19]

Approximately four hours after Elizabeth's fatal assault, her body could finally be moved for an autopsy and identification. It was taken about a half mile overland to St. George's-in-the-East mortuary, which was situated near St. George's-in-the-East Church, in the public gardens, just off Ratcliff Street, St. George Street. PC Lamb, who was helping to move the body, was called back to the yard. A large crowd followed the conveyance, and "here again it was found necessary to take unusual precautions to keep back the crowd." About fifteen minutes later, the search of the area was abandoned, along with the investigation of the club members and the onlookers in the yard, with each one having given his name and address and signed a written statement. PC Lamb finally left the murder scene by the break of dawn, 5:26 A.M., leaving RPC Collins the unenviable task of washing the blood away from the scene. This was common, even though the press had made some criticism of the practice.[20]

The initial search may have been abandoned, but the police were not idle that Sunday. In the morning, Inspector Frederick George Abberline, the officer in charge of the case on the ground, ordered a house-to-house search of the neighborhood. Inspector Reid returned to the yard and saw that the blood had already been removed. He conducted a thorough search of the walls, but found nothing to indicate that someone had climbed over them. Afterwards, he went to the mortuary and wrote down a description of Elizabeth, which was circulated. He estimated her age as forty-two years. She was a relatively short woman, standing only five feet two inches. Her complexion was pale, and she had dark brown curly hair. He raised an eyelid, and found that her eyes were light grey in color. Parting her lips, Inspector Reid found that Elizabeth had lost her front upper teeth. She wore an old black skirt and an old black jacket that was trimmed with fur. She wore a "dark-brown velvet body [bodice]." Attached on the right side of her jacket was a small bunch of flowers, which consisted of a red rose, backed by maiden-hair fern. She had two light serge petticoats, white stockings, and a white chemise that had an insertion in front. Her boots were of the side-spring variety, and she had a black crepe bonnet. In her jacket pocket, Inspector Reid found two pocket-handkerchiefs, a thimble, and a piece of wool on a card.[21]

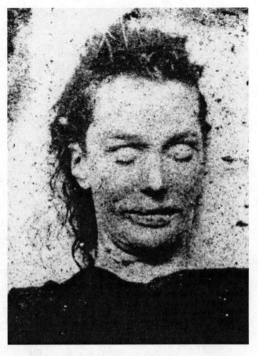

Mortuary photograph of Elizabeth Stride (courtesy Evans/Skinner Crime Archive).

Investigation of the immediate neighborhood resulted in several witnesses who testified at the inquest. But not everyone who spoke to police or reporters was called to give evidence at the Coroner's Court. Among the police who were questioning local citizens was Sergeant Stephen White of H Division, CID. By 9 A.M., the thirty-something sergeant knocked upon the door of Matthew Packer, the elderly greengrocer.

When did you close up shop? quizzed the sergeant.

"Half past twelve, in consequence of the rain it was no good for me to keep open," replied the fruiterer.

Did you see a man or woman go into Dutfield's Yard or stand about the street when you closed up shop? inquired Sergeant White.

"I saw no one standing about neither did I see anyone go up the yard. I never saw anything suspicious or heard the slightest noise. And knew nothing about the murder until I heard of it this morning," came the retort.

With Packer closing up shop and retiring to bed before the murder, the questioning was short. Sergeant White then interviewed the other members of the household: Mrs. Packer, Harry Douglas, and Sarah Harrison. But none of them could shed light on what had happened. Apparently like another neighbor, Kentorrich, Packer and his household must have been deep sleepers despite the commotion that had gone on for the previous eight hours.[22]

Every effort was being made to apprehend the killer. The police conducted house-to-house interviews, rapping their knuckles on more than eighty neighborhood doors that morning just in Berner Street alone, in an effort to find out what the residents saw, heard, or thought they knew. They also knocked on doors in Fairclough Street. The result of this afforded the authorities some success in producing witnesses who testified at the inquest, like Marshall and Brown. And while not everyone testified at the inquest, those who did not appear in court gladly told reporters what they thought.[23]

Mrs. Mortimer informed the *Daily News* reporter what she saw, expressing her views as to how the killer escaped.

> I was standing at the door of my house nearly the whole time between half-past twelve and one o'clock this (Sunday) morning, and did not notice anything unusual. I had just gone indoors, and was preparing to go to bed, when I heard a commotion outside, and immediately ran out, thinking that there was another row at the Socialists' Club close by. I went to see what was the matter, and was informed that another dreadful murder had been committed in the yard adjoining the clubhouse, and on going inside I saw the body of a woman lying huddled up just inside the gates with her throat cut from ear to ear. A man [Spooner] touched her face, and said it was quite warm, so that the deed must have been done while I was standing at the door of my house. There was certainly no noise made, and I did not observe anyone enter the gates. It was just after one o'clock when I went out, and the only man whom I had seen pass through the street previously was a young man [Goldstein] carrying a black shiny bag, who walked very fast down the street from the Commercial-road. He looked up at the club, and then went round the corner by the Board School. I was told that the manager or steward of the club [Diemshütz] had discovered the woman on his return home in his pony cart. He drove through the gates, and my opinion is that he interrupted the murderer, who must have made his escape immediately under cover of the cart. If a man had come out of the yard before one o'clock I must have seen him. It was almost incredible to me that the thing could have been done without the steward's wife hearing a noise, for she was sitting in the kitchen from which a window opens four yards from the spot where the woman was found. The body was lying slightly on one side, with the legs a little drawn up as if in pain, the clothes being slightly disarranged, so that the legs were partly visible. The woman appeared to me to be respectable, judging by her clothes, and in her hand were found a bunch of grapes and some sweets. A young man and his sweetheart were standing at the corner of the street, about 20 yards away, before and after the time the woman must have been murdered, but they told me they did not hear a sound.[24]

However, others added to Mortimer's story in their own retelling of what they knew. According to the *Evening News*, Charles Letchford stated:

> I passed through the street at half-past 12 and everything seemed to me to be going on as usual, and my sister was standing at the door at ten minutes to one,

but did not see any one pass by. I heard the commotion when the body was found, and heard the policeman's whistles, but did not take any notice of the matter, as disturbances are very frequent at the club, and I thought it was only another row.

Possibly talking to the same reporter as Letchford, the young girl of the couple, who was seen by Mortimer, said that she had been "standing in a bisecting thoroughfare [junction of Berner and Fairclough] not fifty yards from the spot where the body was found" when the alarm was raised. According to her, she had been "standing there for about twenty minutes, talking with her sweetheart, but neither of them heard any unusual noises." She then went on to describe what Mrs. Mortimer had apparently told her.

A woman [Mortimer] who lives two doors from the club has made an important statement. It appears that shortly before a quarter to one o'clock she heard the measured, heavy tramp of a policeman passing the house on his beat. Immediately afterwards she went to the street-door, with the intention of shooting the bolts, though she remained standing there ten minutes before she did so. During the ten minutes she saw no one enter or leave the neighbouring yard, and she feels sure that had any one done so she could not have overlooked the fact. The quiet and deserted character of the street appears even to have struck her at the time. Locking the door, she prepared to retire to bed, in the front room on the ground floor, and it so happened that in about four minutes' time she heard Diemschitz's [sic] pony cart pass the house, and remarked upon the circumstance to her husband."[25]

Being the man who discovered the body, Diemschütz was readily sought out by the media, and he had this to say.

I should think the woman was about 27 or 28 years old. She was of light complexion. (This turns out to be an incorrect description, but the man appears to have been too frightened to make a careful examination.) It seemed to me that her clothes were in perfect order. I could see that her throat was fearfully cut. She had dark clothes on, and wore a black crape bonnet. Her hands were clenched, and when the doctor opened them I saw that she had been holding grapes in one hand and sweetmeats in the other. I could not say whether or not she was an unfortunate, but if she was I should judge her to be of a rather better class than the women we usually see about this neighbourhood.

For the *East Morning Advertiser*, Diemschütz added that Elizabeth was "a little better dressed, I should say, then the woman who was last murdered ... I had never seen her before."[26]

The media took every opportunity to interview other residents and neighbors following the body's removal. Barnett Kentorrich, who knew nothing until he was finally woken by the noise at three in the morning. Abraham Heahbury, who commented that Diemshütz remarked he thought the body was his wife. Jospeh Lave, who said he was outside either in the yard or in the street between 12:30 and 12:40. One unknown neighborhood wife, who lived just opposite the scene, told a *Star* reporter that "she was waiting up for her husband and listening for his coming, and she heard nothing to arouse her suspicion."

Some gave interviews in addition to testifying at the inquest. Krantz stated that had there been any noise he would have heard it, but he heard nothing until Diemschütz came into the yard. Wess had seen that "the gates were open, and thought about closing them," but he remembered that the steward was out with his cart, so he "left them open to allow him to come in easily." Eagle stated that "I frequent this club, and I was passing into it so late as twenty minutes to one this [Sunday] morning, which was just twenty minutes before the body was discovered. I had been there earlier in the evening, but left about twelve o'clock, in order to take home my young lady... When I got back to the club ... there was some singing, and after I had been in 20 minutes a man came in and said something about a woman being in the yard." And some people who testified never seemed to have caught the media's attention, like Michael Kidney.[27]

Some of the authorities were also questioned for the papers' readers. The first doctor called to the scene was tracked down and he found enough time to give an interview. According to the *Morning Advertiser*, Dr. Blackwell had this to say about the horrible discovery:

> About ten minutes past one he was called by a policeman to 40 Berner street, where he found the body of the murdered woman. Her head had been almost severed from her body. The body was perfectly warm, and life could not have been extinct more than 20 minutes. It did not appear to him that the woman was Jewess. She was more like an Irish woman. He roughly examined her, and found no other injuries; but this he could not definitely state until he had made a further examination. The deceased had on a black velvet jacket and a black dress; in her hand she held a box of cachous, whilst pinned in her dress was a flower. Altogether, judging from her appearance, he considered that she belonged to the "unfortunate" class. He had no doubt that the same man committed both murders. In his opinion the man is a maniac, but one at least accustomed to use a heavy knife. His belief was that as the woman held the sweets in her left hand her head was dragged back by means of a silk handkerchief, which she wore round her neck, and that her throat was then cut. One of the woman's hands was smeared with blood, and this was evidently done in the struggle. He had, however, no doubt that the woman's windpipe being completely cut through, she was thus rendered unable to make any sound. Dr. Blackwell added that it did not follow that the murderer would be bespattered with blood, for as he was sufficiently cunning in other things, he could contrive to avoid coming in contact with the blood by reaching well forward. The authorities at Leman street police street are very reticent, and stated, in reply to any inquiry late last evening, that they had no further information to impart. It is pretty certain, however, that the murdered woman has been identified.[28]

The staff at the lodging house where Elizabeth lived the several days before her death was also interviewed. Thomas Bates, the night watchman, knew Elizabeth for five or six years, but only by the nickname, "Long Liz." He knew she was Swedish and worked as a charwoman. Elizabeth was a "clean and hardworking woman ... and it was only when driven to extremities that she walked the streets." He was sure that Elizabeth returned to the lodging house on Tuesday, September 25, and he saw her leave Saturday night around seven o'clock. "The fact of her not returning that night was not taken any particular notice of." But when lodging house residents heard rumors of another murder, they became apprehensive. The watchman had been affected by the tragic news and by his retelling of what he knew.

"Lor' bless you," he told the reporter, "when she could get no work she had to do the best she could for her living, but a neater and a cleaner woman never lived."

A bedmaker and fellow lodger, Mrs. Ann Mill, agreed with Bates. "A better hearted, more good natured cleaner woman never lived," she said.[29]

"Files of people were allowed to pass through the mortuary," including occupants of the 32 Flower and Dean Street lodging house. Among the other people and witnesses who were taken to the mortuary to identify the lifeless body was a John Arundell, apparently a fellow lodger, based on accounts. Of those who recognized the body, nearly all said the now dead woman was called "Long Liz." Except for one — Charles Preston. The barber and fellow lodging house resident said she was Elizabeth Stride, and that she had always given him to understand that that was her name. Arguably, Preston was the first known person to identify her correctly. And yet, ironically, he did not let her borrow his clothes brush. More importantly, however, the police and the press no longer had a nameless victim.[30]

Some reporters even caught up with those who viewed the body at the mortuary, and they had "their suspicions raised on Saturday night by the conduct of a man and a woman in Settles-street, Commercial Road." These men were the two laborers and friends, J. Best and John Gardner.

What can you tell our readers, Mr. Best? inquired the *Evening News* reporter.

"I had been to the mortuary, and am almost certain the woman there is the one we saw at the Bricklayers' Arms. She is the same slight woman, and seems the same height. The face looks the same, but a little paler, and the bridge of the nose does not look so prominent," began Best.

The laborer continued. "I was in the Bricklayers' Arms, Settles-street, about two hundred yards from the scene of the murder on Saturday night, shortly before eleven, and saw a man and woman in the doorway. They had been served in the public house, and went out when me and my friends came in. It was raining very fast, and they did not appear willing to go out. He was hugging her and kissing her, and as he seemed a respectably dressed man, we were rather astonished at the way he was going on with the woman, who was poorly dressed. We 'chipped' him, but he paid no attention. As he stood in the doorway he always threw sidelong glances into the bar, but would look nobody in the face. I said to him, 'Why don't you bring the woman in and treat her?' but he made no answer. If he had been a straight fellow he would have told us to mind our own business, or he would have gone away. I was so certain that there was something up that I would have charged him if I could have seen a policeman. When the man could not stand the chaffing any longer he and the woman went off like a shot soon after eleven.

"I should know the man again amongst a hundred," concluded Best. "The man was no foreigner; he was an Englishman right enough."

Would you like to add anything, Mr. Gardner? prompted the reporter.

But Gardner had apparently spoken to the reporter earlier and seemed a bit annoyed by the additional questions.

"Before I got to the mortuary to-day (Sunday) I told you the woman had a flower in her jacket, and that she had a short jacket. Well, I have been to the mortuary, and there she was with the dahlias on the right side of her jacket. I could swear she is the same woman I saw at the Bricklayers' Arms, and she has the same smile on her face now that she had then."[31]

That evening Israel Schwartz presented himself to the Leman Street Police Station. Having heard news of the murder, he wanted to inform the police, through an interpreter, what he had seen.

Israel Schwartz of 22 Helen Street, Backchurch Lane stated that at that hour [12:45 A.M.], turning into Berner Street from Commercial Road, and having gotten as far as the gateway where the murder was committed, he saw a man stop and speak to a woman, who was standing in the gateway. He tried to pull the woman into the street, but he turned her round and threw her down on the footway and the woman screamed three times, but not very loudly. On crossing to the opposite side of the street, he saw a second man lighting his pipe. The man who threw the woman down called out, apparently to the man on the opposite side of the road, "Lipski," and then Schwartz walked away, but finding that he was followed by the second man, he ran as far as the railway arch, but the man did not follow so far. Schwartz cannot say whether the two men were together or known to each other. Upon being taken to the mortuary Schwartz identified the body as that of the woman he had seen.

Schwartz described the first man as about 30 years old, standing 5ft-5in tall, fair complexion, dark hair with a small brown moustache. He had a full face with broad shoulders. He had nothing in his hands, but wore a dark jacket and trousers and a black cap with a peak.

Schwartz then described the second man as 35 years old, standing 5ft-11in tall, fresh complexion with light brown hair. He wore a dark overcoat and an old black hard felt hat with a wide brim. This man had a clay pipe in his hand.[32]

Later on, a "well-known character" called "One-armed Liz" who lived in a common lodging house in Flower and Dean Street was taken to the mortuary by Sergeant Thick. She was an alleged friend of Elizabeth's, and described the deceased as "an unfortunate, living in a common lodging house in the neighbourhood of Flower and Dean street." Despite whatever friendship the two women had, "One-armed Liz," who might have been Elizabeth Burns, did not know the name of the Berner Street victim either, saying she was "Wally Warden" or "Annie Morris." However, she refused to say anything more to the reporter, adding "she had been instructed to keep the matter to herself." While "Liz" identified the body with a completely different name, she was not the only one. At some point between nine and ten that night, another person came to view the body from Berner Street. Her name was Mrs. Mary Malcolm. She lived at 50 Eagle Street, Red Lion Square, and has been described as the "sister from Holborn." She believed the corpse lying in the mortuary was that of her sister, but she had some doubts and was unable to give a good identification.[33]

⌒5⌒

He Saw Liz

Early Monday morning just past midnight, Thomas Coram, a "boy" who worked for a coconut dealer, was walking along Whitechapel Road toward Aldgate. He recently left a friend's house in Brady Street and was heading home. As he was passing near a laundry owned by a Mr. Christmas, at 253 Whitechapel Road, he saw something on the bottom of the two steps that led up to the front door. It was already half-past twelve when Police Constable Joseph William Drage noticed Coram "stooping down to pick up something about twenty yards" away. The object turned out to be a knife with a hand-kerchief tied around it. Seeing what it was, the boy dared not touch it, but readily called to the constable, who was on fixed-point duty.

"Policeman, there is a knife lying here... I was just looking around, and I saw something white."

The young Coram was sober but seemed disturbed by the knife's presence. It appeared to be a foot-long baker's knife. It was a broad blade, about an inch, "flat at the top" and was "discoloured" with what seemed to be blood. The folded handkerchief was tied around the three inch long black handle that was strongly riveted to the blade.

"We hear of such funny things nowadays," commented the young lad, obviously referring to the recent series of killings.

The knife's appearance undoubtedly "created some sensation," since its discovery was not generally known. The constable and lad took the knife to the Leman Street Police Station, so Dr. Phillips could examine it.[1]

With candles and gas lamps burning through the night, the editors took control. Armed with the stories hammered out by exhausted reporters, it did not take long for the media to connect the dots. By dawn, the printing presses were running hard, and London woke to the breaking story of a double-event that horrified two neighborhoods.

According to the *Evening News*:

The East-end fiend is still abroad and two other victims have become his prey. On Sunday morning a woman was found with her throat cut and her body partially mutilated in a court in Berner-street, Whitechapel, close by the International Club situated in that locality. The discovery seems to have been made at one in the morning by Lewis Diemschitz, the steward of the club. Another member of the club, Mr. Morris Eagle, had passed through the court at twenty minutes to one, and had not seen anything unusual near the premises. Even if it was too dark to see the body of this woman it is impossible to suppose that Morris Eagle would not have tripped over it had it been there when he went into the club. The inference is therefore this: if the woman was murdered and mutilated where she was found, the deed was done in the short period of twenty minutes — the deed was done in the time which the police surgeon said a medical expert would take to do it. The residents in the court know nothing about the murder. Neither they nor the people in the club heard or had seen anything that led them to suspect that foul play was going on around them. About three-quarters of an hour after this corpse was found, another was discovered in Mitre-square, Aldgate. It was that of a woman with her throat cut, but in her case the inevitable abdominal mutilation had been accomplished. A watchman was on duty in a counting-house in the square at the time the assassin was operating. Firemen were also on duty at a station close by. Yet nobody heard or saw anything likely to rouse suspicion. The silence and secrecy in which the atrocities were perpetrated wrap them in an impenetrable veil of mystery for the moment. As in former cases the murderer seems to have been almost miraculously successful in securing his retreat. His success in this respect seems to indicate a wonderful power of combination and organisation — an amazing gift for calculating the chances against the success of his schemes or purposes. In fact, the similarity of the murders leads to the conclusion that they have been committed by the one man or the one gang. The worst of it is that we do not know what a 'gang' may mean. It might mean an organisation of great extent, or only the partnership between a criminal and his 'pal.' Recent events seem to suggest that there is more than one individual in the horrid business.[2]

And according to the *Daily News*:

Two dreadful murders were committed yesterday morning in or near the East-end. In one case a woman was found in a yard in Berner-street, Commercial-road, with her head nearly severed from her body. In the other case, a woman was found in Mitre-square, Aldgate, within the City jurisdiction, with her throat cut from ear to ear, and the body mutilated in a way that reproduced the worst features of the murder of Annie Chapman. Both the victims were women of low life.[3]

The *Star*'s account ran thus:

WHAT WE THINK.

THE terror of Whitechapel has walked again, and this time has marked down two victims, one hacked and disfigured beyond discovery, the other with her throat cut and torn. Again he has got away clear; and again the police, with wonderful frankness, confess that they have not a clue. They are waiting for a seventh and an eighth murder, just as they waited for a fifth, to help them to it.

Meanwhile, Whitechapel is half mad with fear. The people are afraid even to talk with a stranger. Notwithstanding the repeated proofs that the murderer has but one aim, and seeks but one class in the community, the spirit of terror has got fairly abroad, and no one knows what steps a practically defenceless community may take to protect itself or avenge itself on any luckless wight who may be taken for the enemy. It is the duty of journalists to keep their heads cool, and not inflame men's passions when what is wanted is cool temper and clear thinking; and we shall try and write calmly about this new atrocity.[4]

The *Star* also got wind of the statement Schwartz made at the Leman Street Police Station. With this tantalizing piece of information, they had sped off a reporter and readily published their interview with the immigrant.

INFORMATION WHICH MAY BE IMPORTANT

was given to the Leman-street police late yesterday afternoon by an Hungarian concerning this murder. This foreigner [Schwartz] was well dressed, and had the appearance of being in the theatrical line. He could not speak a word of English, but came to the police-station accompanied by a friend, who acted as an interpreter. He gave his name and address, but the police have not disclosed them. A *Star* man, however, got wind of his call, and ran him to earth in Backchurch-lane. The reporter's Hungarian was quite as imperfect as the foreigner's English, but an interpreter was at hand, and the man's story was retold just as he had given it to the police. It is, in fact, to the effect that he

SAW THE WHOLE THING.

It seems that he had gone out for the day, and his wife had expected to move, during his absence, from their lodgings in Berner-street to others in Backchurch-lane. When he came homewards about a quarter before one he first walked down Berner-street to see if his wife had moved. As he turned the corner from Commercial-road he noticed some distance in front of him a man walking as if partially intoxicated. He walked on behind him, and presently he noticed a woman standing in the entrance to the alley way where the body was afterwards found. The half-tipsy man halted and spoke to her. The Hungarian saw him put his hand on her shoulder and push her back into the passage, but, feeling rather timid of getting mixed up in quarrels, he crossed to the other side of the street. Before he had gone many yards, however, he heard the sound of a quarrel, and turned back to learn what was the matter, but just as he stepped from the kerb

A SECOND MAN CAME OUT

of the doorway of the public-house a few doors off, and shouting out some sort of warning to the man who was with the woman, rushed forward as if to attack the intruder. The Hungarian states positively that he saw a knife in this second man's hand, but he waited to see no more. He fled incontinently, to his new lodgings. He described

THE MAN WITH THE WOMAN

as about 30 years of age, rather stoutly built, and wearing a brown moustache. He was dressed respectably in dark clothes and felt hat. The man who came at him with a knife he also describes, but not in detail. He says he was taller than the other, but not so stout, and that his moustaches were red. Both men seem to belong to the same grade of society. The police have arrested one man answering the description the Hungarian furnishes. This prisoner has not been charged, but is held for inquiries to be made. The truth of the man's statement is not wholly accepted.[5]

By ten o'clock that morning, it was announced in the *Daily Telegraph* that the Whitechapel Vigilance Committee, getting nowhere with the Home Office, decided to take its petition for a reward straight to the top.

A Reign of Terror is setting in over the East-end of London, and people there have formed themselves into an organisation with a view of securing closer protection than the police have been able to afford. In a district where the population is so diverse and varied both in nationality and religion, this is a work of some difficulty, but the Vigilance Committee have already made good headway, and at several meetings which its members have held a great deal of information has been gathered which may be useful to the police. During the whole of yesterday almost frantic excitement prevailed. Thousands of people visited both Mitre-street and Berner-street, and journals containing details of the crimes were bought up by crowds of men and women in Whitechapel, Stepney, and Spitalfields. The Vigilance Committee, of which Mr. George Lusk is chairman, report that, among all the respectable residents in Whitechapel, the greatest indignation prevails at what they regard as the apathy of the Home Secretary in face of these appalling outrages. When, after the fourth murder, Mr. Matthews was asked to offer a reward for the apprehension of the criminal, he replied, through his secretary, that the "Secretary of State is satisfied that there is nothing in the present case to justify a departure from the rule" not to offer any reward as from the Government. The committee maintain that the nature and number of the crimes removed them from the ordinary category, and demanded more than usual consideration on the part of the Home Office. Yesterday's occurrences have confirmed them in that opinion, and intensified the feeling of discontent at the Home Secretary's inaction. To make up for it as far as possible, the committee determined to offer a reward themselves. Many of the leading residents have assisted them, and they have received promises of subscriptions amounting to about £300. In addition to this Mr. Montagu, M.P., has offered £100, and a similar sum has been forthcoming from another private source. But it is felt that these sums will not have the same effect as a reward offered on the authority of the Government, and accordingly it was suggested at the committee that as the Home Secretary declined to do anything, the Queen herself should be asked to authorise the issue of a reward. Mr. Lusk drew up the following petition, which on Saturday night — of course before the knowledge of these new atrocities — was sent to her Majesty:

"To her Most Gracious Majesty the Queen. The humble petition of George Lusk, of Alderney-road, in the parish of Mile-end Old Town, Middlesex, a member of the Metropolitan Board of Works, vestryman of the above-named parish, and president of the Vigilance Committee formed for the purposes hereunder mentioned, your petitioner acting under the authority and on behalf of the inhabitants of the East-end of London, humbly showeth: 1. That your Majesty's Secretary of State for the Home Department has for some years past discontinued the old practice of granting a Government reward for the apprehension and conviction of those offenders against your Sovereign Majesty, your Crown and dignity, who have escaped detection for the crime of murder. 2. That in the course of the present year no less than four murders of your Majesty's subjects have taken place within a radius of half a mile from one point in the said district. 3. That, notwithstanding the constitution of the Scotland-yard Detective Office, and the efforts of the trained detectives of such office, the perpetrator or perpetrators of these outrages against your Majesty still remain undiscovered. 4. That, acting under the direction of your Majesty's liege subjects, your petitioner caused to be sent to the Secretary of State for the Home Department a suggestion that he should revert to the original system of a Government reward, looking at the fact that the present series of murders was probably the work of one hand, and that the third and fourth were certainly the work of that one hand, and that, in as much as the ordinary means of detection had failed, and that the murderer would in all probability commit other murders of a like nature, such offer of a reward at the earliest opportunity was absolutely necessary for securing your Majesty's subjects from death at the hands of the above one undetected assassin. 5. That, in reply to such suggestion, your petitioner received from the Secretary of State above named a letter of which the following is a copy, viz.: 'Sir — I am directed by the Secretary of State to acknowledge the receipt of your letter of the 16th inst. [this month] with reference to the question of the offer of a reward for the discovery of the perpetrators of the recent murders in Whitechapel, and I am to inform you that, had the Secretary of State considered the case a proper one for the offer of a reward, he would at once have offered one on behalf of the Government, but that the practice of offering rewards for the discovery of criminals was discontinued some years ago, because experience showed that such offers of reward tended to produce more harm than good, and the Secretary of State is satisfied that there is nothing in the present case to justify a departure from this rule. — I am, Sir, your obedient servant, G. LEIGH PEMBERTON.' 6. That the reply above quoted was submitted to the inhabitants of the East-end of London in meeting assembled, and provoked a considerable amount of hostile criticism, and such criticism was repeated throughout your Majesty's dominions, not only by the public at large but, with one or two exceptions, by the entire Press of Great Britain. Your petitioner therefore humbly prays your Majesty as follows: That your Majesty will graciously accede to the prayer of your petitioner, preferred originally through the Secretary of State for the Home Department, and direct that a Government reward, sufficient in amount to meet the peculiar exigencies of the case, may immediately be offered, your petitioner, and those loyal subjects of your Majesty whom he represents, being convinced that without such reward the murderer or murderers of the above four victims will not only remain undetected, but will sooner or later commit other crimes of a like nature. And your petitioner will ever pray, &c."

It is probable that other petitions of a similar character will be forwarded. There was a rumour in Whitechapel last night that certain information was forthcoming from citizens who have been investigating the facts surrounding the whole of the outrages, that the crimes were organised by a gang of four or five men, and that a careful watch which is being kept on persons supposed to be connected with the band may soon lead to the arrest of one or more of them. As yet, however, there is nothing beyond suspicion. In the meantime the terror and indignation of the inhabitants of the East-end are steadily increasing.

But the *Daily Telegraph* made another announcement that morning, one dealing with a victim of the recent double-event, one that would impact the inquest. "The woman murdered in Berner-street has been identified as Elizabeth Stride, who, it seems, had been leading a gay life, and had resided latterly in Flower and Dean-street. She was identified by a sister living in Holborn."[6]

An hour later, "at the Vestry Hall in Cable-street, St. George-in-the-East, Mr. Wynne E. Baxter, coroner for East Middlesex, opened an inquest on the body of the woman who was found dead, with her throat cut, at one o'clock on Sunday morning, in Berner-street, Commercial-road East. At the outset of the inquiry the deceased was described as Elizabeth Stride, but it subsequently transpired that she had not yet been really identified. A jury of twenty-four having been empanelled, they proceeded to view the body at the St. George's Mortuary.

"The room in which the inquiry was held is extremely spacious, and afforded ample accommodations for the jury, the representatives of the Press, who mustered in strong force, and members of the general public, who, however, were only sparingly admitted. The most intense excitement naturally reigns, this morning, throughout the whole district of St. George's-in-the-East, but the coroner's arrangements for preventing anything like over-crowding in the Vestry Hall were admirable." The following evidence was taken, while "Detective-inspector E. Reid, H Division, watched the case on behalf of the Criminal Investigation Department."

William Wess, who affirmed instead of being sworn, was the first witness examined, and, in reply to the coroner, he said: I reside at No. 2, William-street, Cannon-street-road, and am overseer in the printing office attached to No. 40, Berner-street, Commercial-road, which premises are in the occupation of the International Working Men's Education Society, whose club is carried on there. On the ground floor of the club is a room, the door and window of which face the street. At the rear of this is the kitchen, whilst the first floor consists of a large room which is used for our meetings and entertainments, I being a member of the club. At the south side of the premises is a courtyard, to which entrance can be obtained through a double door, in one section of which is a smaller one, which is used when the larger barriers are closed. The large doors are generally closed at night, but sometimes remain open. On the left side of the yard is a house, which is divided into three tenements, and occupied, I believe, by that number of families. At the end is a store or workshop belonging to Messrs. Hindley and Co., sack manufacturers. I do not know that a way out exists there. The club premises and the printing-office occupy the entire length of the yard on the right side. Returning to the club-house, the front room on the ground floor is used for meals. In the kitchen is a window which faces the door opening into the yard. The intervening passage is illuminated by means of a fanlight over the door. The printing-office, which does not communicate with the club, consists of two rooms, one for compositors and the other for the editor. On Saturday the compositors finished their labors at two o'clock in the afternoon. The editor concluded earlier, but remained at the place until the discovery of the murder.

CORONER: How many members are there in the club?

WESS: From seventy-five to eighty. Working men of any nationality can join.

CORONER: Is any political qualification required of members?

WESS: It is a political — a Socialist — club.

CORONER: Do the members have to agree with any particular principles?

WESS: A candidate is proposed by one member and seconded by another, and a member would not nominate a candidate unless he knew that he was a supporter of Socialist principles. On Saturday last I was in the printing-office during the day and in the club during the evening. From nine to half-past ten at night I was away seeing an English friend home, but I was in the club again till a quarter-past midnight. A discussion was proceeding in the lecture-room, which has three windows overlooking the courtyard. From ninety to 100 persons attended the discussion, which terminated soon after half-past eleven, when the bulk of the members left, using the street door, the most convenient exit. From twenty to thirty members remained, some staying in the lecture-room and the others going downstairs. Of those upstairs a few continued the discussion, while the rest were singing. The windows of the lecture-room were partly open.

CORONER: How do you know that you finally left at a quarter-past twelve o'clock?

WESS: Because of the time when I reached my lodgings. Before leaving I went into the yard, and thence to the printing-office, in order to leave some literature there, and on returning to the yard I observed that the double door at the entrance was open. There is no lamp in the yard, and none of the street lamps light it, so that the yard is only lit by the lights through the windows at the side of the club and of the tenements opposite. As to the tenements, I only observed lights in two first-floor windows. There was also a light in the printing-office, the editor being in his room reading.

CORONER: Was there much noise in the club?

WESS: Not exactly much noise; but I could hear the singing when I was in the yard.

CORONER: Did you look towards the yard gates?

WESS: Not so much to the gates as to the ground, but nothing unusual attracted my attention.

CORONER: Can you say that there was no object on the ground?

WESS: I could not say that.

CORONER: Do you think it possible that anything can have been there without your observing it?

WESS: It was dark, and I am a little shortsighted, so that it is possible. The distance from the gates to the kitchen door is 18 ft.

CORONER: What made you look towards the gates at all?

WESS: Simply because they were open. I went into the club, and called my brother, and we left together by the front door.

CORONER: On leaving did you see anybody as you passed the yard?

WESS: No.

CORONER: Or did you meet any one in the street?

WESS: Not that I recollect. I generally go home between twelve and one o'clock.

CORONER: Do low women frequent Berner-street?

WESS: I have seen men and women standing about and talking to each other in Fairclough-street.

CORONER: But have you observed them nearer the club?

WESS: No.

CORONER: Or in the club yard?

WESS: I did once, at eleven o'clock at night, about a year ago. They were chatting near the gates. That is the only time I have noticed such a thing, nor have I heard of it.

Morris Eagle, who also affirmed, said: I live at No. 4, New-road, Commercial-road, and travel in jewelry. I am a member of the International Workmen's Club, which meets at 40, Berner-street. I was there on Saturday, several times during the day, and was in the chair during the discussion in the evening. After the discussion, between half-past eleven and a quarter to twelve o'clock, I left the club to take my young lady home, going out through the front door. I returned about twenty minutes to one. I tried the front door, but, finding it closed, I went through the gateway into the yard, reaching the club in that way.

CORONER: Did you notice anything lying on the ground near the gates?

EAGLE: I did not.

CORONER: Did you pass in the middle of the gateway?

EAGLE: I think so. The gateway is 9 ft. 2 in. wide. I naturally walked on the right side, that being the side on which the club door was.

CORONER: Do you think you are able to say that the deceased was not lying there then?

EAGLE: I do not know, I am sure, because it was rather dark. There was a light from the upper part of the club, but that would not throw any illumination upon the ground. It was dark near the gates.

CORONER: You have formed no opinion, I take it, then, as to whether there was anything there?

EAGLE: No.

CORONER: Did you see anyone about in Berner-street?

EAGLE: I dare say I did, but I do not remember them.

CORONER: Did you observe any one in the yard?

EAGLE: I do not remember that I did.

Contemporary sketch of Morris Eagle (courtesy Evans/Skinner Crime Archive).

CORONER: If there had been a man and woman there you would have remembered the circumstance?

EAGLE: Yes; I am sure of that.

CORONER: Did you notice whether there were any lights in the tenements opposite the club?

EAGLE: I do not recollect.

CORONER: Are you often at the club late at night?

EAGLE: Yes, very often.

CORONER: In the yard, too?

EAGLE: No, not in the yard.

CORONER: And you have never seen a man and woman there?

EAGLE: No, not in the yard; but I have close by, outside the beershop, at the corner of Fairclough-street. As soon as I entered the gateway on Saturday night I could hear a friend of mine singing in the upstairs room of the club. I went up to him. He was singing in the Russian language, and we sang together. I had been there twenty minutes when a member named Gidleman [Gilleman] came upstairs, and said "there is a woman dead in the yard." I went down in a second and struck a match, when I saw a woman lying on the ground in a pool of blood, near the gates. Her feet were towards the gates, about six or seven feet from them. She was lying by the side of and facing the club wall. When I reached the body and struck the match another member was present.

CORONER: Did you touch the body?

EAGLE: No. As soon as I struck the match I perceived a lot of blood, and I ran away and called the police.

CORONER: Were the clothes of the deceased disturbed?

EAGLE: I cannot say. I ran towards the Commercial-road, Dienishitz [sic], the club steward, and another member going in the opposite direction down Fairclough-street. In Commercial-road I found two constables at the corner of Grove-street. I told them that a woman had been murdered in Berner-street, and they returned with me.

CORONER: Was any one in the yard then?

EAGLE: Yes, a few persons — some members of the club and some strangers. One of the policemen turned his lamp on the deceased and sent me to the station for the inspector, at the same time telling his comrade to fetch a doctor. The onlookers seemed afraid to go near and touch the body. The constable, however, felt it.

CORONER: Can you fix the time when the discovery was first made?

EAGLE: It must have been about one o'clock. On Saturday nights there is free discussion at the club, and among those present last Saturday were about half a dozen women, but they were those we knew — not strangers. It was not a dancing night, but a few members may have danced after the discussion.

CORONER: If there was dancing and singing in the club you would not hear the cry of a woman in the yard?

EAGLE: It would depend upon the cry.

CORONER: The cry of a woman in great distress — a cry of "Murder"?

EAGLE: Yes, I should have heard that.

Lewis Diemshitz [Louis Diemschütz], having affirmed, deposed: I reside at No. 40 Berner-street, and am steward of the International Workmen's Club. I am married, and my wife lives at the club too, and assists in the management. On Saturday I left home about half-past eleven in the morning, and returned exactly at one o'clock on Sunday morning. I noticed the time at the baker's shop at the corner of Berner-street. I had been to the market near the Crystal Palace, and had a barrow like a costermonger's, drawn by a pony, which I keep in George-yard Cable-street. I drove home to leave my goods. I drove into the yard, both gates being wide open. It was rather dark there. All at once my pony shied at some object on the right. I looked to see what the object was, and observed that there was something unusual, but could not tell what. It was a dark object. I put my whip handle to it, and tried to lift it up, but as I did not succeed I jumped down from my barrow and struck a match. It was rather windy, and I could only get sufficient light to see that there was some figure there. I could tell from the dress that it was the figure of a woman.

Contemporary sketch of Louis Diemschütz (courtesy Evans/ Skinner Crime Archive).

CORONER: You did not disturb it?

DIEMSCHÜTZ: No. I went into the club and asked where my wife was. I found her in the front room on the ground floor.

CORONER: What did you do with the pony?

DIEMSCHÜTZ: I left it in the yard by itself, just outside the club door. There were several members in the front room of the club, and I told them all that there was a woman lying in the yard, though I could not say whether she was drunk or dead. I then got a candle and went into the yard, where I could see blood before I reached the body.

CORONER: Did you touch the body?

DIEMSCHÜTZ: No, I ran off at once for the police. I could not find a constable in the direction which I took, so I shouted out "Police!" as loudly as I could. A man Spooner: whom I met in Grove-street returned with me, and when we reached the yard he took hold of the head of the deceased. As he lifted it up I saw the wound in the throat.

CORONER: Had the constables arrived then?

DIEMSCHÜTZ: At the very same moment Eagle and the constables arrived.

CORONER: Did you notice anything unusual when you were approaching the club?

DIEMSCHÜTZ: No.

CORONER: You saw nothing suspicious?

DIEMSCHÜTZ: Not at all.

CORONER: How soon afterwards did a doctor arrive?

DIEMSCHÜTZ: About twenty minutes after the constables came up. No one was allowed by the police to leave the club until they were searched, and then they had to give their names and addresses.

CORONER: Did you notice whether the clothes of the deceased were in order?

DIEMSCHÜTZ: They were in perfect order.

CORONER: How was she lying?

DIEMSCHÜTZ: On her left side, with her face towards the club wall.

CORONER: Was the whole of the body resting on the side?

DIEMSCHÜTZ: No, I should say only her face. I cannot say how much of the body was sideways. I did not notice what position her hands were in, but when the police came I observed that her bodice was unbuttoned near the neck. The doctor said the body was quite warm.

CORONER: What quantity of blood should you think had flowed from the body?

DIEMSCHÜTZ: I should say quite two quarts.

CORONER: In what direction had it run?

DIEMSCHÜTZ: Up the yard from the street. The body was about one foot from the club wall. The gutter of the yard is paved with large stones, and the centre with smaller irregular stones.

CORONER: Have you ever seen men and women together in the yard?

DIEMSCHÜTZ: Never.

CORONER: Nor heard of such a thing?

DIEMSCHÜTZ: No.

A JUROR: Could you in going up the yard have passed the body without touching it?

DIEMSCHÜTZ: Oh, yes.

CORONER: Any person going up the centre of the yard might have passed without noticing it?

DIEMSCHÜTZ: I, perhaps, should not have noticed it if my pony had not shied. I had passed it when I got down from my barrow.

CORONER: How far did the blood run?

DIEMSCHÜTZ: As far as the kitchen door of the club.

CORONER: Was any person left with the body while you ran for the police?

DIEMSCHÜTZ: Some members of the club remained; at all events, when I came back they were there. I cannot say whether any of them touched the body.

INSPECTOR REID (interposing): When the murder was discovered the members of the club were detained on the premises, and I searched them, whilst Dr. Phillips examined them.

A JUROR: Was it possible for anybody to leave the yard between the discovery of the body and the arrival of the police?

WITNESS: Oh, yes — or, rather, it would have been possible before I informed the members of the club, not afterwards.

CORONER: When you entered the yard, if any person had run out you would have seen them in the dark?

DIEMSCHÜTZ: Oh, yes, it was light enough for that. It was dark in the gateway, but not so dark further in the yard.

CORONER: The body has not yet been identified?

INSPECTOR REID: Not yet.

THE FOREMAN: I do not quite understand that. I thought the inquest had been opened on the body of one Elizabeth Stride.

THE CORONER: That was a mistake. Something is known of the deceased, but she has not been fully identified. It would be better at present to describe her as a woman unknown. She has been partially identified. It is known where she lived. It was thought at the beginning of the inquest that she had been identified by a relative, but that turns out to have been a mistake.

The inquest was then adjourned until 2 o'clock tomorrow afternoon.

In spite what might have seemed to be the obvious and Baxter's correct statement, the court had no legal choice but to entertain Malcolm's initial identification. Because of her asserted kinship to the victim, it took legal precedence until proven otherwise.[7]

Even though the inquest had started, press interviews with the neighboring residents were not finished.

> With reference to the murder in Berner-street, Mrs. Diemschütz, the stewardess of the Socialist Club in that thoroughfare, has made the following statement: "Just about 1 o'clock on Sunday morning I was in the kitchen on the ground floor of the club and close to the side entrance. I am positive I did not hear any screams or sound of any kind." The servant at the club strongly corroborates the statement made by her mistress, and is equally convinced that there were no sounds coming from the yard between 20 minutes to 1 and 1 o'clock.[8]

During the course of the investigation into the murders, the police literally received countless correspondence from Londoners and from all over the country. Many gave suggestions on how to capture the killer or about who the killer might be — whether animal or person. But among these hundreds, if not thousands of writings, one of them stood out. The press, the *Daily News* among others, published a letter that has since been dubbed "Dear Boss." It was simply addressed to "The Boss, Central News Office, London City" with a postmark of September 27. Written in red ink with a red crayon postscript, it was dated "25 Sept. 1888." The letter was handed over to the police on September 29. But it was not until the double-event that it was made public. The letter was signed "Jack the Ripper."

Sept. 25, 1888.

> Dear Boss — I keep on hearing the police have caught me, but they won't fix me just yet. I have laughed when they look so clever and talk about being on the right track. Great joke about Leather Apron. Gave me real fits. I am down on whores, and I shan't quit ripping them till I do get buckled. Grand work the last job was. I gave the lady no time to squeal. How can they catch me now? I love my work and want to start again. You will soon hear of me, with my funny little games. I saved some of the proper red stuff in a ginger beer bottle over the last job to write with, but it went thick, like glue, and I can't use it. Red ink is fit enough, I hope. Ha, ha! The next job I do I shall clip the lady's ears off and send to the police officers, just for jolly, wouldn't you?
> Keep this letter back till I do a bit more work, then give it out straight. My

knife's so nice and sharp. I want to get to work right away if I get a chance. Good luck — Yours truly,

Jack the Ripper.

Don't mind me giving the trade name.
Wasn't good enough to post this before I got all the red ink off my hands; curse it. No luck yet. They say I'm a doctor now. Ha, ha!

This is the first recognized letter to use the signature "Jack the Ripper," but it was not the last. That same day, Central News received a second correspondence. This time, a post card with a London E postmark, and possibly written in red crayon.

I was not codding dear old Boss when I gave you the tip, you'll hear about saucy Jack s work tomorrow double event this time number one squealed a bit couldn't finish straight off. Had no time to get ears for police thanks for keeping last letter back till I got to work again.

Jack the Ripper

The press, including the police, considered the "Saucy Jack" post card, as it is known, and its sister letter to be a hoax. Decades later, a journalist claimed responsibility, having written the letters in order to "keep the business alive." While these two correspondences gave a name to London's infamous serial killer, it would not be long before other copycat communications were sent to the police, merely as intentional cranks, which ultimately got the sender into trouble.[9]

That day "in the neighbourhood of Berner-street the excitement of the inhabitants continues unabated, and during the whole of yesterday [Monday] a large number of spectators took delight in gazing at the premises of the International Working Man's Constitutional Club, whose committee are making profit out of the notoriety the premises have acquired by charging curiosity-hunters a small sum for admission, the money thus obtained being devoted to the 'propaganda fund' of Socialism." And as the day wore on, more people came to the mortuary to view and hopefully identify the body, including William Marshall and Michael Kidney. There Michael met Mrs. Malcolm, who had returned for a second and third viewing, finally deciding that she was indeed looking at her poor unfortunate sister, based on what appeared to be an old adder bite on her leg. But not everyone visited the mortuary or the murder scene. Leon Goldstein went to the Leman Street Police Station. There, he identified himself as the man carrying the black bag seen by Mortimer, as reported in the papers. Being satisfied with his account, the police attached no suspicion to him, and he was free to go.[10]

Despite the letters, informants, and the parade of people going through the mortuary, Drs. Blackwell and Phillips conducted the post-mortem at three in the afternoon. Mr. Johnston assisted while a Dr. Reigate attended for only a portion of the autopsy. With "Dr. Blackwell kindly consenting to make the dissection," Dr. Phillips took notes. Elizabeth's body temperature was 55 degrees. Rigor mortis was still firmly marked even after thirty-eight hours (on average, full rigor sets in after about twelve hours and eventually subsides to full relaxation after about thirty-six hours). Mud was on her face and on the left side of her head and matted on the hair and her left side. After the clothes were removed, they found the body to be fairly nourished. Over both shoulders, especially the right, from the front aspect under collarbones and in front of chest there was a bluish discoloration. On the neck, from the victim's left to her right, there was a clean-cut incision that was six inches in length. This single incision started two and a half inches in a straight line below the angle of the left jaw. The wound ran three-quarters of an inch over undivided muscle, then became deeper, about an inch in depth, dividing the sheath and the vessels and ascending a little, and then it grazed the muscle outside the cartilage on the left side of the neck. The left carotid artery, along with the other vessels contained in the sheath, was cut through, except for the posterior portion of the artery, to a line about ½th of an inch in extent, which prevented the separation of the upper and lower portion of the artery. The cut through the tissues on the right side of the cartilage was more superficial, and tailed off to about two inches below the right angle of the jaw. It was evident that the hemorrhage, which produced death, was caused through the partial severance of the left carotid artery. There was a deformity in the lower fifth of the bones of the right leg, which were not straight. They bowed forward, and there was a "thickening" above the left ankle. There the bones were straighter. Except for the neck, there was no recent external injury. Although thoroughly healed, the lower left ear lobe had been torn, as if by the forcible removal of or wearing through by an earring. The right ear was pierced for an earring, but it had not been injured like the left; there was no earring. Scalp removal showed no sign of bruising or blood between it and the skullcap. The skull was about one-sixth of an inch in thickness with a dense texture. The brain was fairly normal. Both lungs were unusually pale. The heart was small; left ventricle was absolutely empty and firmly contracted, while the right full of dark clot and less contracted. The stomach contents consisted of partially digested cheese, potato, and "farinaceous edibles" (flour-based foods). The teeth on her left lower jaw were missing.[11]

That evening, Police Constable Walter Frederick Stride, nephew of Elizabeth's estranged and now dead husband, John Stride, viewed the mortuary photo of the Berner Street victim. It is unknown why he did not view the body itself; however, he recognized the woman in the photo as the one who married his uncle. But having seen the body, a distraught Michael Kidney was getting drunk. And when he had his fill, he headed for the Leman Street Police Station. Once he got there, Michael told the inspector on duty, Inspector Pinhorn, that he had information which could readily capture the assailant at any time. And with a young, strong detective, he could trap the killer. The inspector refused to assign a detective to a civilian, especially one that was noticeably intoxicated. At this refusal of police assistance, Kidney told the duty inspector that "he was uncivil," and left without further incident.[12]

—6—

She Said Watts

It had been just over forty-seven hours since Elizabeth's fatal assault, and yet the start of October 2nd saw no definitive signs of the killer. Catching an elusive murderer is a daunting task, but the police were not intimidated, as they intensely pursued every avenue. They knocked on doors, had extensive patrols, distributed thousands of fliers, circulated descriptions, and followed every possible lead whether it came from a letter, an interview, or an observation. But despite these efforts, the Whitechapel Vigilance Committee and the *Evening News*, possibly along with other papers, decided to put their own detectives on the Berner Street case. They were Messrs. Batchelor and Le Grand, and commissioned to uncover what the police failed to see.[1]

They were not in Berner Street long, before the detectives approached an unimportant location next door to the corner beer house. It was the "second house from the spot at which the body was found." There, they came upon an elderly businessman of small means, doing his best to eke out an existence among the urbanized hustle and bustle of industrialized London. The shopkeeper, Packer, readily spoke to the two investigators and even willingly signed a statement.

THE WHITECHAPEL MURDERS.
TWO PRIVATE DETECTIVES ON THE TRACK OF THE ASSASSIN.
HIS PERSONAL APPEARANCE.
WHERE HE BOUGHT THE GRAPES FOUND BESIDE THE
MURDERED WOMAN.
MATTHEW PACKER'S STORY.
INTERVIEW WITH THE MAN WHO SPOKE TO THE MURDERER.

We are enabled to present our readers this morning in the columns of the Evening News with the most startling information that has yet been made public in relation to the Whitechapel murderer, and the first real clue that has been obtained to his identity. The chain of evidence in our possession has been pieced together by two gentlemen connected with the business of private inquiries, who, starting on the track of the assassin without any pet "theory" to substantiate, and contenting themselves with ascertaining and connecting a series of the simplest facts, have succeeded in arriving at a result of the utmost importance. There are no suppositions or probabilities in the story we have to tell; we put forward nothing but simple facts, each substantiated by the evidence of credible witnesses. What they go to establish is that the perpetrator of the Berner street crime was seen and spoken to whilst in the company of his victim, within forty minutes of the commission of the crime and only passed from the sight of a witness

TEN MINUTES BEFORE THE MURDER

and within ten yards of the scene of the awful deed. We proceed to give hereunder the story of the two detectives, Messrs. Grand and J.H. Batchelor, of 283 Strand: When they began their quest, almost from the first place at which they sought evidence from No. 44 Berner street, the second house from the spot at which the body was found. This is the residence of a man named Mathew Packer, who carries on a small business as a greengrocer and fruiterer. His shop is an insignificant place, with a half window in front, and most of his dealings are carried on through the lower part of the window case, in which his fruit is exposed for sale. Mathew Packer had valuable information to give, and after two or three interviews on the subject, made and signed a statement in writing, the substance of which is as follows:

On the 29th ult. [last month], about 11.45 P.M., a man and woman came to his shop window, and asked for some fruit.

DESCRIPTION OF THE MURDERER.

The man was middle aged, perhaps 35 years; about five feet seven inches in height; was stout, square built; wore a wide awake hat and dark clothes; had the appearance of a clerk; had a rough voice and a quick, sharp way of talking.

THE WHITE FLOWER.

The woman was middle aged, wore a dark dress and jacket, and had a white flower in her bosom. It was a dark night and the only light was afforded by an oil lamp which Packer had burning inside his window, but he obtained a sufficiently clear view of the faces of the two people as they stood talking close in front of the window, and his attention was particularly caught by the white flower which the woman wore, and which showed out distinctly against the dark material of her jacket. The importance attached to this flower will be seen afterwards.

BUYING THE GRAPES.

The man asked his companion whether she would have black or white grapes; she replied "black."

"Well, what's the price of the black grapes, old man?" he inquired.

"The black are sixpence and the white fourpence," replied Packer.

"Well then, old man, give us half a pound of the black," said the man.

Packer served him with the grapes, which he handed to the woman. They then crossed the road and stood on the pavement almost directly opposite to the shop for a long time more than half an hour. It will be remembered that the night was very wet, and Packer naturally noticed the peculiarity of the couple's standing so long in the rain. He observed to his wife, "What fools those people are to be standing in the rain like that."

At last the couple moved from their position, and Packer saw them cross the road again and come over to the club, standing for a moment in front of it as though listening to the music inside. Then he lost sight of them. It was then ten or fifteen minutes past twelve o'clock, Packer, who was about to close his shop, noting the time by the fact that the public houses had been closed.

After Packer finished providing his "valuable information," Batchelor and Le Grand obtained permission to take him to the Golden Lane mortuary, where Catherine Eddowes's body lay. In the process, they led the elderly greengrocer into thinking that he was about to see the Berner Street victim. Upon seeing the body, Packer declared, at once, that it was not the same woman he saw Saturday night. Satisfied with the fruiterer's "honesty," the detectives returned to Berner Street and continued with their sleuthing.[2]

At the corner of Sander Street, toward the northern end of the road, the investigators came upon two sisters, Mrs. Rosenfield and Miss Eva Harstein, who lived at 14 Berner Street. They claimed that on early Sunday morning, Rosenfield "passed the spot where the body had lain." On the ground close by was a "grape stalk stained with blood." Her sister affirmed this, adding "after the removal of the body of the murdered woman she saw a few small petals of a white natural flower lying quite close to the spot where the body had rested." With this tidbit of information, the detectives wasted no time in hurrying to Dutfield's. Knowing that the blood had already been washed away, Batchelor and Le Grand deduced that the stalk was in the drain along with the blood and dirt. Searching the "sink," they found a grape stalk "amidst a heap of heterogeneous filth."[3]

It was two in the afternoon when Coroner Baxter "resumed the inquiry into the circumstances attending the death of the woman who was found with her throat cut in a yard adjoining the clubhouse of the International Working Men's Education Society, No. 40, Berner-street, Commercial-road East, at one o'clock on Sunday morning last." The following evidence was presented while "Detective-inspector E. Reid, H Division, watched the case on behalf of the Criminal Investigation Department."

Constable Henry Lamb, 252 H division, examined by the coroner, said: Last Sunday morning, shortly before one o'clock, I was on duty in Commercial-road, between Christian-street and Batty-street, when two men came running towards me and shouting. I went to meet them, and they called out, "Come on, there has been another murder." I asked where, and as they got to the corner of Berner-street they pointed down and said, "There." I saw people moving some distance down the street. I ran, followed by another constable — 426 H. Arriving at the gateway of No. 40 I observed something dark lying on the ground on the right-hand side. I turned my light on, when I found that the object was a woman, with her throat cut and apparently dead. I sent the other constable for the nearest doctor, and a young man who was standing by I dispatched to the police station to inform the inspector what had occurred. On my arrival there were about thirty people in the yard, and others followed me in. No one was nearer than a yard to the body. As I was examining the deceased the crowd gathered round, but I begged them to keep back, otherwise they might have their clothes soiled with blood, and thus get into trouble.

CORONER: Up to this time had you touched the body?

LAMB: I had put my hand on the face.

CORONER: Was it warm?

LAMB: Slightly. I felt the wrist, but could not discern any movement of the pulse. I then blew my whistle for assistance.

CORONER: Did you observe how the deceased was lying?

LAMB: She was lying on her left side, with her left hand on the ground.

CORONER: Was there anything in that hand?

LAMB: I did not notice anything. The right arm was across the breast. Her face was not more than five or six inches away from the club wall.

CORONER: Were her clothes disturbed?

LAMB: No.

CORONER: Only her boots visible?

LAMB: Yes, and only the soles of them. There were no signs of a struggle. Some of the blood was in a liquid state, and had run towards the kitchen door of the club. A little — that nearest to her on the ground — was slightly congealed. I can hardly say whether any was still flowing from the throat. Dr. Blackwell was the first doctor to arrive; he came ten or twelve minutes after myself, but I had no watch with me.

CORONER: Did any one of the crowd say whether the body had been touched before your arrival?

LAMB: No. Dr. Blackwell examined the body and its surroundings. Dr. Phillips came ten minutes later. Inspector Pinhorn arrived directly after Dr. Blackwell. When I blew my whistle other constables came, and I had the entrance of the yard closed. This was while Dr. Blackwell was looking at the body. Before that the doors were wide open. The feet of the deceased extended just to the swing of the gate, so that the barrier could be closed without disturbing the body. I entered the club and left a constable at the gate to prevent any one passing in or out. I examined the hands and clothes of all the members of the club. There were from fifteen to twenty present, and they were on the ground floor.

CORONER: Did you discover traces of blood anywhere in the club?

LAMB: No.

CORONER: Was the steward present?

LAMB: Yes.

CORONER: Did you ask him to lock the front door?

LAMB: I did not. There was a great deal of commotion. That was done afterwards.

THE CORONER: But time is the essence of the thing.

WITNESS: I did not see any person leave. I did not try the front door of the club to see if it was locked. I afterwards went over the cottages, the occupants of which were in bed. I was admitted by men, who came down partly dressed; all the other people were undressed. As to the waterclosets in the yard, one was locked and the other unlocked, but no one was there. There is a recess near the dust-bin.

CORONER: Did you go there?

LAMB: Yes, afterwards, with Dr. Phillips.

THE CORONER: But I am speaking of at the time.

WITNESS: I did it subsequently. I do not recollect looking over the wooden partition. I, however, examined the store belonging to Messrs. Hindley, sack manufacturers, but I saw nothing there.

CORONER: How long were the cottagers in opening their doors?

LAMB: Only a few minutes, and they seemed frightened. When I returned Dr. Phillips and Chief Inspector West had arrived.

CORONER: Was there anything to prevent a man escaping while you were examining the body?

LAMB: Several people were inside and outside the gates, and I should think that they would be sure to observe a man who had marks of blood.

CORONER: But supposing he had no marks of blood?

LAMB: It was quite possible, of course, for a person to escape while I was examining the corpse. Every one was more or less looking towards the body. There was much confusion.

CORONER: Do you think that a person might have got away before you arrived?

LAMB: I think he is more likely to have escaped before than after.

DETECTIVE-INSPECTOR REID: How long before had you passed this place?

WITNESS: I am not on the Berner-street beat, but I passed the end of the street in Commercial-road six or seven minutes before.

CORONER: When you were found what direction were you going in?

LAMB: I was coming towards Berner-street. A constable named Smith was on the Berner-street beat. He did not accompany me, but was the constable who was on fixed-point duty between Grove-street and Christian-street in Commercial-road. Constables at fixed-points leave duty at one in the morning. I believe that is the practice nearly all over London.*

THE CORONER: I think this is important. The Hanbury-street murder was discovered just as the night police were going off duty. (To witness): Did you see anything suspicious?

LAMB: I did not at any time. There were squabbles and rows in the streets, but nothing more.

THE FOREMAN: Was there light sufficient to enable you to see, as you were going down Berner-street, whether any person was running away from No. 40?

LAMB: It was rather dark, but I think there was light enough for that, though the person would be somewhat indistinct from Commercial-road.

---

*The Times *(03 Oct) reported this particular statement by PC Lamb as, "The constable who followed me down is on fixed-point duty from 9 [PM] to 5 [AM] at the end of Grove-street." PC Lamb may have realized this was confusing or misleading, because he clarified it with his next statement. "All the fixed-point men ceased their duty at 1 A.M., and then the men on the beats did the whole duty."*

THE FOREMAN: Some of the papers state that Berner-street is badly lighted; but there are six lamps within 700 feet, and I do not think that is very bad.

THE CORONER: The parish plan shows that there are four lamps within 350 feet, from Commercial-road to Fairclough-street.

WITNESS: There are three, if not four, lamps in Berner-street between Commercial-road and Fairclough-street. Berner-street is about as well lighted as other side streets. Most of them are rather dark, but more lamps have been erected lately.

THE CORONER: I do not think that London altogether is as well lighted as some capitals are.

WITNESS: There are no public-house lights in Berner-street. I was engaged in the yard and at the mortuary all the night afterwards.

Edward Spooner, in reply to the coroner, said: I live at No. 26, Fairclough-street, and am a horse-keeper with Messrs. Meredith, biscuit bakers. On Sunday morning, between half-past twelve and one o'clock, I was standing outside the Beehive Public-house, at the corner of Christian-street, with my young woman. We had left a public-house in Commercial-road at closing time, midnight, and walked quietly to the point named. We stood outside the Beehive about twenty-five minutes, when two Jews came running along, calling out "Murder" and "Police." They ran as far as Grove-street, and then turned back. I stopped them and asked what was the matter, and they replied that a woman had been murdered. I thereupon proceeded down Berner-street and into Dutfield's-yard, adjoining the International Workmen's Club-house, and there saw a woman lying just inside the gate.

CORONER: Was any one with her?

SPOONER: There were about fifteen people in the yard.

CORONER: Was any one near her?

SPOONER: They were all standing round.

CORONER: Were they touching her?

SPOONER: No. One man struck a match, but I could see the woman before the match was struck. I put my hand under her chin when the match was alight.

CORONER: Was the chin warm?

SPOONER: Slightly.

CORONER: Was any blood coming from the throat?

SPOONER: Yes; it was still flowing. I noticed that she had a piece of paper doubled up in her right hand, and some red and white flowers pinned on her breast. I did not feel the body, nor did I alter the position of the head. I am sure of that. Her face was turned towards the club wall.

CORONER: Did you notice whether the blood was still moving on the ground?

SPOONER: It was running down the gutter. I stood by the side of the body for four or five minutes, until the last witness arrived.

CORONER: Did you notice any one leave the yard while you were there?

SPOONER: No.

CORONER: Could any one have left without your observing it?

SPOONER: I cannot say, but I think there were too many people about. I believe it was twenty-five minutes to one o'clock when I arrived in the yard.

CORONER: Have you formed any opinion as to whether the people had moved the body before you came?

SPOONER: No.

THE FOREMAN: As a rule, Jews do not care to touch dead bodies.

WITNESS: The legs of the deceased were drawn up, but her clothes were not disturbed. When Police-constable Lamb came I helped him to close the gates of the yard, and I left through the club.

INSPECTOR REID: I believe that was after you had given your name and address to the police?

SPOONER: Yes.

INSPECTOR REID: And had been searched?

SPOONER: Yes.

INSPECTOR REID: And examined by Dr. Phillips?

SPOONER: Yes.

THE CORONER: Was there no blood on your hands?

SPOONER: No.

CORONER: Then there was no blood on the chin of the deceased?

SPOONER: No.

BY THE JURY: I did not meet any one as I was hastening through Berner-street.

Mary Malcolm was the next witness, and she was deeply affected while giving her evidence. In answer to the coroner she said: I live at No. 50, Eagle-street, Red Lion-square, Holborn, and am married. My husband, Andrew Malcolm, is a tailor. I have seen the body at the mortuary. I saw it once on Sunday and twice yesterday.

CORONER: Who is it?

MALCOLM: It is the body of my sister, Elizabeth Watts.

CORONER: You have no doubt about that?

MALCOLM: Not the slightest.

CORONER: You did have some doubts about it at one time?

MALCOLM: I had at first.

CORONER: When did you last see your sister alive?

MALCOLM: Last Thursday, about a quarter to seven in the evening.

CORONER: Where?

MALCOLM: She came to see me at No. 59, Red Lion-street, where I work as a trousermaker.

CORONER: What did she come to you for?

MALCOLM: To ask me for a little assistance. I have been in the habit of assisting her for five years.

CORONER: Did you give her anything?

MALCOLM: I gave her a shilling and a short jacket — not the jacket which is now on the body.

CORONER: How long was she with you?

MALCOLM: Only a few moments.

CORONER: Did she say where she was going?

MALCOLM: No.

CORONER: Where was she living?

MALCOLM: I do not know. I know it was somewhere in the neighbourhood of the tailoring Jews — Commercial-road or Commercial-street, or somewhere at the East-end.

CORONER: Did you understand that she was living in lodging-houses?

MALCOLM: Yes.

CORONER: Did you know what she was doing for a livelihood?

MALCOLM: I had my doubts.

CORONER: Was she the worse for drink when she came to you on Thursday?

MALCOLM: No, sober.

CORONER: But she was sometimes the worse for drink, was she not?

MALCOLM: That was, unfortunately, a failing with her. She was thirty-seven years of age last March.

CORONER: Had she ever been married?

MALCOLM: Yes.

CORONER: Is her husband alive?

MALCOLM: Yes, so far as I know. She married the son of Mr. Watts, wine and spirit merchant, of Walcot-street, Bath. I think her husband's Christian name was Edward. I believe he is now in America.

CORONER: Did he get into trouble?

MALCOLM: No.

CORONER: Why did he go away?

MALCOLM: Because my sister brought trouble upon him.

CORONER: When did she leave him?

MALCOLM: About eight years ago, but I cannot be quite certain as to the time. She had two children. Her husband caught her with a porter, and there was a quarrel.

CORONER: Did the husband turn her out of doors?

MALCOLM: No, he sent her to my poor mother, with the two children.

CORONER: Where does your mother live?

MALCOLM: She is dead. She died in the year 1883.

CORONER: Where are the children now?

MALCOLM: The girl is dead, but the boy is at a boarding school kept by his aunt.

CORONER: Was the deceased subject to epileptic fits?

WITNESS (sobbing bitterly): No, she only had drunken fits.

CORONER: Was she ever before the Thames police magistrate?

MALCOLM: I believe so.

CORONER: Charged with drunkenness?

MALCOLM: Yes.

CORONER: Are you aware that she has been let off on the supposition that she was subject to epileptic fits?

MALCOLM: I believe that is so, but she was not subject to epileptic fits.

CORONER: Has she ever told you of troubles she was in with any man?

MALCOLM: Oh yes; she lived with a man.

CORONER: Do you know his name?

MALCOLM: I do not remember now, but I shall be able to tell you to-morrow. I believe she lived with a man who kept a coffee-house at Poplar.

INSPECTOR REID: Was his name Stride?

MALCOLM: No; I think it was Dent, but I can find out for certain by to-morrow.

THE CORONER: How long had she ceased to live with that man?

MALCOLM: Oh, some time. He went away to sea, and was wrecked on the Isle of St. Paul, I believe.

CORONER: How long ago should you think that was?

MALCOLM: It must be three years and a half; but I could tell you all about it by to-morrow, even the name of the vessel that was wrecked.

CORONER: Had the deceased lived with any man since then?

MALCOLM: Not to my knowledge, but there is some man who says that he has lived with her.

CORONER: Have you ever heard of her getting into trouble with this man?

MALCOLM: No, but at times she got locked up for drunkenness. She always brought her trouble to me.

CORONER: You never heard of any one threatening her?

MALCOLM: No; she was too good for that.

CORONER: Did you ever hear her say that she was afraid of any one?

MALCOLM: No.

CORONER: Did you know of no man with whom she had relations?

MALCOLM: No.

INSPECTOR REID: Did you ever visit her in Flower and Dean-street?

MALCOLM: No.

CORONER: Did you ever hear her called "Long Liz"?

MALCOLM: That was generally her nickname, I believe.

CORONER: Have you ever heard of the name of Stride?

MALCOLM: She never mentioned such a name to me. I think that if she had lived with any one of that name she would have told me. I have heard what the man Stride has said, but I think he is mistaken.*

THE CORONER: How often did your sister come to you?

MALCOLM: Every Saturday, and I always gave her 2 shillings. That was for her lodgings.

CORONER: Did she come to you at all last Saturday?

MALCOLM: No, I did not see her on that day.

CORONER: The Thursday visit was an unusual one, I suppose?

MALCOLM: Yes.

CORONER: Did you think it strange that she did not come on the Saturday?

MALCOLM: I did.

CORONER: Had she ever missed a Saturday before?

MALCOLM: Not for nearly three years.

CORONER: What time in the day did she usually come to you?

MALCOLM: At four o'clock in the afternoon.

CORONER: Where?

MALCOLM: At the corner of Chancery-lane. I was there last Saturday afternoon from half-past three till five, but she did not turn up.

CORONER: Did you think there was something the matter with her?

MALCOLM: On the Sunday morning when I read the accounts in the newspapers I thought it might be my sister who had been murdered. I had a presentiment [premonition] that that was so. I came down to Whitechapel and was directed to the mortuary; but when I saw the body I did not recognize it as that of my sister.

CORONER: How was that? Why did you not recognize it in the first instance?

---

*By "the man Stride," Malcolm was referring to Michael Kidney, incorrectly assuming that he and Elizabeth were married and that his name was Michael Stride.

MALCOLM: I do not know, except that I saw it in the gaslight, between nine and ten at night. But I recognised her the next day.

CORONER: Did you not have some special presentiment that this was your sister?

MALCOLM: Yes.

CORONER: Tell the jury what it was?

MALCOLM: I was in bed, and about twenty minutes past one on Sunday morning I felt a pressure on my breast and heard three distinct kisses. It was that which made me afterwards suspect that the woman who had been murdered was my sister.

THE CORONER (to the jury): The only reason why I allow this evidence is that the witness has been doubtful about her identification. (To witness) Did your sister ever break a limb?

MALCOLM: No.

CORONER: Never?

MALCOLM: Not to my knowledge.

THE FOREMAN: Had she any special marks upon her?

MALCOLM: Yes, on her right leg there was a small black mark.

THE CORONER: Have you seen that mark on the deceased?

MALCOLM: Yes.

CORONER: When did you see it?

MALCOLM: Yesterday morning.

CORONER: But when, before death, did you see it on your sister?

MALCOLM: Oh not for years. It was the size of a pea. I have not seen it for 20 years.

CORONER: Did you mention the mark before you saw the body?

MALCOLM: I said that I could recognize my sister by this particular mark.

CORONER: What was the mark?

MALCOLM: It was from the bite of an adder. One day, when children, we were rolling down a hill together, and we came across an adder. The thing bit me first and my sister afterwards. I have still the mark of the bite on my left hand.

THE CORONER (examining the mark): Oh, that is only a scar. Are you sure that your sister, in her youth, never broke a limb?

MALCOLM: Not to my knowledge.

CORONER: Has your husband seen your sister?

MALCOLM: Yes.

CORONER: Has he been to the mortuary?

MALCOLM: No; he will not go.

CORONER: Have you any brothers and sisters alive?

MALCOLM: Yes, a brother and a sister, but they have not seen her for years. My brother might recognize her. He lives near Bath. My sister resides at Folkestone. My sister (the deceased) had a hollowness in her right foot, caused by some sort of accident. It was the absence of this hollowness that made me doubt whether the deceased was really my sister. Perhaps it passed away in death. But the adder mark removed all doubt.

CORONER: Did you recognize the clothes of the deceased at all?

MALCOLM: No. (Bursting into tears). Indeed, I have had trouble with her. On one occasion she left a naked baby outside my door.

CORONER: One of her babies?

MALCOLM: One of her own.

CORONER: One of the two children by her husband?

MALCOLM: No, another one; one she had by a policeman, I believe. She left it with me, and I had to keep it until she fetched it away.

INSPECTOR REID: Is that child alive, do you know?

MALCOLM: I believe it died in Bath.

THE CORONER: It is important that the evidence of identification should be unmistakable, and I think that the witness should go to the same spot in Chancery-lane on Saturday next, in order to see if her sister comes.

WITNESS: I have no doubt.

THE CORONER: Still, it is better that the matter should be tested.

WITNESS (in reply to the jury): I did not think it strange that my sister came to me last Thursday instead of the Saturday, because she has done it before. But on previous occasions she has come on the Saturday as well. When she came last Thursday she asked me for money, stating that she had not enough to pay for her lodgings, and I said, "Elizabeth, you are a pest to me."

THE CORONER: Has your sister been in prison?

WITNESS: Yes.

CORONER: Has she never been in prison on a Saturday?

MALCOLM: No; she has only been locked up for the night.

CORONER: Never more?

MALCOLM: No; she has been fined.

A JUROR: You say that before when she has come on the Thursday she has also come on the Saturday as well?

MALCOLM: Always.

THE CORONER: So that the Thursday was an extra. You are quite confident now about the identity?

MALCOLM: I have not a shadow of doubt.

Mr. Frederick William Blackwell [Dr. William P. Blackwell] deposed: I reside at No. 100, Commercial-road, and am a physician and surgeon. On Sunday morning last, at ten minutes past one o'clock, I was called to Berner-street by a policeman. My assistant, Mr. Johnston, went back with the constable, and I followed immediately I was dressed. I consulted my watch on my arrival, and it was 1.16 A.M. The deceased was lying on her left side obliquely across the passage, her face looking towards the right wall. Her legs were drawn up, her feet close against the wall of the right side of the passage. Her head was resting beyond the carriage-wheel rut, the neck lying over the rut. Her feet were three yards from the

Contemporary sketch of Dr. Blackwell (courtesy Evans/Skinner Crime Archive).

gateway. Her dress was unfastened at the neck. The neck and chest were quite warm, as were also the legs, and the face was slightly warm. The hands were cold. The right hand was open and on the chest, and was smeared with blood. The left hand, lying on the ground, was partially closed, and contained a small packet of cachous wrapped in tissue paper. There were no rings, nor marks of rings, on her hands. The appearance of the face was quite placid. The mouth was slightly open. The deceased had round her neck a check silk scarf, the bow of which was turned to the left and pulled very tight. In the neck there was a long incision which exactly corresponded with the lower border of the scarf. The border was slightly frayed, as if by a sharp knife. The incision in the neck commenced on the left side, 2 inches below the angle of the jaw, and almost in a direct line with it, nearly severing the vessels on that side, cutting the windpipe completely in two, and terminating on the opposite side 1 inch below the angle of the right jaw, but without severing the vessels on that side. I could not ascertain whether the bloody hand had been moved. The blood was running down the gutter into the drain in the opposite direction from the feet. There was about 1lb of clotted blood close by the body, and a stream all the way from there to the back door of the club.

CORONER: Were there no spots of blood about?

BLACKWELL: No; only some marks of blood which had been trodden in.

CORONER: Was there any blood on the soles of the deceased's boots?

BLACKWELL: No.

CORONER: No splashing of blood on the wall?

BLACKWELL: No, it was very dark, and what I saw was by the aid of a policeman's lantern. I have not examined the place since. I examined the clothes, but found no blood on any part of them. The bonnet of the deceased was lying on the ground a few inches from the head. Her dress was unbuttoned at the top.

CORONER: Can you say whether the injuries could have been self-inflicted?

BLACKWELL: It is impossible that they could have been.

CORONER: Did you form any opinion as to how long the deceased had been dead?

BLACKWELL: From twenty minutes to half an hour when I arrived. The clothes were not wet with rain. She would have bled to death comparatively slowly on account of vessels on one side only of the neck being cut and the artery not completely severed.

CORONER: After the infliction of the injuries was there any possibility of any cry being uttered by the deceased?

BLACKWELL: None whatever. Dr. Phillips came about twenty minutes to half an hour after my arrival. The double doors of the yard were closed when I arrived, so that the previous witness must have made a mistake on that point.

A JUROR: Can you say whether the throat was cut before or after the deceased fell to the ground?

BLACKWELL: I formed the opinion that the murderer probably caught hold of the silk scarf, which was tight and knotted, and pulled the deceased backwards, cutting her throat in that way. The throat might have been cut as she was falling, or when she was on the ground. The blood would have spurted about if the act had been committed while she was standing up.

THE CORONER: Was the silk scarf tight enough to prevent her calling out?

BLACKWELL: I could not say that.

CORONER: A hand might have been put on her nose and mouth?
BLACKWELL: Yes, and the cut on the throat was probably instantaneous.
The inquest was then adjourned until tomorrow afternoon.[4]

That day, Dr. Phillips returned to the mortuary for an additional look at the body. He found that the total circumference of the neck was twelve inches. In the pocket of Elizabeth's underskirt he found a padlock-type key, a comb, a broken piece of comb, a metal spoon, half a dozen large buttons, one small button, a piece of muslin, a small piece of lead pencil, one or two small pieces of paper, and a hook, as if off a dress. When he examined her jacket, he "found that although there was a slight amount of mud on the right side, the left was well plastered with mud."[5]

7

I Need a Detective

On Wednesday, October 3, "at St. George's Vestry Hall, Cable-street, Mr. Wynne E. Baxter, coroner for East Middlesex, again resumed the inquiry into the circumstances attending the death of the woman who was found with her throat cut at one o'clock on Sunday morning last in a yard adjoining the International Working Men's Club, Berner-street, Commercial-road East." It was one o'clock in the afternoon, and "Detective-Inspector E. Reid, H Division, again watched the case on behalf of the Criminal Investigation Department." The following evidence was presented.

Elizabeth Tanner, examined by the Coroner, said: I am deputy of the common lodging-house, No. 32, Flower and Dean-street, and am a widow. I have seen the body of the deceased at St. George's Mortuary, and recognize it as that of a woman who has lodged in our house, on and off, for the last six years.

CORONER: Who is she?

TANNER: She was known by the nick-name of "Long Liz."

CORONER: Do you know her right name?

TANNER: No.

CORONER: Was she an English woman?

TANNER: She used to say that she was a Swedish woman. She never told me where she was born. She said that she was married, and that her husband and children were drowned in the Princess Alice.

CORONER: When did you last see her alive?

TANNER: Last Saturday evening, at half-past six o'clock.

CORONER: Where was she then?

TANNER: With me in a public-house, called the Queen's Head, in Commercial-street.

CORONER: Did she leave you there?

TANNER: She went back with me to the lodging-house. At that time she had no bonnet or cloak on. She never told me what her husband was.

CORONER: Where did you actually leave her?

TANNER: She went into the kitchen, and I went to another part of the building.

CORONER: Did you see her again?

TANNER: No, until I saw the body in the mortuary to-day.

88

CORONER: You are quite certain it is the body of the same woman?

TANNER: Quite sure. I recognize, beside the features, that the roof of her mouth is missing. Deceased accounted for this by stating that she was in the Princess Alice when it went down, and that her mouth was injured.

CORONER: How long had she been staying at the lodging-house?

TANNER: She was there last week only on Thursday and Friday nights.

CORONER: Had she paid for her bed on Saturday night?

TANNER: No.

CORONER: Do you know any of her male acquaintances?

TANNER: Only of one.

CORONER: Who is he?

TANNER: She was living with him. She left him on Thursday to come and stay at our house, so she told me.

CORONER: Have you seen this man?

TANNER: I saw him last Sunday.

DETECTIVE-INSPECTOR REID: He is present to-day [Kidney].

WITNESS: I do not know that she was ever up at the Thames Police-court, or that she suffered from epileptic fits. I am aware that she lived in Fashion-street, but not that she has ever resided at Poplar. I never heard of a sister at Red Lion-square. I never heard of any relative except her late husband and children.

CORONER: What sort of a woman was she?

TANNER: Very quiet.

CORONER: A sober woman?

TANNER: Yes.

CORONER: Did she use to stop out late at night?

TANNER: Sometimes.

CORONER: Do you know if she had any money?

TANNER: She cleaned two rooms for me on Saturday, and I paid her 6d for doing it. I do not know whether she had any other money.

CORONER: Are you able to say whether the two handkerchiefs now at the mortuary belonged to the deceased?

TANNER: No.

CORONER: Do you recognize her clothes?

TANNER: Yes. I recognize the long cloak which is hanging up in the mortuary. The other clothes she had on last Saturday.

CORONER: Did she ever tell you that she was afraid of any one?

TANNER: No.

CORONER: Or that any one had ever threatened to injure her?

TANNER: No.

CORONER: The fact of her not coming back on Saturday did not surprise you, I suppose?

TANNER: We took no notice of it.

CORONER: What made you go to the mortuary, then?

TANNER: Because I was sent for. I do not recollect at what hour she came to the lodging-house last Thursday. She was wearing the long cloak then. She did not bring any parcel with her.

BY THE JURY: I do not know of any one else of the name of Long Liz. I never heard of her sister allowing her any money, nor have I heard the name of Stride mentioned in connection with her. Before last Thursday she had been away from my house about three months.*

THE CORONER: Did you see her during that three months?

TANNER: Yes, frequently; sometimes once a week, and at other times almost every other day.

CORONER: Did you understand what she was doing?

TANNER: She told me that she was at work among the Jews, and was living with a man in Fashion-street.

CORONER: Could she speak English well?

TANNER: Yes, but she spoke Swedish also.

CORONER: When she spoke English could you detect that she was a foreigner?

TANNER: She spoke English as well as an English woman. She did not associate much with Swedish people. I never heard of her having hurt her foot, nor of her having broken a limb in childhood. I had no doubt that she was what she represented herself to be—a Swede.

Catherine Lane: I live in Flower and Dean-street, and am a charwoman and married. My husband is a dock laborer, and is living with me at the lodging house of which the last witness is deputy. I have been there since last February. I have seen the body of the deceased at the mortuary.

THE CORONER: Did you recognize it?

LANE: Yes, as the body of Long Liz, who lived occasionally in the lodging-house. She came there last Thursday.

CORONER: Had you ever seen her before?

LANE: I have known her for six or seven months. I used to see her frequently in Fashion-street, where she lived, and I have seen her at our lodging-house.

CORONER: Did you speak to her last week?

LANE: On Thursday and Saturday.

CORONER: At what time did you see her first on Thursday?

LANE: Between ten and eleven o'clock.

CORONER: Did she explain why she was coming back?

LANE: She said she had had a few words with the man she was living with.

CORONER: When did you see her on Saturday?

LANE: When she was cleaning the deputy's room.

CORONER: And after that?

LANE: I last saw her in the kitchen, between six and seven in the evening. She then had on a long cloak and a black bonnet.

CORONER: Did she say where she was going?

LANE: No. I first saw the body in the mortuary on Sunday afternoon, and I recognised it then.

CORONER: Did you see her leave the lodging-house?

LANE: Yes; she gave me a piece of velvet as she left, and asked me to mind it until she came back. (The velvet was produced, and proved to be a large piece, green in color.)

CORONER: Had she no place to leave it?

LANE: I do not know why she asked me, as the deputy would take charge of

---

*Living off and on at a lodging house, even for a regular customer, is a good example of how transient even the locals could be. (Refer also to MEPO 3/140, f20.)

anything. I know the deceased had sixpence when she left; she showed it to me, stating that the deputy had given it to her.

CORONER: Had she been drinking then?

LANE: Not that I am aware of.

CORONER: Do you know of any one who was likely to have injured her?

LANE: No one.

CORONER: Have you heard her mention any person but this man she was living with?

LANE: No. I have heard her say she was a Swede, and that at one time she lived in Devonshire-street, Commercial-road — never in Poplar.

CORONER: Did you ever hear her speak of her husband?

LANE: She said he was dead. She never said that she was afraid, or that any one had threatened her life. I am satisfied the deceased is the same woman.

BY THE JURY: I could tell by her accent that she was a foreigner. She did not bring all her words out plainly.

CORONER: Have you ever heard of her speaking to any one in her own language?

LANE: Yes; with women for whom she worked. I never heard of her having a sister, or of her having left a child at her sister's door.

Charles Preston deposed: I live at No. 32, Flower and Dean-street, and I am a barber. I have been lodging at my present address for eighteen months, and have seen the deceased there. I saw the body on Sunday last, and am quite sure it is that of Long Liz.

THE CORONER: When did you last see her alive? — On Saturday morning between six and seven o'clock.

CORONER: Where was she then?

PRESTON: In the kitchen of the lodging-house.

CORONER: Was she dressed to go out?

PRESTON: Yes, and asked me for a brush to brush her clothes with, but I did not let her have one.

CORONER: What was she wearing?

PRESTON: The jacket I have seen at the mortuary, but no flowers in the breast. She had the striped silk handkerchief round her neck.

CORONER: Do you happen to have seen her pocket-handkerchiefs?

PRESTON: No.

CORONER: You cannot say whether she had two?

PRESTON: No.

CORONER: Do you know anything about her?

PRESTON: I always understood that she was born at Stockholm, and came to England in the service of a gentleman.

CORONER: Did she ever tell you her age?

PRESTON: She said once that she was thirty-five.

CORONER: Did she ever tell you that she was married?

PRESTON: Yes; and that her husband and children went down in the Princess Alice — that she had been saved while they were lost.

CORONER: Did she ever state what her husband was?

PRESTON: I have some recollection that she said he was a seafaring man, and that he had kept a coffee-house in Chrisp-street, Poplar.

CORONER: Did she ever tell you that she was taken to the Thames Police-court?

PRESTON: I only remember her having been taken into custody for being drunk and disorderly at the Ten Bells public-house, Commercial-street, one Sunday morning from four to five months ago.

CORONER: Do you know of any one who was likely to have injured her?
PRESTON: No.

CORONER: Did she ever state that she was afraid of any one?
PRESTON: Never.

CORONER: Did she say where she was going on Saturday?
PRESTON: No.

CORONER: Or when she was coming back?
PRESTON: No.

CORONER: Did she say whether she was coming back?
PRESTON: She never said anything about it. She always gave me to understand that her name was Elizabeth Stride. She never mentioned any sister. She stated that her mother was still alive in Sweden. She apparently spoke Swedish fluently to people who came into the lodging-house.*

Michael Kidney said: I live at No. 38, Dorset-street, Spitalfields, and am a waterside laborer. I have seen the body of the deceased at the mortuary.

THE CORONER: Is it the woman you have been living with?
KIDNEY: Yes.

CORONER: You have no doubt about it?
KIDNEY: No doubt whatever.

CORONER: What was her name?
KIDNEY: Elizabeth Stride.

CORONER: How long have you known her?
KIDNEY: About three years.

CORONER: How long has she been living with you?
KIDNEY: Nearly all that time.

CORONER: What was her age?
KIDNEY: Between thirty-six and thirty-eight years.

CORONER: Was she a Swede?
KIDNEY: She told me that she was a Swede, and I have no doubt she was. She said she was born three miles from Stockholm, that her father was a farmer, and that she first came to England for the purpose of seeing the country; but I have grave doubts about that. She afterwards told me that she came to England in a situation with a family.

CORONER: Had she got any relatives in England?
KIDNEY: When I met her she told me she was a widow, and that her husband had been a ship's carpenter at Sheerness.

CORONER: Did he ever keep a coffee-house?
KIDNEY: She told me that he had.

CORONER: Where?
KIDNEY: In Chrisp-street, Poplar.

CORONER: Did she say when he died?

*It has been suggested that "Swedish" was actually a misprint or mishearing of "Yiddish."

KIDNEY: She informed me that he was drowned in the Princess Alice disaster.

CORONER: Was the roof of her mouth defective?

KIDNEY: Yes.

CORONER: You had a quarrel with her on Thursday?

KIDNEY: I did not see her on Thursday.

CORONER: When did you last see her?

KIDNEY: On the Tuesday, and I then left her on friendly terms in Commercial-street. That was between nine and ten o'clock at night, as I was coming from work.

CORONER: Did you expect her home?

KIDNEY: I expected her home half an hour afterwards. I subsequently ascertained that she had been in and had gone out again, and I did not see her again alive.

CORONER: Can you account for her sudden disappearance? Was she the worse for drink when you last saw her?

KIDNEY: She was perfectly sober.

CORONER: You can assign no reason whatever for her going away so suddenly?

KIDNEY: She would occasionally go away.

CORONER: Oh, she has left you before?

KIDNEY: During the three years I have known her she has been away from me about five months altogether.

CORONER: Without any reason?

KIDNEY: Not to my knowledge. I treated her the same as I would a wife.

CORONER: Do you know whether she had picked up with any one?

KIDNEY: I have seen the address of the brother of the gentleman with whom she lived as a servant, somewhere near Hyde Park, but I cannot find it now.

CORONER: Did she have any reason for going away?

KIDNEY: It was drink that made her go on previous occasions. She always came back again. I think she liked me better than any other man. I do not believe she left me on Tuesday to take up with any other man.

CORONER: Had she any money?

KIDNEY: I do not think she was without a shilling when she left me. From what I used to give her I fancy she must either have had money or spent it in drink.

CORONER: You know of nobody whom she was likely to have complications with or fall foul of?

KIDNEY: No, but I think the police authorities are very much to blame, or they would have got the man who murdered her. At Leman-street Police-station, on Monday night, I asked for a detective to give information to get the man.

CORONER: What information had you?

KIDNEY: I could give information that would enable the detectives to discover the man at any time.

CORONER: Then will you give us your information now.

KIDNEY: I told the inspector on duty at the police-station that I could give information provided he would let me have a young, strange [sic] detective to act on it, and he would not give me one.

CORONER: What do you think should be inquired into?

KIDNEY: I might have given information that would have led to a great deal if I had been provided with a strange young detective.

INSPECTOR REID: When you went to Leman-street and saw the inspector on duty, were you intoxicated?

KIDNEY: Yes; I asked for a young detective, and he would not let me have one, and I told him that he was uncivil. (Laughter.)

CORONER: You have been in the army, and I believe have a good pension?

KIDNEY: Only the reserve.

A JUROR: Have you got any information for a detective?

KIDNEY: I am a great lover of discipline, sir. (Laughter.)

THE CORONER: Had you any information that required the service of a detective?

KIDNEY: Yes. I thought that if I had one, privately, he could get more information than I could myself. The parties I obtained my information from knew me, and I thought someone else would be able to derive more from them.

INSPECTOR REID: Will you give me the information directly, if you will not give it to the coroner?

KIDNEY: I believe I could catch the man if I had a detective under my command.

THE CORONER: You cannot expect that. I have had over a hundred letters making suggestions, and I dare say all the writers would like to have a detective at their service. (Laughter.)

WITNESS: I have information which I think might be of use to the police.

THE CORONER: You had better give it, then.

WITNESS: I believe that, if I could place the policeman myself, the man would be captured.

THE CORONER: You must know that the police would not be placed at the disposal of a man the worse for drink.

WITNESS: If I were at liberty to place 100 men about this city the murderer would be caught in the act.

INSPECTOR REID: But you have no information to give to the police?

WITNESS: No, I will keep it to myself.*

A JUROR: Do you know of any sister who gave money to the deceased?

KIDNEY: No. On Monday I saw Mrs. Malcolm, who said the deceased was her sister. She is very like the deceased.

CORONER: Did the deceased have a child by you?

KIDNEY: No.

CORONER: Or by a policeman?

KIDNEY: She told me that a policeman used to court her when she was at Hyde Park, before she was married to Stride. Stride and the policeman courted her at the same time, but I never heard of her having a child by the policeman. She said she was the mother of nine children, two of whom were drowned with her husband in the Princess Alice, and the remainder were either in a school belonging to the Swedish Church on the other side of London Bridge, or with the husband's friends. I thought she was telling the truth when she spoke of Swedish people. I understood that the deceased and her husband were employed on the Princess Alice.

The exchange between Coroner Baxter, Inspector Reid, and Michael Kidney over Kidney's alleged information demonstrates the public's belief that it can do something better than the professionals.

Mr. Edward Johnson [Johnston]: I live at 100, Commercial-road, and am assistant to Drs. Kaye and Blackwell. On Sunday morning last, at a few minutes past one o'clock, I received a call from Constable 436 H [426H]. After informing Dr. Blackwell, who was in bed, of the case, I accompanied the officer to Berner-street, and in a courtyard adjoining No. 40 I was shown the figure of a woman lying on her left side.

THE CORONER: Were there many people about?

JOHNSTON: There was a crowd in the yard.

CORONER: And police?

JOHNSTON: Yes.

CORONER: Was any one touching the deceased?

JOHNSTON: No.

CORONER: Was there much light?

JOHNSTON: Very little.

CORONER: What light there was, where did it come from?

JOHNSTON: From the policeman's lantern. I examined the woman and found an incision in the throat.

CORONER: Was blood coming from the wound?

JOHNSTON: No, it had stopped bleeding. I felt the body and found all warm except the hands, which were quite cold.

CORONER: Did you undo the dress?

JOHNSTON: The dress was not undone when I came. I undid it to see if the chest was warm.

CORONER: Did you move the head at all?

JOHNSTON: I left the body precisely as I found it. There was a stream of blood down to the gutter; it was all clotted. There was very little blood near the neck; it had all run away. I did not notice at the time that one of the hands was smeared with blood. The left arm was bent, away from the body. The right arm was also bent, and across the body.

CORONER: Can you say whether any one had stepped into the stream of blood?

JOHNSTON: There was no mark of it.

CORONER: Did you look for any?

JOHNSTON: Yes. I had no watch with me, but Dr. Blackwell looked at his when he arrived, and the time was 1.16 A.M. I preceded him by three or four minutes. The bonnet of the deceased was lying three or four inches beyond the head on the ground. The outer gates were closed shortly after I came.

Thomas Coram: I live at No. 67, Plummer's-road, and work for a cocoanut dealer. On Monday shortly after midnight I left a friend's house in Bath-gardens, Brady-street. I walked straight down Brady-street and into Whitechapel-road towards Aldgate. I first walked on the right side of Whitechapel-road, and afterwards crossed over to the left, and when opposite No. 253 I saw a knife lying on the doorstep.

CORONER: What is No. 253?

CORAM: A laundry. There were two steps to the front door, and the knife was on the bottom step. The production of the knife created some sensation, its discovery not having been generally known. It was a knife such as would be used by a baker in his trade, it being flat at the top instead of pointed, as a butcher's knife would be. The blade, which was discoloured with something resembling blood, was quite a foot long and an inch broad, whilst the black handle was six inches in length, and strongly riveted in three places.

WITNESS (continuing): There was a handkerchief round the handle of the knife, the handkerchief having been first folded and then twisted round the blade. A policeman coming towards me, I called his attention to the knife, which I did not touch.

CORONER: Did the policeman take the knife away?

CORAM: Yes, to the Leman-street station, I accompanying him.

CORONER: Were there many people passing at the time?

CORAM: Very few. I do not think I passed more than a dozen from Brady-street to where I found the knife. The weapon could easily be seen; it was light there.

CORONER: Did you pass any policeman between Brady-street and where the knife was?

CORAM: I passed three policemen.

Constable Joseph Drage, 282 H Division: On Monday morning at half-past twelve o'clock I was on fixed point duty opposite Brady-street, Whitechapel-road, when I saw the last witness stooping down to pick up something about twenty yards from me. As I went towards him he beckoned with his finger, and said, "Policeman, there is a knife lying here." I then saw a long-bladed knife on the doorstep. I picked up the knife, and found it was smothered with blood.

CORONER: Was it wet?

DRAGE: Dry. A handkerchief, which was also blood-stained, was bound round the handle and tied with a string. I asked the lad how he came to see it, and he said, "I was just looking around, and I saw something white." I asked him what he did out so late, and he replied, "I have been to a friend's in Bath-gardens." I took down his name and address, and he went to the police-station with me. The knife and handkerchief are those produced. The boy was sober, and his manner natural. He said that the knife made his blood run cold, adding, "We hear of such funny things nowadays." I had passed the step a quarter of an hour before. I could not be positive, but I do not think the knife was there then. About an hour earlier I stood near the door, and saw the landlady let out a woman. The knife was not there then. I handed the knife and handkerchief to Dr. Phillips on Monday afternoon.

Mr. George Baxter Phillips [Dr. George Bagster Phillips]: I live at No. 2, Spital-square, and am surgeon of the H Division of police. I was called on Sunday morning last at twenty past one to Leman-street Police-station, and was sent on to Berner-street, to a yard at the side of what proved to be a club-house. I found Inspector Pinhorn and Acting-Superintendent West in possession of a body, which had already been seen by Dr. Blackwell, who had arrived some time before me. The body was lying on its left side, the face being turned towards the wall, the head towards the yard, and the feet toward the street. The left arm was extended from elbow, and a packet of cachous was in the hand. Similar ones were in the gutter. I took them from the hand and gave them to Dr. Blackwell. The right arm was lying over the body, and the back of the hand and wrist had on them clotted blood. The legs were drawn up, feet close to wall, body still warm, face warm, hands cold, legs quite warm, silk handkerchief round throat, slightly torn (so is my note, but I since find it is cut). I produce the handkerchief. This corresponded to the right angle of the jaw. The throat was deeply gashed, and there was an abrasion of the skin, about an inch and a quarter in diameter, under the right clavicle. On Oct. 1, at three P.M., at St. George's Mortuary, present Dr. Blackwell and for part of the time Dr. Reigate and Dr. Blackwell's assistant; temperature being about 55 degrees, Dr. Blackwell and I made a post-mortem examination, Dr. Blackwell kindly consenting to make the dissection, and I took the following note:

Rigor mortis still firmly marked. Mud on face and left side of the head. Matted on the hair and left side. We removed the clothes. We found the body fairly nourished. Over both shoulders, especially the right, from the front aspect under collar bones and in front of chest there is a bluish discolouration which I have watched and seen on two occasions since. On neck, from left to right, there is a clean cut incision six inches in length; incision commencing two and a half inches in a straight line below the angle of the jaw. Three-quarters of an inch over undivided muscle, then becoming deeper, about an inch dividing sheath and the vessels, ascending a little, and then grazing the muscle outside the cartilages on the left side of the neck. The carotid artery on the left side and the other vessels contained in the sheath were all cut through, save the posterior portion of the carotid, to a line about 1–12th of an inch in extent, which prevented the separation of the upper and lower portion of the artery. The cut through the tissues on the right side of the cartilages is more superficial, and tails off to about two inches below the right angle of the jaw. It is evident that the haemorrhage which produced death was caused through the partial severance of the left carotid artery. There is a deformity in the lower fifth of the bones of the right leg, which are not straight, but bow forward; there is a thickening above the left ankle. The bones are here straighter. No recent external injury save to neck. The lower lobe of the ear was torn, as if by the forcible removing or wearing through of an earring, but it was thoroughly healed. The right ear was pierced for an earring, but had not been so injured, and the earring was wanting. On removing the scalp there was no sign of bruising or extravasation of blood between it and the skull-cap. The skull was about one-sixth of an inch in thickness, and dense in texture. The brain was fairly normal. Both lungs were unusually pale. The heart was small; left ventricle firmly contracted, right less so. Right ventricle full of dark clot; left absolutely empty. Partly digested food, apparently consisting of cheese, potato, and farinaceous edibles. Teeth on left lower jaw absent.

On Tuesday, at the mortuary, I found the total circumference of the neck 12 inches. I found in the pocket of the underskirt of the deceased a key, as of a padlock, a small piece of lead pencil, a comb, a broken piece of comb, a metal spoon, half a dozen large and one small button, a hook, as if off a dress, a piece of muslin, and one or two small pieces of paper. Examining her jacket I found that although there

Contemporary sketch of Dr. Phillips (courtesy Stephen Ryder/Casebook).

was a slight amount of mud on the right side, the left was well plastered with mud.

A JUROR: You have not mentioned anything about the roof of the mouth. One witness said part of the roof of the mouth was gone.

WITNESS: That was not noticed.

THE CORONER: What was the cause of death?

PHILLIPS: Undoubtedly the loss of blood from the left carotid artery and the division of the windpipe.

CORONER: Did you examine the blood at Berner-street carefully, as to its direction and so forth?

PHILLIPS: Yes. The blood near to the neck and a few inches to the left side was well clotted, and it had run down the waterway to within a few inches of the side entrance to the club-house.

CORONER: Were there any spots of blood anywhere else?

PHILLIPS: I could trace none except that which I considered had been transplanted — if I may use the term — from the original flow from the neck. Roughly estimating it, I should say there was an unusual flow of blood, considering the stature and the nourishment of the body.

BY A JUROR: I did notice a black mark on one of the legs of the deceased, but could not say that it was due to an adder bite.

Before the witness had concluded his evidence the inquiry was adjourned until Friday.[1]

With the amazing information dug up by Batchelor and Le Grand, the *Evening News* sent its correspondent to personally interview Packer that evening. To them, this unassuming greengrocer held the key to the assassin's identity. The newspaper had no doubt about the elderly fruiterer's importance.

WHERE THE MURDERER BOUGHT THE GRAPES.

INTERVIEW WITH THE MAN WHO TALKED WITH HIM.

(BY OUR SPECIAL COMMISSIONER.)

Last evening [Oct. 3] was far advanced when I [interviewer] walked into the greengrocer's little shop where the murdered woman was "treated" to some grapes, late on Saturday night, by the inhuman monster who shortly afterwards shed her blood with that revolting brutality peculiar to those now notorious murders. This shop is at No. 44 Berner street, and is kept by a quiet intelligent fruiterer named Matthew Packer, and his wife. They are both a little past the prime of life, and are known as respectable, hard working people. Their unpretending premises are situated just two doors from the scene of the murder, and the presumption of any mind of ordinary intelligence would be that it was the very first place at which the detectives and the police would have made their inquiries. They did nothing of the sort, as the man's simple, straightforward narrative will show.

MATHEW PACKER'S STORY.

"Now, Mr. Packer, I want you to tell me all that you know about the events of Saturday night last," I said as I took the seat he offered me.

"Well, that's soon told," was his answer.

"I had been out with my barrow most of the day, but hadn't done much business; and as the night came on wet I went home and took the place of the 'missus' in the shop here."

THE MURDERER AT THE WINDOW.

"Some time between half past eleven and twelve a man and woman came up Berner street from the direction of Ellen street, and stopped outside my window looking at the fruit. The man was about thirty to thirty five years of age, medium height, and with rather a dark complexion. He wore a black coat and a black, soft felt hat. He looked to me like a clerk or something of that sort. I am certain he wasn't what I should call a working man or anything like us folks that live around here."

WHAT THE WOMAN WAS LIKE.

"Did you notice the woman so that you would know her again?"

"Yes. I saw that she was dressed in dark clothes, looked a middle aged woman, and carried a white flower in her hand. I saw that as plain as anything could be, and I am sure I should know the woman again. I was taken today to the see the dead body of a woman lying in Golden lane mortuary, but I can swear that wasn't the woman that stood at my shop window on Saturday night."

THE SOUND OF THE ASSASSIN'S VOICE.

"Well, they hadn't stood there more than a minute when the man stepped a bit forward, and said, 'I say, old man, how do you sell your grapes.'"

"I answered, 'Sixpence a pound the black 'uns, sir, and fourpence a pound the white 'uns.'" Then he turned to the woman and said, 'Which will you have, my dear, black or white? You shall have whichever you like best.'"

"The woman said, 'Oh, then I'll have the black 'uns, 'cos they look the nicest.'"

"'Give us half a pound of the black ones, then,' said the man. I put the grapes in a paper bag and handed them to him."

"Did you observe anything peculiar about his voice or manner, as he spoke to you?"

"He spoke like an educated man, but he had a loud, sharp sort of voice, and a quick commanding way with him."

"But did he speak like an Englishman or more in this style?" I asked, imitating as well as I could the Yankee twang.

"Yes, now you mention it, there was a sound of that sort about it," was the instantaneous reply.

THE MURDERER LAYING HIS PLANS.

"And what became of them after that?"

"First of all, they stood near the gateway leading into the club for a minute or two, and then they crossed the road and stood right opposite."

"For how long?"

"More than half an hour, I should say; so long that I said to my missus, 'Why, them people must be a couple o' fools to stand out there in the rain eating grapes they bought here, when they might just as well have had shelter!' In fact, sir, me and my missus left 'em standing there when we went to bed."

"And what time was that?"

"I couldn't say exactly, but it must have been past midnight a little bit, for the public houses was shut up."

"And that was positively the last you saw of them?"

"Yes. Standing opposite the yard where the murdered woman was found."

"Well, Mr. Packer, I suppose the police came at once to ask you and your wife what you knew about the affair, as soon as ever the body was discovered."

"The police? No. They haven't asked me a word about it yet!!! A young man in plain clothes came in here on Monday and asked if he might look at the yard at the back of our house, so as to see if anybody had climbed over. My missus lent him some steps. But he didn't put any questions to us about the man and the woman."

"I am afraid you don't quite understand my question, Mr. Packer. Do you actually mean to say that no detective or policeman came to inquire whether you had sold grapes to any one that night? Now, please be very careful in your answer, for this may prove a serious business for the London police [Metropolitan Police]."

"I've only got one answer," said the man "because it's the truth. Except a gentleman who is a private detective. No detective or policeman has ever asked me a single question nor come near my shop to find out if I knew anything about the grapes the murdered woman had been eating before her throat was cut!!!"

MATTHEW PACKER
THE BERNER STREET FRUITERER IDENTIFIES LIZZIE STRIDE.

This afternoon Matthew Packer, the fruiterer, of 44 Berner street, referred to in the above narrative, visited the mortuary of St. George's in the East, and identified the body of Elizabeth Stride as that of the woman for whom the grapes were purchased on the night of the murder.

The *Evening News* waited until October 4 to publish both stories: the one from their special correspondent and that from Batchelor and Le Grand. This was intentional, because of the circulation war that was occurring. No doubt, they wanted to keep this exclusive to themselves, until the last possible minute, and then release this late-breaking story to the world. It is unknown who the plain-clothes detective was that appeared on Monday, but most likely he was a police detective performing his assignment as part of the house-to-house search, ordered by Inspector Abberline.[2]

It was soon Thursday, October 4. Only four days into the murder investigation, the authorities woke to some shocking news — Packer's inflammatory remarks. Because of his accusations of neglect against the police, Chief Inspector Henry Moore (possibly the liaison between Inspector Swanson and Inspector Abberline), sent Sergeant White to re-interview the irrepressible fruiterer, and, if necessary, take him to the mortuary to view the body of the Berner Street victim. Mr. Packer was not home, but Mrs. Packer was. She informed Sergeant White that two detectives had called and took her husband to the mortuary. The sergeant immediately proceeded to St. George's. While on his way there, Sergeant White ran into Packer, who was with a man.

Where have you been? asked White.

"This detective asked me to go to see if I could identify the woman," Packer replied.

"Have you done so?" the sergeant inquired.

"Yes," he said. "I believe she bought some grapes at my shop about 12. oclock on Saturday."

Before long, another man joined them. Sergeant White became curious. He asked this new arrival what they were doing with Packer? Instead of answering the policeman's question, Batchelor and Le Grand both proclaimed that they were detectives. Curiosity gave way to suspicion, and Sergeant White asked for their "authority." One man produced a card from his pocket book, but he would not allow the sergeant to touch it. Possibly realizing the grave issue that was suddenly before them, being viewed as masquerading as policemen, the two men then stated that they were "private detectives." At that, "they then induced Packer to go away with them."[3]

That same day, Mr. Samuel Frederick Langham, City of London coroner, opened the Eddowes inquest at Golden Lane, which was approximately one mile overland to the northeast from Mitre Square, where Eddowes's body was found. "The court was crowded, and much interest was taken in the proceedings, many people standing outside the building during the whole of the day." Mr. Henry Homewood Crawford, the City of London solicitor, sat in on behalf of the Corporation, as responsible for the police, while Major Henry Smith, acting commissioner, City of London Police, and Detective Superintendent Alfred Lawrence Forster, City of London Police, represented the officers engaged in the investigation. Only seven people testified, including Eddowes's boyfriend, John Kelly. After Dr. Frederick Gordon Brown, city police surgeon, gave his evidence, Mr. Langham "was glad to announce that the Corporation had unanimously approved the offer by the Lord Mayor of a reward of £500 for the discovery of the murderer. Several jurymen expressed their satisfaction at the promptness with which the offer was made. The inquest was then adjourned until next Thursday."

Mr. Langham's announcement was welcome news to many people, for the subject of rewards was a major concern to average person in the street. Not only was it readily brought up during the inquests, there were numerous letters to the editor emphasizing the need for a reward. Yet despite the public outcry, the Home Office, which oversaw the metropolitan area of London, maintained its four-year-old policy of no reward in the event of murder. Being a separate jurisdiction, however, the Corporation of London, which governed the one square mile of the city proper, was empowered to offer a reward, whether or not the Home Office agreed with such a practice.[4]

While the coroner's inquest was carried out on Eddowes, Registrar William Armstrong officially registered Elizabeth's death in St. George's-in-the-East. Cause of death — "Violent haemorrhage from severance of blood vessels in the neck by a sharp instrument." Possibly because of Packer's fifteen minutes of fame with the press that day, it would not be until about four in the afternoon when Sergeant White was able to meet up with fruit-seller again. They were in the greengrocer's shop, talking, when detectives Batchelor and Le Grand returned. The two men had arrived in a hansom cab and entered the shop. After they induced Packer to leave with them, Sergeant White asked where they were going. With the shopkeeper entering the cab, the two investigators proclaimed that they were taking him to see Sir Charles Warren. At Scotland Yard, Packer presented the following evidence:

> On Sat. night [September 29] about 11 P.M., a young man from 25–30, about 5 [feet] 7 [inches], with long black coat buttoned up, soft felt hat, kind of Yankee hat, rather broad shoulders, rather quick in speaking, rough voice. I sold him ½ pound black grapes, 3d. A woman came up with him from Back Church end (the lower end of street). She was dressed in black frock & jacket, fur round bottom of jacket, a black crepe bonnet, she was playing with a flower like a geranium white outside & red inside. I identify the woman at the St. George's Mortuary as the one I saw that night.
>
> They passed by as though they were going up [to] Commercial Road, but instead of going up they crossed to the other side of the road to the Board School, & were there for about ½ an hour till I should say 11.30, talking to one another. I then shut up my shutters. Before they passed over opposite to my shop, they went near to the club for a few minutes apparently listening to the music. I saw no more of them after I shut my shutters.[5]

At some point during the day, Dr. Phillips returned to the mortuary with Drs. Blackwell and Brown. The coroner asked them to "make a re-examination of the body of the deceased, especially with regard to the palate." This was done in response to several witnesses claiming that Elizabeth's mouth was injured. The doctors "did not find any injury to, or absence of, any part of either the hard or the soft palate." While there, they also looked at the two handkerchiefs found on Elizabeth's body. The larger of the two seemed to have fruit stains on it. Additionally, "the neckerchief which she had on was not torn, but cut," and what was thought to have been an abrasion on the right side of the neck had disappeared after the skin was washed. It was uninjured.[6]

⁓8⁓

The Swedish Connection

It was already Friday, October 5, and nearly a week had passed since the double event. At two that afternoon, "at the Vestry Hall of St. George-in-the-East, Cable-street, Mr. Wynne E. Baxter, coroner for East Middlesex, resumed the inquiry concerning the death of the woman who was found early on Sunday last with her throat cut, in a yard adjoining the International Working Men's Club, Berner-street, Commercial-road East." It was the fourth session, and "Superintendent T. Arnold and Detective-inspector Reid, H Division, watched the case on behalf of the Criminal Investigation Department." The following evidence was given.

Dr. Phillips, surgeon of the H Division of police, being recalled, said: On the last occasion I was requested to make a re-examination of the body of the deceased, especially with regard to the palate, and I have since done so at the mortuary, along with Dr. Blackwell and Dr. Gordon Brown. I did not find any injury to, or absence of, any part of either the hard or the soft palate. The Coroner also desired me to examine the two handkerchiefs which were found on the deceased. I did not discover any blood on them, and I believe that the stains on the larger handkerchief are those of fruit. Neither on the hands nor about the body of the deceased did I find grapes, or connection with them. I am convinced that the deceased had not swallowed either the skin or seed of a grape within many hours of her death. I have stated that the neckerchief which she had on was not torn, but cut. The abrasion which I spoke of on the right side of the neck was only apparently an abrasion, for on washing it it was removed, and the skin found to be uninjured. The knife [found by Coram] produced on the last occasion was delivered to me, properly secured, by a constable, and on examination I found it to be such a knife as is used in a chandler's shop, and is called a slicing knife. It has blood upon it, which has characteristics similar to the blood of a human being. It has been recently blunted, and its edge apparently turned by rubbing on a stone such as a kerbstone. It evidently was before a very sharp knife.

THE CORONER: Is it such as knife as could have caused the injuries which were inflicted upon the deceased?

PHILLIPS: Such a knife could have produced the incision and injuries to the neck, but it is not such a weapon as I should have fixed upon as having caused the injuries in this case; and if my opinion as regards the position of the body is correct, the knife in question would become an improbable instrument as having caused the incision.

CORONER: What is your idea as to the position the body was in when the crime was committed?

PHILLIPS: I have come to a conclusion as to the position of both the murderer and the victim, and I opine that the latter was seized by the shoulders and placed on the ground, and that the murderer was on her right side when he inflicted the cut. I am of opinion that the cut was made from the left to the right side of the deceased, and taking into account the position of the incision it is unlikely that such a long knife inflicted the wound in the neck.

CORONER: The knife produced on the last occasion was not sharp pointed, was it?

PHILLIPS: No, it was rounded at the tip, which was about an inch across. The blade was wider at the base.

CORONER: Was there anything to indicate that the cut on the neck of the deceased was made with a pointed knife?

PHILLIPS: Nothing.

CORONER: Have you formed any opinion as to the manner in which the deceased's right hand became stained with blood?

PHILLIPS: It is a mystery. There were small oblong clots on the back of the hand. I may say that I am taking it as a fact that after death the hand always remained in the position in which I found it — across the body.

CORONER: How long had the woman been dead when you arrived at the scene of the murder, do you think?

PHILLIPS: Within an hour she had been alive.

CORONER: Would the injury take long to inflict?

PHILLIPS: Only a few seconds — it might be done in two seconds.

CORONER: Does the presence of the cachous in the left hand indicate that the murder was committed very suddenly and without any struggle?

PHILLIPS: Some of the cachous were scattered about the yard.

THE FOREMAN: Do you not think that the woman would have dropped the packet of cachous altogether if she had been thrown to the ground before the injuries were inflicted?

PHILLIPS: That is an inference which the jury would be perfectly entitled to draw.

THE CORONER: I assume that the injuries were not self-inflicted?

PHILLIPS: I have seen several self-inflicted wounds more extensive than this one, but then they have not usually involved the carotid artery. In this case, as in some others, there seems to have been some knowledge where to cut the throat to cause a fatal result.

CORONER: Is there any similarity between this case and Annie Chapman's case?

PHILLIPS: There is very great dissimilarity between the two. In Chapman's case the neck was severed all round down to the vertebral column, the vertebral bones being marked with two sharp cuts, and there had been an evident attempt to separate the bones.

CORONER: From the position you assume the perpetrator to have been in, would he have been likely to get bloodstained?

PHILLIPS: Not necessarily, for the commencement of the wound and the injury to the vessels would be away from him, and the stream of blood — for stream it was — would be directed away from him, and towards the gutter in the yard.

CORONER: Was there any appearance of an opiate or any smell of chloroform?

PHILLIPS: There was no perceptible trace of any anesthetics or narcotic. The absence of noise is a difficult question under the circumstances of this case to account for, but it must not be taken for granted that there was not any noise. If there was an absence of noise I cannot account for it.

THE FOREMAN: That means that the woman might cry out after the cut?

PHILLIPS: Not after the cut.

CORONER: But why did she not cry out while she was being put on the ground?

PHILLIPS: She was in a yard, and in a locality where she might cry out very loudly and no notice be taken of her. It was possible for the woman to draw up her legs after the wound, but she could not have turned over. The wound was inflicted by drawing the knife across the throat. A short knife, such as a shoe-maker's well-ground knife, would do the same thing. My reason for believing that deceased was injured when on the ground was partly on account of the absence of blood anywhere on the left side of the body and between it and the wall.

A JUROR: Was there any trace of malt liquor in the stomach?

PHILLIPS: There was no trace.

Dr. Blackwell [recalled] (who assisted in making the post-mortem examination) said: I can confirm Dr. Phillips as to the appearances at the mortuary. I may add that I removed the cachous from the left hand of the deceased, which was nearly open. The packet was lodged between the thumb and the first finger, and was partially hidden from view. It was I who spilt them in removing them from the hand. My impression is that the hand gradually relaxed while the woman was dying, she dying in a fainting condition from the loss of blood. I do not think that I made myself quite clear as to whether it was possible for this to have been a case of suicide. What I meant to say was that, taking all the facts into consideration, more especially the absence of any instrument in the hand, it was impossible to have been a suicide. I have myself seen many equally severe wounds self-inflicted. With respect to the knife which was found, I should like to say that I concur with Dr. Phillips in his opinion that, although it might possibly have inflicted the injury, it is an extremely unlikely instrument to have been used. It appears to me that a murderer, in using a round-pointed instrument, would seriously handicap himself, as he would be only able to use it in one particular way. I am told that slaughterers always use a sharp-pointed instrument.

THE CORONER: No one has suggested that this crime was committed by a slaughterer.

WITNESS: I simply intended to point out the inconvenience that might arise from using a blunt-pointed weapon.

THE FOREMAN: Did you notice any marks or bruises about the shoulders?

BLACKWELL: They were what we call pressure marks. At first they were very obscure, but subsequently they became very evident. They were not what are ordinarily called bruises; neither is there any abrasion. Each shoulder was about equally marked.

A JUROR: How recently might the marks have been caused?

BLACKWELL: That is rather difficult to say.

CORONER: Did you perceive any grapes near the body in the yard?

BLACKWELL: No.

CORONER: Did you hear any person say that they had seen grapes there?

BLACKWELL: I did not.

Mr. Sven Ollsen [Olsson] deposed: I live at No. 23, Prince's-square, St. George's-in-the-East, and am clerk of the Swedish Church there. I have examined the body of the deceased at the mortuary. I have seen her before.

THE CORONER: Often?

OLSSON: Yes.

CORONER: For how many years?

OLSSON: Seventeen.

CORONER: Was she a Swede?

OLSSON: Yes.

CORONER: What was her name?

OLSSON: Her name was Elizabeth Stride, and she was the wife of John Thomas Stride, carpenter. Her maiden name was Elizabeth Gustafdotter. She was born at Torlands [sic], near Gothenburg, on Nov. 27, 1843.

CORONER: How do you get these facts?

OLSSON: From the register at our church.

CORONER: Do you keep a register of all the members of your church?

OLSSON: Of course. We register those who come into this country bringing a certificate and desiring to be registered.

CORONER: When was she registered?

OLSSON: Her registry is dated July 10, 1866, and she was then registered as an unmarried woman.

CORONER: Was she married at your church?

OLSSON: No.

CORONER: Then how do you know she was the wife of John Thomas Stride?

OLSSON: In the registry I find a memorandum, undated, in the handwriting of the Rev. Mr. Palmayer, in Swedish, that she was married to an Englishman named John Thos. Stride. This registry is a new one, and copied from an older book. I have seen the original, and it was written by Mr. Frost, our pastor, until two years ago. I know the Swedish hymn book produced, dated 1821. I gave it to the deceased.

CORONER: When?

OLSSON: Last winter, I think.

CORONER: Do you know when she was married to Stride?

OLSSON: I think it was in 1869.

CORONER: Do you know when he died?

OLSSON: No. She told me about the time the Princess Alice went down that her husband was drowned in that vessel.

CORONER: Was she in good circumstances then?

OLSSON: She was very poor.

CORONER: Then she would have been glad of any assistance?

OLSSON: Yes.

CORONER: Did you give her some?

OLSSON: I did about that time.

CORONER: Do you remember that there was a subscription raised for the relatives of the sufferers by the Princess Alice?

OLSSON: No.

CORONER: I can tell you that there was, and I can tell you another thing — that no person of the name of Stride made any application. If her story had been true, don't you think she would have applied?

OLSSON: I do not know.

CORONER: Have you any schools connected with the Swedish Church?

OLSSON: No, not in London.

CORONER: Did you not ever hear that this woman had any children?

OLSSON: I do not remember.

CORONER: Did you ever see her husband?

OLSSON: No.

CORONER: Did your church ever assist her before her husband died?

OLSSON: Yes, I think so; just before he died.

CORONER: Where has she been living lately?

OLSSON: I have nothing to show. Two years ago she gave her address as Devonshire-street, Commercial-road.

CORONER: Did she then explain what she was doing?

OLSSON: She stated that she was doing a little work in sewing.

CORONER: Could she speak English well?

OLSSON: Pretty well.

CORONER: Do you know when she came to England?

OLSSON: I believe a little before the register was made, in 1866.

William Marshall, examined by the Coroner, said: I reside at No. 64, Berner-street, and am a laborer at an indigo warehouse. I have seen the body at the mortuary. I saw the deceased on Saturday night last.

CORONER: Where?

MARSHALL: In our street, three doors from my house, about a quarter to twelve o'clock. She was on the pavement, opposite No. 58, between Fairclough-street and Boyd-street.

CORONER: What was she doing?

MARSHALL: She was standing talking to a man.

CORONER: How do you know this was the same woman?

MARSHALL: I recognize her both by her face and dress. She did not then have a flower in her breast.

CORONER: Were the man and woman whom you saw talking quietly?

MARSHALL: They were talking together.

CORONER: Can you describe the man at all?

MARSHALL: There was no gas-lamp near. The nearest was at the corner, about twenty feet off. I did not see the face of the man distinctly.

CORONER: Did you notice how he was dressed?

MARSHALL: In a black cut-away coat and dark trousers.

CORONER: Was he young or old?

MARSHALL: Middle-aged he seemed to be.

CORONER: Was he wearing a hat?

MARSHALL: No, a cap.

CORONER: What sort of a cap?

MARSHALL: A round cap, with a small peak. It was something like what a sailor would wear.

CORONER: What height was he?

MARSHALL: About 5ft. 6in.

CORONER: Was he thin or stout?

MARSHALL: Rather stout.

CORONER: Did he look well dressed?

MARSHALL: Decently dressed.

CORONER: What class of man did he appear to be?

MARSHALL: I should say he was in business, and did nothing like hard work.

CORONER: Not like a dock laborer?

MARSHALL: No.

CORONER: Nor a sailor?

MARSHALL: No.

CORONER: Nor a butcher?

MARSHALL: No.

CORONER: A clerk?

MARSHALL: He had more the appearance of a clerk.

CORONER: Is that the best suggestion you can make?

MARSHALL: It is.

CORONER: You did not see his face. Had he any whiskers?

MARSHALL: I cannot say. I do not think he had.

CORONER: Was he wearing gloves?

MARSHALL: No.

CORONER: Was he carrying a stick or umbrella in his hands?

MARSHALL: He had nothing in his hands that I am aware of.

CORONER: You are quite sure that the deceased is the woman you saw?

MARSHALL: Quite. I did not take much notice whether she was carrying anything in her hands.

CORONER: What first attracted your attention to the couple?

MARSHALL: By their standing there for some time, and he was kissing her.

CORONER: Did you overhear anything they said?

MARSHALL: I heard him say, "You would say anything but your prayers."

CORONER: Different people talk in a different tone and in a different way. Did his voice give you the idea of a clerk?

MARSHALL: Yes, he was mild speaking.

CORONER: Did he speak like an educated man?

MARSHALL: I thought so. I did not hear them say anything more. They went away after that. I did not hear the woman say anything, but after the man made that observation she laughed. They went away down the street, towards Ellen-street. They would not then pass No. 40 (the club).

CORONER: How was the woman dressed?

MARSHALL: In a black jacket and skirt.

CORONER: Was either the worse for drink?

MARSHALL: No, I thought not.

CORONER: When did you go indoors?

MARSHALL: About twelve o'clock.

CORONER: Did you hear anything more that night?

MARSHALL: Not till I heard that the murder had taken place, just after one o'clock. While I was standing at my door, from half-past eleven to twelve, there was no rain at all. The deceased had on a small black bonnet. The couple were standing between my house and the club for about ten minutes.

DETECTIVE-INSPECTOR REID: Then they passed you?

MARSHALL: Yes.

A JUROR: Did you not see the man's face as he passed?

MARSHALL: No; he was looking towards the woman, and had his arm round her neck. There is a gas lamp at the corner of Boyd-street. It was not closing time when they passed me.

James Brown: I live in Fairclough-street, and am a dock laborer. I have seen the body in the mortuary. I did not know deceased, but I saw her about a quarter to one on Sunday morning last.

THE CORONER: Where were you?

BROWN: I was going from my house to the chandler's shop at the corner of the Berner-street and Fairclough-street, to get some supper. I stayed there three or four minutes, and then went back home, when I saw a man and woman standing at the corner of the Board School. I was in the road just by the kerb, and they were near the wall.

CORONER: Did you see enough to make you certain that the deceased was the woman?

BROWN: I am almost certain.

CORONER: Did you notice any flower in her dress?

BROWN: No.

CORONER: What were they doing?

BROWN: He was standing with his arm against the wall; she was inclined towards his arm, facing him, and with her back to the wall.

CORONER: Did you notice the man?

BROWN: I saw that he had a long dark coat on.

CORONER: An overcoat?

BROWN: Yes; it seemed so.

CORONER: Had he a hat or a cap on?

BROWN: I cannot say.

CORONER: You are sure it was not her dress that you chiefly noticed?

BROWN: Yes. I saw nothing light in color about either of them.

CORONER: Was it raining at the time?

BROWN: No. I went on.

CORONER: Did you hear anything more?

BROWN: When I had nearly finished my supper I heard screams of "Murder" and "Police." This was a quarter of an hour after I had got home. I did not look at any clock at the chandler's shop. I arrived home first at ten minutes past twelve o'clock, and I believe it was not raining then.

CORONER: Did you notice the height of the man?

BROWN: I should think he was 5ft. 7in.

CORONER: Was he thin or stout?

BROWN: He was of average build.

CORONER: Did either of them seem the worse for drink?

BROWN: No.

CORONER: Did you notice whether either spoke with a foreign accent?

BROWN: I did not notice any. When I heard screams I opened my window, but could not see anybody. The cries were of moving people going in the direction of Grove-street. Shortly afterwards I saw a policeman standing at the corner of Christian-street, and a man called him to Berner-street.

William Smith, 452 H Division: On Saturday last I went on duty at ten P.M. My beat was past Berner-street, and would take me twenty-five minutes or half an hour to go round. I was in Berner-street about half-past twelve or twenty-five minutes to one o'clock, and having gone round my beat, was at the Commercial-road corner of Berner-street again at one o'clock. I was not called. I saw a crowd outside the gates of No. 40, Berner-street. I heard no cries of "Police." When I came to the spot two constables had already arrived. The gates at the side of the club were not then closed. I do not remember that I passed any person on my way down. I saw that the woman was dead, and I went to the police-station for the ambulance, leaving the other constables in charge of the body. Dr. Blackwell's assistant arrived just as I was going away.

THE CORONER: Had you noticed any man or woman in Berner-street when you were there before?

SMITH: Yes, talking together.

CORONER: Was the woman anything like the deceased?

SMITH: Yes. I saw her face, and I think the body at the mortuary is that of the same woman.

CORONER: Are you certain?

SMITH: I feel certain. She stood on the pavement a few yards from where the body was found, but on the opposite side of the street.

CORONER: Did you look at the man at all?

SMITH: Yes.

CORONER: What did you notice about him?

SMITH: He had a parcel wrapped in a newspaper in his hand. The parcel was about 18in. long and 6in. to 8in. broad.

CORONER: Did you notice his height?

SMITH: He was about 5ft. 7in.

CORONER: His hat?

SMITH: He wore a dark felt deerstalker's hat.

CORONER: Clothes?

SMITH: His clothes were dark. The coat was a cutaway coat.

CORONER: Did you overhear any conversation?

SMITH: No.

CORONER: Did they seem to be sober?

SMITH: Yes, both.

CORONER: Did you see the man's face?

SMITH: He had no whiskers, but I did not notice him much. I should say he was twenty-eight years of age. He was of respectable appearance, but I could not state what he was. The woman had a flower in her breast. It rained very little after eleven o'clock. There were but few about in the bye streets. When I saw the body at the mortuary I recognized it at once.

Michael Kidney, the man with whom the deceased last lived, being recalled, stated: I recognize the Swedish hymn-book produced as one belonging to the

deceased. She used to have it at my place. I found it in the next room to the one
I occupy — in Mrs. Smith's room. Mrs. Smith said deceased gave it to her when
she left last Tuesday — not as a gift, but to take care of. When the deceased and I
lived together I put a padlock on the door when we left the house. I had the key,
but the deceased has got in and out when I have been away. I found she had
been there during my absence on Wednesday of last week — the day after she
left — and taken some things.

CORONER: The Coroner: What made you think there was anything the matter
with the roof of her mouth?

KIDNEY: She told me so.

CORONER: Have you ever examined it?

KIDNEY: No.

CORONER: Well, the doctors say there is nothing the matter with it.

KIDNEY: Well, I only know what she told me.

Philips Krantz (who affirmed) deposed: I live at 40, Berner-street, and am
editor of the Hebrew paper called "The Worker's Friend." I work in a room
forming part of the printing office at the back of the International Working
Men's Club. Last Saturday night I was in my room from nine o'clock until one of
the members of the club came and told me that there was a woman lying in the
yard.

CORONER: Had you heard any sound up to that time?

KRANTZ: No.

CORONER: Any cry?

KRANTZ: No.

CORONER: Or scream?

KRANTZ: No.

CORONER: Or anything unusual?

KRANTZ: No.

CORONER: Was your window or door open?

KRANTZ: No.

CORONER: Supposing a woman had screamed, would you have heard it?

KRANTZ: They were singing in the club, so I might not have heard. When I
heard the alarm I went out and saw the deceased, but did not observe any
stranger there.

CORONER: Did you look to see if anybody was about — anybody who might
have committed the murder?

KRANTZ: I did look. I went out to the gates, and found that some members of
the club had gone for the police.

CORONER: Do you think it possible that any stranger escaped from the yard
while you were there?

KRANTZ: No, but he might have done so before I came. I was afterwards
searched and examined at the club.

Constable Albert Collins, 12 H. R., stated that by order of the doctors, he, at
half-past five o'clock on Sunday morning, washed away the blood caused by the
murder.

Detective-Inspector Reid said: I received a telegram at 1.25 on Sunday morning last at Commercial-street Police-office. I at once proceeded to No. 40,

Berner-street, where I saw several police officers, Drs. Phillips and Blackwell, and a number of residents in the yard and persons who had come there and been shut in by the police. At that time Drs. Phillips and Blackwell were examining the throat of the deceased. A thorough search was made by the police of the yard and the houses in it, but no trace could be found of any person who might have committed the murder. As soon as the search was over the whole of the persons who had come into the yard and the members of the club were interrogated, their names and addresses taken, their pockets searched by the police, and their clothes and hands examined by the doctors. The people were twenty-eight in number. Each was dealt with separately, and they properly accounted for themselves. The houses were inspected a second time and the occupants examined and their rooms searched. A loft close by was searched, but no trace could be found of the murderer. A description was taken of the body, and circulated by wire around the stations. Inquiries were made at the different houses in the street, but no person could be found who had heard screams or disturbance during the night. I examined the wall near where the body was found, but could detect no spots of blood. About half-past four the body was removed to the mortuary.

Having given information of the murder to the coroner I returned to the yard and made another examination and found that the blood had been removed. It being daylight I searched the walls thoroughly, but could discover no marks of their having been scaled. I then went to the mortuary and took a description of the deceased and her clothing as follows: Aged forty-two; length 5ft. 2in; complexion pale; hair dark brown and curly; eyes light grey; front upper teeth gone. The deceased had on an old black skirt, dark-brown velvet body, a long black jacket trimmed with black fur, fastened on the right side, with a red rose backed by a maidenhair fern. She had two light serge petticoats, white stockings, white chemise with insertion, side-spring boots, and black crape bonnet. In her jacket pocket were two handkerchiefs, a thimble, and a piece of wool on a card. That description was circulated. Since then the police have made a house-to-house inquiry in the immediate neighbourhood, with the result that we have been able to produce the witnesses who have appeared before the Court. The investigation is still going on. Every endeavor is being made to arrest the assassin, but up to the present without success.

The inquiry was adjourned to Tuesday fortnight, at two o'clock.[1]

Despite several interviews and a trip to both mortuaries, the media was not finished with the neighborhood greengrocer. Not wanting to be outdone by the *Evening News*, the *Daily Telegraph* sent their own man, Joseph Hall Richardson, to interview the elderly shopkeeper, after the inquest had ended that day. And they took things up a notch with "sketch portraits of the supposed murderer."

The above sketches are presented not, of course, as authentic portraits, but as a likeness which an important witness has identified as that of the man who was seen talking to the murdered woman in Berner-street and its vicinity until within a quarter of an hour of the time when she was killed last Sunday morning. Three men, William Marshall, James Brown, both labourers, and Police-

***Daily Telegraph*'s sketch portraits (courtesy Alex Chisholm).**

constable Smith, have already stated before the coroner that a man and woman did stand in Fairclough-street, at the corner of Berner-street, for some time — that is, from a quarter to twelve o'clock, as stated by Marshall, to a quarter before one A.M., the hour mentioned by Brown. The policeman appears to have seen the same pair in Berner-street at half-past twelve. The evidence of another witness has yet to be taken, and this man seems to have had a better opportunity of observing the appearance of the stranger than any other individual, for it was at his shop that the grapes which other witnesses saw near the body were bought.

This witness, Mathew Packer, has furnished information to the Scotland-yard authorities, and it was considered so important that he was examined in the presence of Sir Charles Warren himself. He has also identified the body of Elizabeth Stride as that of the woman who accompanied the man who came to his shop, not long before midnight on Saturday. In accordance with the general description furnished to the police by Packer and others, a number of sketches were prepared, portraying men of different nationalities, ages, and ranks of life. These were submitted to Packer, who unhesitatingly selected one of these here reproduced — the portrait of the man without the moustache, and wearing the soft felt or American hat.

Further, in order to remove all doubt, and, if possible, to obtain a still better visible guidance, Packer was shown a considerable collection of photographs, and from these, after careful inspection, he picked out one which corresponded in all important respects to the sketch. It was noticed that Packer, as also another important witness, presently to be mentioned, at once rejected the faces of men of purely sensuous type, and that they thus threw aside the portraits of several noted American criminals.

Both witnesses inclined to the belief that the man's age was not more than thirty, in which estimate they were supported by the police-constable, who guessed him to be twenty-eight. If the impressions of two men, who, it may be supposed, have actually conversed with the alleged murderer, be correct, and their recollection of his features can be relied upon, then, in their opinion, at all events, the above sketches furnish a reasonably accurate representation of his general appearance as described and adopted by them. It is possible that, with the aid of these drawings, many persons who may also have met the man may be able to recognise him more easily than by reading the bare particulars of his height, dress, &c., and it is for this reason that we publish them.

A man like the one without the moustache, and wearing the soft black felt deerstalker hat, as drawn, was seen by Mathew Packer, of 44, Berner-street, two doors from the scene of the murder, late on Saturday night, and Packer, as above stated, attests the general accuracy of the likeness given. He describes the incident which brought the man to his notice as follows: On Saturday night about half-past eleven o'clock, this man and the woman he has identified as the deceased came to the fruiterer's shop which he keeps. It was not necessary for them to enter it, as customers usually stand upon the pavement, and make their purchases through the window, which is not a shop front of the ordinary kind.

Packer is certain that the woman, who wore a dark jacket and a bonnet with some crepe stuff in it, was playing with a white flower which she carried. The man was square-built, about 5ft. 7in. in height, thirty years of age, full in the face, dark complexioned, without moustache, and alert-looking. His hair was black. He wore a long black coat and soft felt hat. It seemed to Packer that he was a clerk, and not a working man. He spoke in a quick, sharp manner, and stood in front of the window. The man purchased half a pound of black grapes, which were given to him in a paper bag, and he paid threepence in coppers. The couple then stood near the gateway of the club for a minute or so, and afterwards crossed the road and remained talking by the Board School for some time. They were still there when Packer had had supper and when he went to bed; and Mrs. Packer remarked it as strange that they should remain, for rain was falling at the time.

It is a remarkable circumstance — much more than an ordinary coincidence — that the description of the supposed murderer given by Packer was yesterday confirmed by another man [unknown] who, without being aware of the fact, also chose from the sketches the one which had been already selected by Packer. Search for an individual answering to the description above detailed, but having a small moustache and wearing a black deerstalker felt hat, instead of a soft one, has been made by the police in Whitechapel ever since Saturday, Sept. 1, the day following the Buck's-row tragedy.[2]

⌒9⌒

A Wilful Murder

The following day was October 6, and this was not a typical Saturday. London mournfully started the weekend with the funeral of the first who fell victim in the double event, Elizabeth Stride. Her body was moved from the mortuary and buried in a paupers' grave 15509 at East London Cemetery, Plaistow. For the last time, Elizabeth received subsistence, as Mr. Hawkes, the undertaker, paid for the funeral at the expense of the parish. It had to have been a fairly quiet procession and ceremony, for the funeral was sparsely attended. In spite of the vast number of onlookers who ventured into Berner Street the previous Sunday to view the murder scene and witness the body being moved to the mortuary, their interest had declined, and even the press paid little attention, barely mentioning the somber event.[1]

Whether because of the extensive mutilations or because she died within the city limits, Stride's sister victim, Catherine Eddowes, became a greater loss to London than had Elizabeth. At 1:30 Monday afternoon the body was removed from the mortuary, and "quite a multitude of persons assembled to witness the departure.... Not only was the thoroughfare itself thronged with people, but the windows and roofs of adjoining buildings were occupied by groups of spectators.... As the funeral procession passed through Golden-lane and Old-street the thousands of persons who followed it nearly into Whitechapel rendered locomotion extremely difficult ... and at the cemetery it was awaited by several hundreds, most of whom had apparently made their way thither from the East-end." Eddowes was buried in a polished elm coffin with oak moldings, bearing a plate with an inscription in gold letters. Her unmarked, but public (pauper's) grave 49336 was at City of London Cemetery, Ilford, at Manor Park Cemetery, Sebert Road, Forest Gate. The cortège consisted of a "hearse of improved description, a mourning coach, containing relatives and friends of the deceased, and a brougham conveying representatives of the press.... Mr. G. C. Hawkes, a vestryman of St. Luke's, undertook the responsibility of carrying out the funeral at his own expense,

115

and the City authorities, to whom the burial ground belongs, remitted the usual fees."[2]

On the following day, Tuesday, the *Times* published a letter to the editor from Dr. Thomas Barnardo, a street preacher with a calling. He wrote it the day of Elizabeth's funeral.

THE CHILDREN OF THE COMMON LODGING-HOUSES.
TO THE EDITOR OF THE TIMES.

Sir,—Stimulated by the recently revealed Whitechapel horrors many voices are daily heard suggesting as many different schemes to remedy degraded social conditions, all of which doubtless contain some practical elements. I trust you will allow one other voice to be raised on behalf of the children. For the saddest feature of the common lodging-houses in Whitechapel and other parts of London is that so many of their inmates are children. Indeed, it is impossible to describe the state in which myriads of young people live who were brought up in these abodes of poverty and of crime.

I and others are at work almost day and night rescuing boys and girls from the foul contamination of these human sewers; but while the law permits children to herd in these places, there is little that can be done except to snatch a few here and there from ruin and await patiently those slower changes which many have advocated. Meanwhile, a new generation is actually growing up in them. We want to make it illegal for the keepers of licensed lodging-houses to which adults resort to admit young children upon any pretext whatever. It is also desirable that the existing laws relating to the custody and companionship of the children should be more rigidly enforced. At the same time some provision is urgently required for the shelter of young children of the casual or tramp class, something between the casual wards of the workhouse and the lodging-house itself, places where only young people under 16 would be admitted, where they would be free to enter and as free to depart, and which could be made self-supporting, or nearly so. A few enterprising efforts to open lodging-houses of this class for the young only would do immense good.

Only four days before the recent murders I visited No. 32, Flower and Dean-street, the house in which the unhappy woman Stride occasionally lodged. I had been examining many of the common lodging-houses in Bethnal-green that night, endeavouring to elicit from the inmates their opinions upon a certain aspect of the subject. In the kitchen of No. 32 there were many persons, some of them being girls and women of the same unhappy class as that to which poor Elizabeth Stride belonged. The company soon recognized me, and the conversation turned upon the previous murders. The female inmates of the kitchen seemed thoroughly frightened at the dangers to which they were presumably exposed. In an explanatory fashion I put before them the scheme which had suggested itself to my mind, by which children at all events could be saved from the contamination of the common lodging-houses and the streets, and so to some extent the supply cut off which feeds the vast ocean of misery in this great city.

The pathetic part of my story is that my remarks were manifestly followed with deep interest by all the women. Not a single scoffing voice was raised in ridicule or opposition. One poor creature, who had evidently been drinking, exclaimed somewhat bitterly to the following effect:—"We're all up to no good, and no one cares what becomes of us. Perhaps some of us will be killed next!" And then she added, " If anybody had helped the likes of us long ago we would never have come to this!"

Impressed by the unusual manner of the people, I could not help noticing their appearance somewhat closely, and I saw how evidently some of them were moved. I have since visited the mortuary in which were lying the remains of the poor woman Stride, and I at once recognized her as one of those who stood around me in the kitchen of the common lodging-house on the occasion of my visit last Wednesday week.

In all the wretched dens where such unhappy creatures live are to be found hundreds, if not thousands, of poor children who breathe from their very birth an atmosphere fatal to all goodness. They are so heavily handicapped at the start in the race of life that the future is to most of them absolutely hopeless. They are continually surrounded by influences so vile that decency is outraged and virtue becomes impossible.

Surely the awful revelations consequent upon the recent tragedies should stir the whole community up to action and to the resolve to deliver the children of to-day who will be the men and women of to-morrow from so evil an environment.

I am, Sir, your obedient servant,
THOS. J. BARNARDO.
18 to 26, Stepney-causeway, E., Oct. 6.[3]

Two days later on Thursday, October 11, Mr. Langham resumed the Eddowes inquest. Mr. Crawford, the city solicitor, again watched the case on behalf of the police. Fifteen people gave evidence including Eddowes's daughter, Annie Phillips. After reviewing the Goulston Street graffito, a chalked, anti–Semitic writing found in Goulston Street, "the coroner said he considered a further adjournment unnecessary, and the better plan would be for the jury to return their verdict and then leave the matter in the hands of the police." Following a brief summation, the coroner "presumed that the jury would return a verdict of wilful murder against some person or persons unknown, and then the police could freely pursue their inquiries and follow up any clue they might obtain. A magnificent reward had been offered, and that might be the means of setting people on the track and bringing to speedy justice the creature who had committed this atrocious crime." The coroner reevaluated his words, and stated, "Perhaps it would be sufficient to return a verdict of wilful murder against some person unknown, inasmuch as the medical evidence conclusively demonstrated that only one person could be implicated." The jury agreed and returned the verdict. Having had only one adjournment, the inquest ended after the jury "presented their fees to Annie Phillips, daughter of the deceased."[4]

Elizabeth had been buried for thirteen days without a definitive suspect attached to her death, but the police were not backing down in their pursuit of the killer. They remained vigilant.

The force of police, dressed in private clothes, who have been told off to make a house-to-house search in Whitechapel and Spitalfields, were busily engaged yesterday. At every house or tenement visited they left a copy of the subjoined police notice: 'To the Occupier.— On the mornings of Friday, Aug. 31, Saturday, 8th, and Sunday, Sept. 30, 1888, women were murdered in or near Whitechapel, supposed by some one residing in the immediate neighbourhood. Should you know of any person to whom suspicion is attached, you are earnestly requested to communicate at once with the nearest police-station.' The police have everywhere been received with the greatest good-feeling, even in the poorest districts, and have had no difficulty in obtaining information.

Actions readily speak louder than words and the police easily demonstrated their willingness and desire to capture the elusive killer. Nor were they the oppressors of the poor as portrayed by some, in an attempt to merely serve their own means.[5]

Commenting on this due diligence, Chief Inspector Donald Sutherland Swanson, in charge of the Whitechapel murder investigations for the Metropolitan Police, wrote a summary of the investigation that was sent to the Home Office:

8,000 pamphlets to occupier were issued and a house to house enquiry made not only involving the result of enquiries from the occupiers but also a search by police & with a few exceptions — but not such as convey suspicion — covered the area bounded by the City Police boundary on the one hand, Lamb St. Commercial St. Great Eastern Railway & Buxton St. then by Albert St. Dunk St. Chicksand St. & Great Garden St. to Whitechapel Rd. and then to the City boundary, under this head also Common Lodging Houses were visited & over 2000 lodgers were examined.

Enquiry was also made by Thames Police as to sailors on board ships in Docks on river & extended enquiry as to Asiatics present in London, about 80 persons have been detained at the different police stations in the Metropolis & their statements taken and verified by police & enquiry has been made into the movements of a number of persons estimated at upwards of 300 respecting whom communications were received by police & such enquiries are being continued.

Seventy six Butchers & Slaughterers have been visited & the characters of the men employed enquired into, this embraces all servants who had been employed for the past six months.

Enquiries have also been made as to the alleged presence in London of Greek Gipsies, but it was found that they had not been in London during the times of the various murders.

Three of the persons calling themselves Cowboys who belonged to the American Exhibition were traced & satisfactorily accounted for themselves.

Up to date although the number of letters daily is considerably lessened, the other enquiries respecting alleged suspicious persons continues as numerous.

There are now 994 Dockets besides police reports.

The inspector also reflected on several witnesses, revealing some of the internal thinking at that time.

***The description of the man seen by the P.C. was circulated amongst police by wire, & by authority of Commissioner it was also given to the press. On the evening of 30th the man Schwartz gave the description of the men he had seen ten minutes later than the P.C. and it was circulated by wire. It will be observed that allowing for differences of opinion between the P.C. & Schwartz as to apparent age & height of the man each saw with the woman whose body they both identified there are serious differences in the description of dress — thus the P.C. describes the dress of the man whom he saw as black diagonal coat, hard felt hat, while Schwartz describes the dress of the man he saw as dark jacket black cap with peak, so that at least it is rendered doubtful whether they are describing the same man.

If Schwartz is to be believed, and the police report of his statement casts no doubt upon it, it follows if they are describing different men that the man Schwartz saw & described is the more probable of the two to be the murderer, for a quarter of an hour afterwards the body is found murdered. At the same time account must be taken of the fact that the throat only of the Victim was cut in this instance which measured by time, considering meeting (if with a man other than Schwartz saw) the time for the agreement & the murderous action would I think be a question of so many minutes, five at least, ten at most, so that I respectfully submit it is not clearly proved that the man that Schwartz saw is the murderer although it is clearly the more probable of the two. Before concluding in dealing with the descriptions of these two men I venture to insert here for the purpose of comparison with these two descriptions, the description of a man seen with a woman in Church Passage close to Mitre Square at 1.35 A.M. 30th ult. by two men coming out of a club close by :- age 30 ht. 5ft. 7 or 8 in. comp. fair, fair moustache medium build, dress pepper & salt color loose jacket, grey cloth cap with peak of same color, reddish handkerchief tied in a knot, round neck, appearance of a sailor. In this case I understand from the City Police that Mr. Lewin [Joseph Lawende] one of the men identified the clothes only of the murdered woman Eddowes, which is a serious drawback to the value of the description of the man. Ten minutes afterwards the body is found horribly mutilated & it is therefore reasonable to believe that the man he saw was the murderer, but for purposes of comparison, this description is nearer to that given by Schwartz than to that given by the P.C.

The body was identified as that of Elizabeth Stride, a prostitute, & it may be shortly stated that the enquiry into her history did not disclose the slightest pretext for a motive on behalf of friends or associates or anybody who had known her.

***This is rather confused — If the man whom the P.C. saw at 12.30 is not the same as the man whom Schwartz saw at 12.45 then it is clearly more probable that the man who Schwartz saw was the murderer, because Schwartz saw his man a quarter of an hour later than the P.C. But I understand the Inspector to suggest that Schwartz' man need not have been the murderer. For only 15 minutes elapsed between 12.45 when Schwartz saw the man & 1.0 when the woman was found murdered on the same spot — But the suggestion is that Schwartz' man may have left her, she being; a prostitute then accosted or was accosted by another man, & there was time enough for this to take place & for this other man to Murder her before 1.0. The Police apparently do not suspect the 2nd man whom Schwartz saw on the other side of the Street & who followed Schwartz.

Inspector Swanson's account was a summary presented to the Home Office. He submitted several such reports to his superiors during the course of the investigations, covering various aspects of each murder and the police activities that occurred. These were not intended as full-blown transcripts, detailing every witness, etc., but gave an overview or a recap of actions taken or being taken.[6]

That same day, October 19, the *Police Gazette* refuted the sketches published with the J. Hall Richardson interview of Packer and presented the official descriptions.

APPREHENSIONS SOUGHT.

MURDER.

METROPOLITAN POLICE DISTRICT.

The woodcut sketches, purporting to resemble the persons last seen with the murdered women, which have appeared in the "Daily Telegraph," were not authorised by Police. The following are the descriptions of the persons seen:—

At 12.35 A.M., 30 September, with Elizabeth Stride, found murdered at 1 A.M., same date, in Berner-street—A MAN, age 28, height 5 ft. 8 in., complexion dark, small dark moustache; dress, black diagonal coat, hard felt hat, collar and tie; respectable appearance. Carried a parcel wrapped up in newspaper.

At 12.45 A.M., 30th, with same woman, in Berner-street—A MAN, age about 30, height 5 ft. 5 in., complexion fair, hair dark, small brown moustache, full face, broad shoulders; dress, dark jacket and trousers, black cap with peak.

At 1.35 A.M., 30 September, with Catherine Eddows, in Church-passage, leading to Mitre-square, where she was found murdered at 1.45 A.M., same date—A MAN, age 30, height 5 ft. 7 or 8 in., complexion fair, moustache fair, medium build; dress, pepper-and-salt colour loose jacket, grey cloth cap with peak of same material, reddish neckerchief tied in knot; appearance of a sailor.

Information to be forwarded to the Metropolitan Police Office, Great Scotland-yard, London, S.W.[7]

Four days later, on October 23, Coroner Baxter resumed the Stride inquest. It was the fifth and final day of the inquiry. Detective-Inspector Reid, H Division, watched the case on behalf of the Criminal Investigation Department. The following evidence was presented; afterwards, the coroner gave a tallying summation.

Detective-Inspector Edmund Reid, recalled, said,—I have examined the books of the Poplar and Stepney Sick Asylum, and find therein the entry of the death of John Thomas William Stride, a carpenter, of Poplar. His death took place on the 24th day of October, 1884. Witness then said that he had found Mrs. Watts, who would give evidence.

Constable Walter Stride stated that he recognised the deceased by the photograph as the person who married his uncle, John Thomas Stride, in 1872 or 1873. His uncle was a carpenter, and the last time witness saw him he was living in the East India Dock-road, Poplar.

Elizabeth Stokes, 5, Charles-street, Tottenham, said,— My husband's name is Joseph Stokes, and he is a brickmaker. My first husband's name was Watts, a wine merchant of Bath. Mrs. Mary Malcolm, of 15, Eagle-street, Red Lion-square, Holborn, is my sister. I have received an anonymous letter from Shepton Mallet, saying my first husband is alive. I want to clear my character. My sister I have not seen for years. She has given me a dreadful character. Her evidence is all false. I have five brothers and sisters.

A JURYMAN: Perhaps she refers to another sister.

INSPECTOR REID: She identified the deceased person as her sister, and said she had a crippled foot. This witness has a crippled foot.

WITNESS: This has put me to a dreadful trouble and trial. I have only a poor crippled husband, who is now outside. It is a shame my sister should say what she has said about me, and that the innocent should suffer for the guilty.

THE CORONER: Is Mrs. Malcolm here?

INSPECTOR REID: No, Sir.

The Coroner, in summing up, said the jury would probably agree with him that it would be unreasonable to adjourn this inquiry again on the chance of something further being ascertained to elucidate the mysterious case on which they had devoted so much time. The first difficulty which presented itself was the identification of the deceased. That was not an unimportant matter. Their trouble was principally occasioned by Mrs. Malcolm, who, after some hesitation, and after having had two further opportunities of viewing again the body, positively swore that the deceased was her sister — Mrs. Elizabeth Watts, of Bath. It had since been clearly proved that she was mistaken, notwithstanding the visions which were simultaneously vouchsafed at the hour of the death to her and her husband. If her evidence was correct, there were points of resemblance between the deceased and Elizabeth Watts which almost reminded one of the Comedy of Errors. Both had been courted by policemen; they both bore the same Christian name, and were of the same age; both lived with sailors; both at one time kept coffee-houses at Poplar; both were nick-named "Long Liz;" both were said to have had children in charge of their husbands' friends; both were given to drink; both lived in East-end common lodging-houses; both had been charged at the Thames Police-court; both had escaped punishment on the ground that they were subject to epileptic fits, although the friends of both were certain that this was a fraud; both had lost their front teeth, and both had been leading very questionable lives.

Whatever might be the true explanation of this marvelous similarity, it appeared to be pretty satisfactorily proved that the deceased was Elizabeth Stride, and that about the year 1869 she was married to a carpenter named John Thomas Stride. Unlike the other victims in the series of crimes in this neighbourhood — a district teeming with representatives of all nations — she was not an Englishwoman. She was born in Sweden in the year 1843, but, having resided in this country for upwards of 22 years, she could speak English fluently and without much foreign accent. At one time the deceased and her husband kept a coffee-house in Poplar. At another time she was staying in Devonshire-street, Commercial-road, supporting herself, it was said, by sewing and charing. On and off for the last six years she lived in a common lodging-house in the notorious lane called Flower and Dean-street. She was there known only by the nickname of "Long Liz," and often told a tale, which might have been apocryphal, of her husband and children having gone down with the Princess Alice. The deputy of the lodging-house stated that while with her she was a quiet and sober woman, although she used at times to stay out late at night — an offence very venial, he suspected, among those who frequented the establishment.

For the last two years the deceased had been living at a common lodging-house in Dorset-street, Spitalfields, with Michael Kidney, a waterside laborer, belonging to the Army Reserve. But at intervals during that period, amounting altogether to about five months, she left him without any apparent reason, except a desire to be free from the restraint even of that connexion, and to obtain greater opportunity of indulging her drinking habits. She was last seen alive by Kidney in Commercial-street on the evening of Tuesday, September 25. She was sober, but never returned home that night. She alleged that she had some words with her paramour, but this he denied.

The next day she called during his absence, and took away some things, but, with this exception, they did not know what became of her until the following Thursday, when she made her appearance at her old quarters in Flower and Dean-street. Here she remained until Saturday, September 29. On that day she cleaned the deputy's rooms, and received a small remuneration for her trouble. Between 6 and 7 o'clock on that evening she was in the kitchen wearing the jacket, bonnet, and striped silk neckerchief which were afterwards found on her. She had at least 6d. in her possession, which was possibly spent during the evening. Before leaving she gave a piece of velvet to a friend to take care of until her return, but she said neither where she was going nor when she would return. She had not paid for her lodgings, although she was in a position to do so. They knew nothing of her movements during the next four or five hours at least — possibly not till the finding of her lifeless body.

But three witnesses spoke to having seen a woman that they identified as the deceased with more or less certainty, and at times within an hour and a-quarter of the period when, and at places within 100 yards of the spot where she was ultimately found. William Marshall, who lived at 64, Berner-street, was standing at his doorway from half-past 11 till midnight. About a quarter to 12 o'clock he saw the deceased talking to a man between Fairclough-street and Boyd-street. There was every demonstration of affection by the man during the ten minutes they stood together, and when last seen, strolling down the road towards Ellen-street, his arms were round her neck. At 12 30 P.M. the constable on the beat (William Smith) saw the deceased in Berner-street standing on the pavement a few yards from Commercial-street, and he observed she was wearing a flower in her dress. A quarter of an hour afterwards James Brown, of Fairclough-street, passed the deceased close to the Board school. A man was at her side leaning against the wall, and the deceased was heard to say, "Not to-night, but some other night." Now, if this evidence was to be relied on, it would appear that the deceased was in the company of a man for upwards of an hour immediately before her death, and that within a quarter of an hour of her being found a corpse she was refusing her companion something in the immediate neighbourhood of where she met her death.

But was this the deceased? And even if it were, was it one and the same man who was seen in her company on three different occasions? With regard to the identity of the woman, Marshall had the opportunity of watching her for ten minutes while standing talking in the street at a short distance from him, and she afterwards passed close to him. The constable feels certain that the woman he observed was the deceased, and when he afterwards was called to the scene of the crime he at once recognized her and made a statement; while Brown was almost certain that the deceased was the woman to whom his attention was attracted. It might be thought that the frequency of the occurrence of men and women being seen together under similar circumstances might have led to mistaken identity; but the police stated, and several of the witnesses corroborated the statement, that although many couples are to be seen at night in the Commercial-road, it was exceptional to meet them in Berner-street.

With regard to the man seen, there were many points of similarity, but some of dissimilarity, in the descriptions of the three witnesses; but these discrepancies did not conclusively prove that there was more than one man in the company of the deceased, for every day's experience showed how facts were differently observed and differently described by honest and intelligent witnesses. Brown, who saw least in consequence of the darkness of the spot at which the two were standing, agreed with Smith that his clothes were dark and that his height was about 5ft. 7in., but he appeared to him to be wearing an overcoat nearly down to his heels; while the description of Marshall accorded with that of Smith in every respect but two. They agreed that he was respectably dressed in a black cut away coat and dark trousers, and that he was of middle age and without whiskers. On the other hand, they differed with regard to what he was wearing on his head. Smith stated he wore a hard felt deer stalker of dark colour; Marshall that he was wearing a round cap with a small peak, like a sailor's. They also differed as to whether he had anything in his hand. Marshall stated that he observed nothing. Smith was very precise, and stated that he was carrying a parcel, done up in a newspaper, about 18in. in length and 6in. to 8in. in width. These differences suggested either that the woman was, during the evening, in the company of more than one man — a not very improbable supposition — or that the witness had been mistaken in detail. If they were correct in assuming that the man seen in the company of deceased by the three was one and the same person it followed that he must have spent much time and trouble to induce her to place herself in his diabolical clutches.

They last saw her alive at the corner of Fairclough-street and Berner-street, saying "Not to-night, but some other night." Within a quarter of an hour her lifeless body was found at a spot only a few yards from where she was last seen alive. It was late, and there were few people about, but the place to which the two repaired could not have been selected on account of its being quiet or unfrequented. It had only the merit of darkness. It was the passage-way leading into a court in which several families resided. Adjoining the passage and court there was a club of Socialists, who, having finished their debate, were singing and making merry. The deceased and her companion must have seen the lights of the clubroom, and the kitchen, and of the printing office. They must have heard the music and dancing, for the windows were open. There were persons in the yard but a short time previous to their arrival. At 40 minutes past 12, one of the members of the club, named Morris Eagle, passed the spot where the deceased drew her last breath, passing through the gateway to the back door, which opened into the yard.

At 1 o'clock the body was found by the manager of the club. He had been out all day, and returned at the time. He was in a two-wheeled barrow drawn by a pony, and as he entered the gateway his pony shied at some object on his right. There was no lamp in the yard, and having just come out of the street it was too dark to see what the object was and he passed on further down the yard. He returned on foot, and on searching found the body of deceased with her throat cut. If he had not actually disturbed the wretch in the very act, at least he must have been close on his heels; possibly the man was alarmed by the sound of the approaching cart, for the death had only just taken place. He did not inspect the body himself with any care, but blood was flowing from the throat, even when Spooner reached the spot some few minutes afterwards, and although the bleeding had stopped when Dr. Blackwell's assistant arrived, the whole of her body and the limbs, except her hands, were warm, and even at 16 minutes past 1 A.M. Dr. Blackwell found her face slightly warm, and her chest and legs quite warm.

In this case, as in other similar cases which had occurred in this neighbourhood, no call for assistance was noticed. Although there might have been some noise in the club, it seemed very unlikely that any cry could have been raised without its being heard by some one of those near. The editor of a Socialist paper Krantz: was quietly at work in a shed down the yard, which was used as a printing office. There were several families in the cottages in the court only a few yards distant, and there were 20 persons in the different rooms of the club. But if there was no cry, how did the deceased meet with her death? The appearance of the injury to her throat was not in itself inconsistent with that of a self-inflicted wound. Both Dr. Phillips and Dr. Blackwell have seen self-inflicted wounds more extensive and severe, but those have not usually involved the carotid artery. Had some sharp instrument been found near the right hand of the deceased this case might have had very much the appearance of a determined suicide. But no such instrument was found, and its absence made suicide an impossibility.

The death was, therefore, one by homicide, and it seemed impossible to imagine circumstances which would fit in with the known facts of the case, and which would reduce the crime to manslaughter. There were no signs of any struggle; the clothes were neither torn nor disturbed. It was true that there were marks over both shoulders, produced by pressure of two hands, but the position of the body suggested either that she was willingly placed or placed herself where she was found. Only the soles of her boots were visible. She was still holding in her left hand a packet of cachous, and there was a bunch of flowers still pinned to her dress front. If she had been forcibly placed on the ground, as Dr. Phillips opines, it was difficult to understand how she failed to attract attention, as it was clear from the appearance of the blood on the ground that the throat was not cut until after she was actually on her back. There were no marks of gagging, no bruises on the face, and no trace of any anesthetic or narcotic in the stomach; while the presence of the cachous in her hand showed that she did not make use of it in self-defense. Possibly the pressure marks may have had a less tragical origin, as Dr. Blackwell says it was difficult to say how recently they were produced.

There was one particular which was not easy to explain. When seen by Dr. Blackwell her right hand was lying on the chest, smeared inside and out with blood. Dr. Phillips was unable to make any suggestion how the hand became soiled. There was no injury to the hand, such as they would expect if it had been raised in self-defense while her throat was being cut. Was it done intentionally by her assassin, or accidentally by those who were early on the spot? The evidence afforded no clue. Unfortunately the murderer had disappeared without leaving the slightest trace. Even the cachous were wrapped up in unmarked paper, so that there was nothing to show where they were bought. The cut in the throat might have been effected in such a manner that bloodstains on the hands and clothes of the operator were avoided, while the domestic history of the deed suggested the strong probability that her destroyer was a stranger to her. There was no one among her associates to whom any suspicion had attached. They had not heard that she had had a quarrel with any one — unless they magnified the fact that she had recently left the man with whom she generally cohabited; but this diversion was of so frequent an occurrence that neither a breach of the peace ensued, nor, so far as they knew, even hard words.

There was therefore in the evidence no clue to the murderer and no suggested motive for the murder. The deceased was not in possession of any valuables. She was only known to have had a few pence in her pocket at the beginning of the evening. Those who knew her best were unaware of any one likely to injure her. She never accused any one of having threatened her. She never expressed any fear of anyone, and, although she had outbursts of drunkenness, she was generally a quiet woman. The ordinary motives of murder — revenge, jealousy, theft, and passion — appeared, therefore, to be absent from this case; while it was clear from the accounts of all who saw her that night, as well as from the postmortem examination, that she was not otherwise than sober at the time of her death. In the absence of motive, the age and class of woman selected as victim, and the place and time of the crime, there was a similarity between this case and those mysteries which had recently occurred in that neighbourhood.

There had been no skilful mutilation as in the cases of Nichols and Chapman, and no unskillful injuries as in the case in Mitre-square — possibly the work of an imitator; but there had been the same skill exhibited in the way in which the victim had been entrapped, and the injuries inflicted, so as to cause instant death and prevent blood from soiling the operator, and the same daring defiance of immediate detection, which, unfortunately for the peace of the inhabitants and trade of the neighbourhood, had hitherto been only too successful. He himself was sorry that the time and attention which the jury had given to the case had not produced a result that would be a perceptible relief to the metropolis — the detection of the criminal; but he was sure that all had used their utmost effort to accomplish this object, and while he desired to thank the gentlemen of the jury for their kind assistance, he was bound to acknowledge the great attention which Inspector Reid and the police had given to the case. He left it to the jury to say, how, when, and by what means the deceased came by her death.

The Jury, after a short deliberation, returned a verdict of "Wilful murder against some person or persons unknown."[8]

✑—10—✑

The Mysterious Liz

Elizabeth Stride was not unique among the Victorian East Enders. She emigrated to London like many foreigners. In fact the Old City's migrant population tripled between 1850 and 1888. Even her poor lifestyle was fairly common, and such abject poverty was well known to about 175,000 of her fellowmen who lived in Spitalfields, Whitechapel, St. George's, Bow, Poplar, Bethnal Green, and the Mile End. Yet several thousands more were actually worse off and in a chronic state of want. Despite having a husband who had a good trade while attempting a middle-class life as a shopkeeper, and a boyfriend that had a job, Elizabeth seemed almost to jinx herself by her apparent desire for more.

Those who have little sometimes dream of a better life, while others work to achieve it. In this respect, she was not unique. When things did not work out, she ran away, like many. Maybe like some, Elizabeth simply wanted her ship to come in. After all, she paid for it with a rough life. There is no doubt that she had a hard life compared to many: she lost her mother and only child at an early age; in her mid-thirties, she lost her father; and she separated from her husband and became a widow before she turned forty. At an age when most modern people either attend school or hold down a job, Elizabeth took to the streets and became a prostitute, subjecting herself to police questioning and medical exams, and that was the better part of it. She moved from location to location with "bouts of drunkenness" added to the mix, and she had a rocky relationship for the last three years of her life.

Nevertheless, Elizabeth's life was unique — unique in the sense of her death. She was at the wrong place at the wrong time. And for that, she paid with her life. Elizabeth was not the first in that grisly circumstance, and sadly she will not be the last. But unlike many that had a similar fate, Elizabeth's tragic end propelled her onto the world stage for over a century. Yet because of her murder, many people know Elizabeth better in death than those who knew her while she lived. It's surprising, considering the stories she told her compatriots. They say time heals all wounds. Maybe, but in this case, time has afforded a better view.

Pregnancy and Prostitution

When, how or why Elizabeth entered prostitution is interesting to ponder. Pregnancy was either the result or the cause of her becoming a streetwalker. The first thing to consider, however, is under what circumstances Elizabeth left her various residences over the years.

Her sister, Anna, left the family home at the age of seventeen and moved to Gothenburg, where she eventually settled down with a husband and had five children.

Contemporary impression of Elizabeth Stride (courtesy Stephen Ryder/Casebook).

Elizabeth was only fourteen when her sister struck out on her own, and her two brothers were nine and six. With one less hand to help out, Anna's chores would most likely have passed to Elizabeth, while Carl and Svante began to come into their own as sons of a farmer. Farm life is not easy with its early rising and long, sometimes thankless hours. But Elizabeth would have been expected to leave, if for no other reason than to get married and have her own family; moreover, her mother worked as domestic servant when she was a teenager in order to help support the family. So following in the footsteps of her mother and sister, Elizabeth headed to Gothenburg just before she turned seventeen. It would not be hard to imagine that she wanted what her sister ultimately had — a family. Anything less would probably have given her a questionable character, or worse, labeled her as a spinster. (I am being somewhat facetious with the term "spinster," however in such older societies young women were traditionally expected to marry and not remain single.)

There is no current information as to what she was doing for her first four months in Gothenburg. But one innocent possibility is that Gustaf and Beata might have sent their second daughter to live with their eldest. Anna was already established, presumably, having been in the city for about three years, and that would be a good place for Elizabeth to stay until she landed a job. Like her mother, Elizabeth obtained work as a domestic servant. The Olofsson family must have provided a rather decent situation. Mr. and Mrs. Olofsson were in their early thirties and only had two children. But almost three years to the day after she was hired, something happened that made Elizabeth want to leave, and leave in a hurry. Apart from possible domestic issues, the previous year, 1863, might provide a clue. That year, Mrs. Olofsson gave birth to what was actually their fourth child. (The eldest had died in 1860.) The other two children, Carl and Johan, were seven and six respectively. This paints a very similar picture to Elizabeth's own family after her sister left home. In all likelihood, she had to help with the younger ones, as part of her duties. This was a duty she had already fulfilled once before on the farm. When she hastily left the Olofssons' in 1864, Elizabeth was only twenty and might have had enough of other people's kids.

She might have gone back to live with her sister, which would seem to be a natural thing to do. Chances are Elizabeth could not have gone home again, because leaving her job suddenly would have been a disgrace to her mother and father, especially in a society where scripture and its teachings are ranked very high, and "honor thy father" and "honor thy mother" are at the top of the list. In any era, losing a job, whether through quitting or being fired, is detrimental, and six months is a long time to go without any type of income. This conjures up images of Elizabeth walking the streets, but the police did not take notice of her until March the following year, and even then she was only listed as "registered." So if the police did not really know of her, then what? Elizabeth became pregnant around September of 1864, and her mother died the month before. This in itself is suggestive. If she had been living with Anna, perhaps six months had been too long, especially when she learned of Beata's death. If Elizabeth was afraid to go back home, even to say good-bye to her departed mother then that might have been the final straw. With nowhere else to go or any means of support, Elizabeth possibly felt she had no other choice. She took to the streets, and before long she was expecting a child.

Thanks to the kindly assistance of Maria Wiesners and her husband Carl, Elizabeth seemed to revert back to a normal life. But even that soon ended. The May–December couple was expecting its first child. Possibly remembering what she had gone through helping to raise her own brothers and the Olofsson children, Elizabeth may have wanted no part of it. She also would have been reminded of the loss of her only child. But she also seemed determined to not wander the streets again, since she stayed until after receiving her mother's inheritance. A month or so later, she was bound for England — free at last.[1]

Servant or Tourist?

Elizabeth gave two explanations for her initial presence in England. To see the country and, later, to work as a domestic servant. Had she really been in London merely to view the scenery, it is very doubtful that she would have left her job and submitted a permanent change of residence. She would probably have spent her sixty-five Swedish crowns and then returned to her homeland like other visitors. Chances are she wanted a permanent change and a better situation. She probably had a desire to stay away from prostitution, but her mother had recently died, she had had a bad pregnancy, and within six months her new mistress would have a child, a situation she apparently wanted to avoid.

Elizabeth's departure from Sweden has been described as leaving "disgrace and misery." There is little doubt that she felt both, yet she could have escaped by simply leaving Gothenburg; she was, after all, removed from the prostitutes' register. However, there is a possible explanation for Elizabeth leaving Sweden completely, not just the area where she grew up. The year following Elizabeth's arrival in London saw the start of a major influx of Swedes going to America. The last year of the rule of King Charles XIV John of Sweden was 1844. He was unpopular because he was a foreigner, and his reign was characterized by conflict. Yet in spite of the economic reforms of his successor, Oscar I, nearly 500,000 Swedes emigrated to the U.S. due to food and job shortages between 1867 and 1886. Such migrations due to economic hard times are common throughout history. The Irish Potato Famine of 1845–1850 is a good example. Even England saw its share of internal migration as a result of the Confederacy losing the American Civil War, which resulted in a major downturn for Britain's cotton industry, and many of the displaced went to London seeking a better life. It is not difficult to imagine that the Swedes talked often enough about their King's economic reforms, their ailing country, and a land of opportunity prior 1867. But America was not the only game in town, and like many other impoverished Europeans, Elizabeth saw London as the best chance for a fresh start in life.

It seems apparent that Elizabeth wanted to start over. Two other primary points refute the tourist theory — her certificate of altered residence and the clerk for the Swedish Church, who readily stated that all church members were registered if they entered England "bringing a certificate *and desiring* to be registered [my emphasis]." Neither would have occurred if Elizabeth were merely there for a visit. But one question that arises from this is what did Elizabeth do between the time she landed and when she finally registered at the church?

We do know that she had some money, but depending on how she lived, it is uncertain as to how long that might have sustained her. Elizabeth told Charles Preston "she came to England in the service of a gentleman," which is similar to what she eventually told Michael Kidney, "she came to England in a situation with a family [as a servant]." It is possible, but it is also suspect, because of when she told these stories — nineteen years later. At that time, she was also telling people of her tragic family loss with the *Princess Alice*. A more likely explanation is that she came to England by herself, simply enjoying her newly found freedom as an immigrant. Around the time she managed to secure employment was most likely when she registered with the church. The latter explanation has merit and gives a good illustration of the various stories that Elizabeth ultimately told. The truth probably lies somewhere in between.

One question that invariably comes to mind, however, regarding Elizabeth's early British life, revolves around her living at or near Hyde Park, which is approximately three-quarters of a mile to the south of Regent's Park, the area where John Stride lived when he and Elizabeth were married. This comes from Michael Kidney when he first spoke at the inquest on October 3. However, Kidney never said Elizabeth's employer lived at or near that park. The *Daily Telegraph* reported his comment as, "I have seen the address of the brother of the gentleman with whom she lived as a servant, somewhere near Hyde Park, but I cannot find it now." While most grammar teachers might cringe over such a mixture of pronouns and possessives, it was the employer's brother who lived at or near the park, not the employer. The *Times* corroborates this with its awkward version: "I have seen the address of some one with the family she was living with at Hyde Park; but I cannot find it." While this one reads more like her employer's residence, the address belonged to "someone with the family," and it was that "someone" who lived at Hyde Park. And yet she apparently did spend some time in the Hyde Park area according to Kidney. For when John Stride courted her, so did a policeman, "when she was at Hyde Park, before she was married to Stride." But based on Kidney's previous Hyde Park address comment, it seems that the policeman who dated Elizabeth lived in Hyde Park and that he was the relative or friend of the family or gentleman who employed her.[2]

What's in a Name?

When Elizabeth married, her maiden name was listed as "Gustifson." Such a surname change from "Gustafsdotter" is fairly common in the genealogical world, even if it can be frustrating. The reason was the immigration official. These people did not necessarily speak another language nor did they really take the time to be accurate. The officials had a tendency to spell a foreign surname phonetically as they heard it, explaining the change from pronounced "Goo'staf..." to written "Gu'stif...." Yet this does not really explain the other aspect of the name change, from "...sdotter" to "...son," even though it does explain the slight change in her given name, from Elisabeth to Elizabeth. My own last name is a good example of this. The original German spelling is Jost, but different American immigration officials gave it a variety of spellings based on how it sounded to them at the time, providing a nice selection: Yost, Youst, and Yoast are among the more common versions. (The changes in surnames from generation to generation may seem a bit odd, since we no longer live in an era where in some European countries the last names change in accordance to the father's first name and sex of the child. Russians once did this, and had I been born there at that time, my last name would have been Thurmanovich.)

But getting to England was only part of the difficulties. Ship voyages for women in the 1900's tended to be a bit quirky. For example, British officials would not generally permit an unattended female to travel to America, especially if she was expecting. (I am *not* implying that Elizabeth was). The woman had to have a male relative with her. This man might merely be a family friend or he might not even know the woman, but he would be commonly listed as the woman's uncle. (My own ancestor had such an experience when she traveled from England to America.) If this were the circumstance for Elizabeth when she finally boarded the ship bound for Great Britain, then in all likelihood, her uncle's last name was "Gustafsson." The immigration official heard "Gustifson" and affixed that as the surname for the entire family. This may seem rather convoluted but such things actually happened. While it does support the basic stories that Elizabeth told to Preston and Kidney, there may be a simpler explanation.

In April 1865, Elizabeth gave birth to a stillborn girl. She gave her only daughter the surname of "Gustafsson." Elizabeth did this out of respect for her own father, as a clue as to the baby's "unknown" father, or for some other reason. It is more than likely that the young Elizabeth used her baby's last name, "Gustafsson" when she boarded the ship bound for England. Upon landing, the immigration official was told "Elisabeth Gustafsson" and recorded her name as "Elizabeth Gustifson." Her letter of employment from Maria also supports this. Fortunately for us, her certificate of altered residence had her correct name, which is what was she presented to the church on July 10.[3]

Marital Address

At the time of their marriage, John Stride lived at 21 Munster Street, Hampstead Road, just west of Regent Park, and Elizabeth recorded her residence as 67 Gower Street. (It is questioned, however, if John's 1869 address was actually Munster Square, instead of Munster Street, since contemporary maps only list Munster Square within the vicinity of Hampstead Road.) Their nuptial location, St. Giles Church, was within a half-mile to the south of Gower. This may seem to be a rather curious address for Elizabeth, considering it is virtually on the opposite side of London proper from the Swedish Church area. It is doubtful that she moved to Gower simply as a result of being courted by or engaged to John.

She was permitted to live where she wanted, but Gower Street consisted primarily of the middle class and those who earned a comfortable living. By comparison, Hampstead Road and its environs were a mixture of the middle class and comfortable with the predominant presence of the poor, and less-than-poor. This alone indicates that Elizabeth continued as a domestic servant, with a middle-class employer, possibly the aforementioned policeman's friend or relative. This also supports the essence of what she told Preston and Kidney, and since Elizabeth was no longer dating the policeman, she used her employer's address, 67 Gower. Being a fairly local artisan, John's services may have been contracted by Elizabeth's employer. If so, then the employer might have unknowingly introduced the future Mr. and Mrs. Stride.[4]

Chrisp Street Address

There is significant doubt about the Chrisp Street address being the first location of John's java emporium. In order to be listed in Kelly's Directory for 1870, the shop would had to have been established before the fall of 1869, indicating that the initial location was indeed Upper North Street. Kelly's London Post Office Directory began its annual publication in the fall, preceding its published year. Thus the 1870 version was being published by the autumn of 1869. Granted there are roughly six months between the autumn of 1869 and the Strides' wedding date. But Upper North Street being the first location is further evidenced by Chrisp Street itself. No Strides are recorded as living there, and 1869 only saw two coffee shops there: John Phillips at No.7 and William Green at No.106. There is little if any doubt that the Chrisp Street coffee shop was an embellishment on Elizabeth's part, and we will have a glimpse as to why. The only real support for Chrisp Street comes from John's nephew, PC Stride, when he stated at the inquest that "he recognised the deceased by the photograph as the person who married his uncle, John Thomas Stride, in 1872 or 1873. His uncle was a carpenter, and the last time witness saw him he was living in the East India Dock-road, Poplar." Unfortunately PC Stride's incorrect years(s) for his uncle's marriage is the only date given and that is not necessarily when he last saw his uncle, especially since he did not indicate that he saw his uncle and aunt, but only his uncle.[5]

Loss of the Coffee Shop

According to the research carried out by Adrian Phypers, about 1,600 coffee shops existed within the capital by 1841. They commonly charged 1 pence or 2 pence per cup and even sold buns, pastries, and snacks. With Victorians becoming more prosperous and moving towards sobriety, as a society coffee emerged as a drink of choice for an ever-expanding base of consumers. With a ready-made market and being located within blocks of what could amount to hundreds of laborers, railway workers, and merchant sailors, one would think that the shop should have been a success. Yet apparently it was not.

The most likely reason that Dale took over the coffee shop was financial hardship. John had to sell it. The question becomes why was John's business not profitable? An obvious possibility, but assuredly not the only one, is Elizabeth herself. In 1874 she turned 32 and had already been in the workforce since age sixteen, primarily as a domestic servant. Despite any formal education she might have received from family, her husband, previous employers, or the church, Elizabeth's background does not suggest that she could have properly run a business. As a domestic servant (i.e., maid or charwoman), Elizabeth would have been more familiar with cleaning rooms than handling ledger accounts, and in all likelihood, it would have been her brothers who would have been taught the farm finances. John may have been able to properly deal with business finances, but according to him, he was still a carpenter.

And it is possible that John moved his family closer to the docks in order to continue plying his previous trade. This coincides with what he told the census taker and might also explain why they were able to remain at Poplar High Street for three years — living on earnings from his carpentry plus from the coffee shop. John obviously could not be in two places at once, especially with the hours that both occupations required. There seems to be no doubt, therefore, that Elizabeth ran the shop. But without John's assistance with the day-to-day operations, Elizabeth possibly ran the business into the ground.

A more tragic explanation, a more personal reason might also explain John's apparent financial demise, which ultimately left him in the poor house. By early September 1873, John's father died. The 1874 edition of Kelly's Directory lists John Dale as owner of the coffee shop, which means that Dale had to obtain the business from Stride in or around the fall of 1873. This is highly suggestive that John sold the shop to Dale, in part, as a result of his father's death. Whether they were distraught over the personal loss or possibly encumbered by unknown financial obligations left behind, neither Elizabeth nor John could keep up with the proper management of the shop. The loss of the coffee shop seems to be a culmination of events and not necessarily the result of any one action. In an odd way, this could explain why Elizabeth eventually told acquaintances that the coffee shop was in Chrisp Street.[6]

Elizabeth and the Princess Alice

Oddly enough, a *Woolwich* news article at the time of the disaster made a reference to a woman, her destroyed family, and how her husband heroically died while trying to save one of their children. This report was subsequently re-counted as part of Elizabeth's life in several papers on October 8, 1888, two days after Elizabeth was buried. (Woolwich is the location where the deceased from the wreck were laid out and is approximately three and a half miles east of Poplar.) Subscriptions were raised as a relief fund for the victims' families, but "no person of the name of Stride made any application." In fact, a search of the British Death Index for 1837–1983 has shown a number of women and men with the last name of Stride who died before and after the *Princess Alice* disaster (as well as several who also died in 1888). But so far only one has been found who had a recorded death around the time of the colliding ships, and she was 66 years old. (An interesting side note is that there were several Elizabeth Strides residing not just in England, but in London, according to the 1871 and 1881 census records. Fortunately, only one of them came from Sweden.) Elizabeth did receive a small assistance from the Swedish Church at around that time, but it was no different than any other time she asked for financial aid from the church.

Demonstrably, Elizabeth lied about her involvement with the *Princess Alice*, even though acquaintances such as Sven Olsson, Elizabeth Tanner, Charles Preston, Michael Kidney, and perhaps others may have listened with sadness and empathy and recounted her tale of woe. Sympathy was the name of the game, and this seems to have been her demeanor after she and John moved to Poplar. It was how she described her past, even claiming to census takers that she was from Stockholm, which is way more exciting than Torslanda. Her citing Sweden's capital as her birth city may be another indication of how she wanted to remove her past.

In a way, who could blame her? While in Gower Street, she most likely lived in comfortable surroundings, and possibly wore a decent uniform, all at her employer's expense. This obviously ended after the young couple set up the coffee shop. While Elizabeth lied about her circumstances in order to obtain money from the church, there's little doubt that she and John were poorly off.

These tidbits can be hashed and rehashed with every new or seasoned student of the subject. Yet these stories are delightful in a way. It is almost like listening to your grandmother spin yarns about the good old days. We might not always appreciate having to hear the stories, but they do give us some insight into the person telling them. For Elizabeth, however, the days might have been old, but they were not good, and these remembrances might have been her way of dealing with her past.[7]

Elizabeth's Absence

Thomas Bates, the night watchman, claimed that Elizabeth "returned to the [lodging] house on Tuesday last [Sept. 25], after a prolonged absence, and remained there until Saturday night," indicating that she rented a bed for those four nights. There is some corroboration to this claim from Dr. Thomas Barnardo, an East End street preacher who opened the first shelter for destitute boys and commonly visited doss houses to speak to prostitutes. In a letter to the *Times*, Dr. Barnardo stated that he saw Elizabeth in that lodging house kitchen on the Wednesday before her death, while he "had been examining many of the common lodging-houses in Bethnal-green that night." Later, he recognized her body in the mortuary.

But considering the many lodging houses Barnardo visited and the vast number of women he spoke to, it is unlikely that Elizabeth stood out in any particular way. And he himself commented on how similar the women were that night. "In the kitchen of No. 32 there were many persons, some of them being girls and women of the same unhappy class as that to which poor Elizabeth Stride belonged." Barnardo never claimed to have spoken to Elizabeth directly. Nor did he write his letter until after Elizabeth's name was mentioned in the papers as the Berner Street victim (which was on October 1). It was not until the day of Elizabeth's funeral (October 6) that he wrote his letter to the *Times*, and he was probably creating a memory out of his desire to help the poor and destitute.

Other lodging house residences refuted Bates's claim. Tanner, the house deputy who befriended Elizabeth, saw her frequently, sometimes every day, and Lane, who also knew her, saw her frequently. According to them, Elizabeth did not show up until two days later. "She was there last week only on Thursday and Friday nights," according to Tanner. And Lane agreed, "She came there last Thursday." Conclusively, Elizabeth did not rent a room at the lodging house on Tuesday or Wednesday night.

Yet she was not with Michael Kidney. He did "not see her on Thursday." Instead he last saw her "on the Tuesday," leaving her in Commercial Street on friendly terms between 9 and 10 P.M. Even Coroner Baxter recognized this. "The next day [Wednesday] she called during his [Kidney's] absence, and took away some things, but, with this exception, they [Elizabeth's associates] did not know what became of her until the following Thursday, when she made her appearance at her old quarters in Flower and Dean-street." Given the circumstances of the inquest, Kidney might have had a reason to sugar coat *how* he and Elizabeth parted ways, but he had no reason to lie about *when* they parted company. Additionally, Elizabeth gave her hymnbook to Mrs. Smith, a next-door neighbor, to watch over. That was when Elizabeth "left last Tuesday," and later Elizabeth went back to the Devonshire lodgings on Wednesday to retrieve a few items. So where was Elizabeth for two days?

According to Lane, she "frequently" saw Elizabeth in Fashion Street, and Tanner accepted that Elizabeth's man lived in Fashion Street — her "man" being Kidney, whom Tanner saw only once, "last Sunday." However, no known information puts Kidney's residence in Fashion Street; he still resided in Devonshire Street, nearly a mile away. In looking back at the Chrisp Street address for the coffee shop, this is almost a case of déjà vu. The coffee shop existed, so did Chrisp Street, but John Stride's coffee shop was not in Chrisp Street. So either the man in Fashion Street was an embellishment of Kidney or Elizabeth had business there. Business was either a new tryst or work "among the Jews." Both are likely, and a combination of these would explain much.

In all probability, Elizabeth met a man who lived in Fashion Street, possibly while performing her duties as a charwoman. Tanner merely concluded, as most would, that Kidney was this person. After leaving him in Commercial Street, Elizabeth went to her nearby tryst. Several days later, they "had a few words." While Lane's comment has at times been described as "had a row," which literally means "had an argument," the term "row" has been used to imply an assault. However, there is nothing in Lane's statement to indicate any kind of altercation. Because of this disagreement, Elizabeth went to the lodging house. Yet it seems she expected to see the man in Fashion Street again, as indicated by her actions that Saturday night.[8]

The Many Faces of Liz

Over the years, several people offered their views of what Elizabeth looked like, including what has been described as an "unflattering artist's conception," drawn for the *Illustrated Police News* after her death. Going years back, one of the first glimpses comes from the Gothenburg Police when she was roughly 22 years of age. Blue eyes, brown hair, a straight nose, an oval face, and a slender build.

It would be a further twenty-three years before John Gardner and J. Best saw her. And like many who saw Elizabeth that night, they were more concerned about her young man. The two laborers said she was poorly dressed, wearing a short jacket with a dahlia on the right side. She was a slight woman with a somewhat prominent nose. She had the same face and height when she was alive as she did in death, but she was a little paler. Gardner and Best may have mistaken Elizabeth's dark brown velvet bodice that was noted by Inspector Reid at the mortuary, for their described short dark jacket, what Packer ultimately called a "black frock."

Surprisingly perhaps, Matthew Packer did not really change his description of Elizabeth that much from interview to interview. For Batchelor and Le Grand, he described her as middle aged, wearing a dark dress and jacket, with a white flower in her bosom. But for the *Evening News's* special correspondent, the flower slightly adjusted; she was now carrying the white flower. While at Scotland Yard, Packer added the detail of black frock and jacket with fur round the bottom of the jacket. She wore a black crepe bonnet, and played with a flower like a geranium that was white on the outside and red inside. During Packer's last interview, he remained fairly consistent for J. Hall Richardson. Elizabeth "wore a dark jacket and a bonnet with some crepe stuff in it," and she was "playing with a white flower which she carried." Based on how the news account reads, Packer gave his description of Elizabeth to Batchelor and Le Grand before he saw the body at the mortuary.

When Marshall described Elizabeth for the Coroner's Court, he did not give much of a description, except to say that the woman he saw that Sunday morning was the same as the woman in the mortuary. He did comment that she wore a small black crepe bonnet, black jacket and black skirt, and he did not notice anything in her hands. He also made a somewhat ambiguous statement, "she did not then have a flower in her breast." While the *Times* never reported this comment, it can have a dual meaning. "Then" meaning when he saw the body in the mortuary or meaning when he first saw her that Sunday morning.

> CORONER: How do you know this was the same woman [as the one in the mortuary]?
> MARSHALL: I recognize her both by her face and dress. She did not then have a flower in her breast.

But the timing can be reconciled, because the flower was indeed on her jacket when the body lay in the mortuary, thanks to Inspector Reid's description. So Marshall's "then" is when he saw Elizabeth in Berner Street.

In addition to the inquest evidence, Diemschütz provided his thoughts about Elizabeth to several news reporters. For the *Times*, he gave the following (the description, as reported in the *Times*, is so detailed that it appears to originate more from the news reporter, who obviously viewed the body in the mortuary, instead of solely on the club steward's memory):

> The woman appears to be about 30 years of age. Her hair is very dark, with a tendency to curl, and her complexion is also dark. Her features are sharp and somewhat pinched, as though she had endured considerable privations recently. She wore a rusty black dress of a cheap kind of sateen with a velveteen bodice, over which was a black diagonal worsted jacket, with fur trimming. Her bonnet, which had fallen from her head when she was found in the yard, was of black crape. In her right hand were tightly clasped some grapes, and in her left she held a number of sweetmeats. Both the jacket and the bodice were open towards the top, but in other respects the clothes were not disarranged. The linen was clean and in tolerably good repair. The cut in the woman's throat, which was the cause of death, had evidently been effected with a very sharp instrument. The weapon had apparently been drawn across the throat obliquely from left to right, and it had severed both the windpipe and the jugular vein. As the body lies in the mortuary the head seems to be almost severed, the gash being about three inches long, and nearly the same depth. In the pocket of the woman's dress were discovered two pocket-handkerchiefs, a brass thimble, and a skein of black darning worsted.

By comparison, the *Daily News* presented Diemschütz's description as "The woman was about 27 or 28 years old. She was of light complexion... She had dark clothes on, and wore a black crape bonnet." And for the *East Morning Advertiser* he added very little: "The woman seemed to be about twenty seven or twenty eight years old... She had a flower in the bosom of her dress." Similarly, Mortimer merely described her as, "appeared respectable." Being more concerned with the situation, PC Lamb could only state that "her clothes were not disturbed and only the soles of her boots were visible." Heahbury simply described her as "a short dark young woman."

Inspector Reid and Drs. Blackwell and Phillips provided the most detail while the body was at the mortuary. Elizabeth was about 42 years old and 5 feet, 2 inches tall. She had a pale complexion with dark curly brown hair and grey eyes. Some of her teeth were gone, but the soft and hard palates were intact. She wore an old black skirt, a dark-brown velvet body [bodice], and a long black jacket that was trimmed with black fur. On the right side of the jacket was a red rose with backed with a maidenhair fern. Underneath she wore two light serge petticoats, white stockings, and a white chemise with insertion. She also wore side-spring boots and a black crepe bonnet. She carried two handkerchiefs, a thimble, and a piece of wool on a card as well as a padlock-type key, a small piece of lead pencil, and one or two small pieces of paper. She also carried a comb, a broken piece of comb, and a metal spoon, six large buttons and one small button, along with what appeared to be a dress hook, and a piece of muslin.

There are several obvious differences such as age, for it seems most of the civilian eyewitnesses viewed Elizabeth as being almost sixteen years younger than what she actually was. The other major distinction was her complexion. Diemschütz said light, and the news reporter disagreed with him. Inspector Reid said pale, while most others (who mentioned it) said she had a dark complexion. The mortuary photo does not readily show this, but one thing is certain, people look different in death than they do in life. The pale or light description might have been a natural result of viewing a dead body not touched up by a mortician.[9]

Six Pence

The one thing not mentioned in any of the descriptions was the 6 pence Tanner gave her. According to several witnesses, Elizabeth had the six pence when she went out for the night — after she and Tanner returned from the pub. Considering the number of bystanders in the yard, the hundreds of onlookers that lined the streets, and the files of people who viewed her body at the mortuary, it can be certain that no one in authority took the money. A club member did not take it, since they had a propensity for not wanting to touch a corpse, and Spooner was being observed when he knelt down to check out her injuries. If anyone else had tried to rifle through her belongings, it would have been easily noticed and reported privately at the police station, if not when the police and doctors examined each onlooker that morning. Since there were four hours between her leaving the lodging house and her next sighting at the Bricklayer's Arms, Elizabeth obviously spent it during the course of the evening, most likely on supper and possibly on a drink or two. A dinner with vegetables would have cost 4 pence and drinks would easily have consumed the rest, and we know that she did eat that night, having cheese, potato, and some type of flour-based foods in her digestive system. She may also have used the money to buy the cachous she was carrying.[10]

Teeth

One aspect that seems to differ in two descriptions of Elizabeth comes not from the civilian eyewitnesses, but from the authorities themselves. This is not the issue of a damaged soft or hard palate, which is the roof of the mouth. (Tanner's description was apparently a misnomer, saying "the roof of her mouth is missing" when she meant the teeth.) Dr. Phillips readily examined that, and Elizabeth's mouth was not damaged as she claimed to her friends and associates. The ambiguity here is the missing teeth. At the inquest on October 3rd, after having performed the autopsy October 1, Dr. Phillips stated that the teeth on the left lower jaw were absent. Two days later at the Coroner's Court, Inspector Reid, who took a description of the body that Sunday, stated that he noticed that the front upper teeth were missing. Either Elizabeth had several sets of teeth missing or someone erred in his observation. Given the extensive examination at the post-mortem, and the fact that Dr. Phillips re-examined the mouth at the court's request because of the comments made about the palate, then Dr. Phillips' statement about the missing lower left teeth, and none other, would be the correct version.[11]

Flower Power

There are several descriptions of the flower Elizabeth had that night. At around 11 P.M., Best and Gardner claimed it was a dahlia and pinned on the right side of her jacket. Next, Packer claimed, at first and almost emphatically, that it was a white flower pinned on her jacket. Then he said Elizabeth held the white flower. The flower then became a kind of geranium that was white outside and red inside, and finally Packer simply said she carried a white flower. By 11:45 P.M., Marshall never saw a flower, but almost forty-five minutes later, PC Smith had seen it pinned to her jacket. Yet the constable never said what type of flower it was.

After the discovery of her body, others noticed Elizabeth's flower. Diemschütz merely said it was pinned on her dress. Kozebrodski could only say that there was a "little bunch of flowers stuck above her right bosom." Spooner, who had a better view, described it as "some red and white flowers pinned on her breast." After the body was removed, Harstein said she saw "a few small petals of a white natural flower lying quite close to the spot where the body had rested." However, Harstein's comment, while not suggestive, is suspect considering the number of people who had already tramped through the yard. While at the mortuary, Inspector Reid recorded Elizabeth's personal effects and her description, stating that "fastened on the right side [of her jacket], was a red rose backed by a maidenhair fern."

A most likely explanation for these variations starts with Inspector Reid: a red rose backed with maidenhair fern. Obviously Best, Gardner, and Packer's observations, which led to their descriptions of "dahlia" and a "geranium type flower," were wrong. But what about the "white?" If a sufficient amount of baby's breath had also been used with the maidenhair fern, then to the unobservant, it would appear to be white outside and red inside, and the "white" would have stood out more against a black jacket. (This could also account for Harstein's comments.) Additionally, it can be asserted that when Packer saw the couple, Elizabeth unpinned the flower, held it, and then reattached it to her jacket later on. This explains Packer's different descriptions for the flower's position and why Marshall never readily noticed it, which he himself stated, "I did not take much notice whether she was carrying anything in her hands." It is possible that Elizabeth bought this in order to look nice for her young man, but it is more likely than he bought it for her.[12]

Long Liz

We know Elizabeth's appearance only through one known photo and the description provided for her from the various accounts. At the time of her death, she was five foot two tall with a bowed right leg and a "thickening" above her left ankle. A lean woman, with a slender build, who died nearly two months shy of her 45th birthday. Her blue eyes eventually turned hazel or "grey" (which does happen to eyes that are not true blue). She had an oval face with a prominent nose, a dark complexion, and teeth missing on her lower left jaw. Her features have been described as sharp and pinched. She had somewhat curly or wavy dark brown hair ("somewhat curly, or wavy" is based on the photo, to better indicate that the curls or waves were neither tight nor extensive such as one might expect from a perm). Both ears were pierced, but the left lobe was injured as if torn or worn through by an earring. She wore a small black crepe bonnet and a checked silk scarf. She wore a long black diagonal worsted jacket, with black fur trimming; pinned on the right side was a red rose backed by maidenhair fern and baby's breath. She had a black skirt and a dark-brown velvet bodice. Underneath she wore two light serge petticoats and a white chemise. On her feet she wore white stockings and side-spring boots. She owned an 1821 Swedish hymnbook, given to her by the clerk of the Swedish Church, Mr. Olsson, which she gave to a neighbor, Mrs. Smith, for safe-keeping, and a large piece of green velvet, which was being watched by Catherine Lane. She carried with her two pocket-handkerchiefs, a brass thimble, and a skein of black darning worsted (a piece of wool on a card). She had a padlock-type key, for the Devonshire Street residence. She had a small piece of lead pencil, and one or two small pieces of paper, a comb, a broken piece of comb, and a metal spoon, six large buttons, one small button, along with what appeared to be a dress hook, and a piece of muslin.

And yet Elizabeth was more than the mere sum of what she looked like or what she owned. She was a runaway, a prostitute, a live-in lover, but also a widow, an aunt, an orphan, a sister, and, tragically, a mother that never was. She was a farmer's daughter brought up with religious values — a country girl, and yet a city street-wise woman. She was also a maid, a wife, apparently sometimes a drunk, a part-time dosser, a poverty inmate, an immigrant, a store manager, and a storyteller. Elizabeth was many things, as we all are. No one can be truly described by a single word or psychological term. No matter what she was to her friends, family, employers, or herself, history will remember Elizabeth for what happened in Berner Street that early Sunday morning on September 30, 1888.

❧ 11 ❧

Packer and the Grapes

The enigmatic discrepancies of Matthew Packer's various statements might lead some to exclude him from any discussion of Elizabeth's death. This is understandable, and indeed some prefer to exclude all witnesses no matter how valuable or valueless they might appear. In the figurative sense, "all witnesses" might simply refer to all civilian witnesses. In a literal sense, this would also apply to the medical and police professionals. Unfortunately, devaluing all witnesses actually leaves very little in the way of information, and tends to produce as many issues as does elevating a particular witness (as Packer was elevated by the media for instance), because it is the witness who fills in many of the gaps, such as when something happened, or possibly even how an event took place. Was someone running away from the scene or merely sauntering past? Such details can only be obtained from an eyewitness and can have a big impact on how the entire story plays out. Granted some witnesses are more reliable than others, and for good reason. A policeman, for instance, would be expected to be more observant than a casual passerby.

The problem with Packer is not his apparent willingness to alter the times for when he did or did not do something, such as close up shop, or even his adjustments in his recollections of what Elizabeth or her young man looked like. The trouble with Packer stems primarily from the media, loudly proclaiming that the shopkeeper saw the assassin — during their circulation-war for the best story, and somewhat from the authorities, who might be viewed as barely acknowledging his presence, by comparison. And yet considering Inspector Swanson's comments, Scotland Yard's reaction was understandable, and it seems that even the authorities were disappointed by the whole ordeal: "Packer who is an elderly man, has unfortunately made different statements so that apart from the fact of the hour at which he saw the woman (and she was seen afterwards by the P.C. & Schwartz as stated) any statement he made would be rendered almost valueless as evidence."

Had Packer remained consistent with his time, however, he might have been afforded more than press interviews. He might have had an invitation to the Coroner's Court.

There is little if any doubt that Packer can be classified as one of the most colorful witnesses associated with the Berner Street case. While his antics may tend toward the annoying at times, he does provide some good interjections, even though he ostensibly adds little value to what he already said. So why spend so much time on a fifty-eight-year-old fruit-seller who seemed more interested in the attention he was getting than on being as factual as possible for the interviewer? Actually Packer is not the only one to amuse or confound his contemporaries or modern-day people. Ted Stanley is another good example: "When you talk to me, Sir, you talk to an honest man." Stanley's retort was in reply to Coroner Baxter's questioning about being "the Pensioner." Stanley initially admitted to the nickname, but he would never

actually admit to being the person named by others, and refused to state whether or not he actually was a pensioner. This banter brought some needed laughter to the court, as did Michael Kidney when he claimed to be a lover of discipline after acknowledging that he showed up drunk at the Leman Street Police Station. And yet despite their human failings and personal faults, these two and others like them have not been banished to a witness graveyard. And so it should be with Packer.

Packer's value lies not in being able to determine who the killer was, but in establishing a more complete view of what might have happened after Elizabeth and her young man left the Bricklayer's Arms. This in itself has value by indicating what route Elizabeth and her young man possibly took after they left Settles Street. True, Packer did view the body and

Contemporary impression of Matthew Packer (courtesy Stephen Ryder/Casebook).

claimed she was the woman he saw that night, but his shifts in time made it difficult even for the police to accept his account(s), despite what the *Evening News* thought. In the end, it might not matter to some since others obviously saw Elizabeth after Packer had. But establishing a greater understanding for the whole affair nags at us, and Packer, along with the mystical grapes, are a part of that. (For those with a sense of historical accuracy, if not irony, Elizabeth is the only known victim where grapes were involved, despite what some modern theatrics or novels have portrayed.)[1]

Time After Time

The best place to begin is at the beginning. When did Packer take his barrow and head for home? Packer informed the special commissioner for the *Evening News* that "I had been out with my barrow most of the day, but hadn't done much business; and as the night came on wet I went home and took the place of the 'missus' in the shop here." This statement was made during Packer's third interview. According to the official meteorological records, there was a 100 percent cloud cover that Saturday with a sudden heavy rain at "9.5 P.M." ("9.5" can be easily misconstrued for 9:30, but this actually means 9:50.) Camden Square is the location where the official weather recordings for London were taken. Since this location is some miles northeast of Whitechapel, it could not have been later than 9:50 when most of the East End saw the rain, and in fact it was much sooner, which will be explained later. Now Packer never said where he was with his barrow trying to sell his wares, but it is reasonable to assume that he had hoped for a good day of selling, as do all proprietors, especially the small businessman, because they in particular cannot afford any significant loss. So he most likely would have been close enough to return home in order to re-supply, if need be, and then head back out again. He probably moved at a pace slower than a modern-day hiker, especially with the chill and the dampness, say maybe two miles an hour. Because he would not want to spend a great deal of travel time going between the shop and his usual location(s), his walking distance from the shop could be estimated at one to two miles. By comparison, Diemschütz traveled a greater distance, about five miles overland, but the jewelry trader had a pony and cart and could afford to be farther away. Packer might have been a roaming vendor, or perhaps he had a spot at the Spitalfields Market off Commercial Street, which is the more likely of the two. (Had Packer been at the market, he might not have wanted to leave, risking losing his spot to another vendor.) Since he left no later than around 9:50 that night, wheeling his barrow at most two miles, there seems little doubt that the greengrocer was back in the shop to relieve his wife by no later than 11 PM, if not before.

Packer was home in plenty of time to have seen Elizabeth and her young man once they were in Berner Street. Yet despite this, he has been criticized over his recollection of times causing many, including the authorities, to generally discount him as an eyewitness of virtually anything. From the morning of September 30 to Friday, October 5, Packer talked to at least six people, resulting in five recorded interviews. Sergeant White saw and/or spoke with him on three occasions. Batchelor and Le Grand caught up with the greengrocer three times as well. The *Evening News* and the *Daily Telegraph* had their shot at him, and Scotland Yard finally had him, after his unsubstantiated remarks about the police. To better understand the problem, it is important to review what he said and when he said it.

About four hours after Elizabeth's body was removed from Dutfield's Yard on Sunday, Sergeant White interviewed the greengrocer as part of the house-to-house search ordered by Inspector Abberline. Packer's response to the sergeant was curt: "Closed up: 'Half past twelve, in consequence of the rain.' Saw: 'No one standing about.' Saw: No one going up into the yard. Saw: Nothing 'suspicious or heard the slightest noise.'"

This interview may seem overly short, but it is understandably so. Packer, who seemed to dislike the sergeant's interruption, stated that he closed up and went to bed, seeing no one in the general vicinity. Similar to Barnett Kentorrich, he was apparently enough of a deep sleeper to not have been woken by the commotion outside. (Either that or he did not want to get involved.) But there are several things of importance to consider. While it was unknown at the time of this interview, around 12:30–12:35 is when PC Smith turned onto Berner Street, where he saw Elizabeth and her young man standing by the Board School. So obviously someone could have been standing about at that time. But it is possible for Packer to have closed up before PC Smith came into view, so his statement to Sergeant White would not necessarily be wrong. This also indicates that Elizabeth and her young man were no longer in view when he shut his shutters, and Packer might not have made the connection of a murdered woman and a man buying grapes. An aside on Packer's first answer is that the official weather recording for the London area states that the rain lasted until after midnight, giving this statement a certain amount of credibility — up front.

Two days later, on October 2nd, the second session of the inquest took place and private detectives Batchelor and Le Grand arrived upon the scene. (Tom Wescott's evaluation of their report suggests that the two private inquiry men were originally in Berner Street the morning after the murder.) There, they obtained an interview with Packer. According to the juicy headline, the greengrocer is "the man who spoke to the murderer." What follows is Packer's second account of what he witnessed, and as can be seen, the *Evening News* wasted no time in using Packer to its advantage:

> On the 29th ult. [last month], about 11.45 P.M., a man and woman came to his shop window, and asked for some fruit.
>
> ...
>
> The man was middle aged, perhaps 35 years; about five feet seven inches in height; was stout, square built; wore a wide awake hat and dark clothes; had the appearance of a clerk; had a rough voice and a quick, sharp way of talking.
>
> ...
>
> The woman was middle aged, wore a dark dress and jacket, and had a white flower in her bosom ... his attention was particularly caught by the white flower which the woman wore, and which showed out distinctly against the dark material of her jacket.
>
> ...
>
> Packer served him with the grapes, which he handed to the woman. They then crossed the road and stood on the pavement almost directly opposite to the shop for a long time more than half an hour ... Packer naturally noticed the peculiarity of the couple's standing so long in the rain. He observed to his wife, "What fools those people are to be standing in the rain like that."
> At last the couple moved from their position, and Packer saw them cross the road again and come over to the club, standing for a moment in front of it as though listening to the music inside. Then he lost sight of them. It was then ten or fifteen minutes past twelve o'clock, Packer, who was about to close his shop, noting the time by the fact that the public houses had been closed.

This is a rather interesting tale, because it seems to contradict what he told Sergeant White. The good Sergeant asked Packer when he closed up shop. The shopkeeper said 12:30, and when he did close up no one was standing about. Packer did not necessarily lie, but he never expanded on anything either. And Sergeant White never asked if the greengrocer saw anyone within the half-hour before he closed up shop. So the worst thing Packer did was possibly withhold information, assuming he actually remembered something before Sergeant White departed from his household. But the right questions, apparently, seemed to have jogged Packer's memory.

According to what Batchelor and Le Grand presented to the *Evening News*, the small businessman saw the couple from about 11:45 to 12:10, maybe 12:15, and supposedly it was still raining at that time. The couple moved on, and Packer closed up before PC Smith came into view. This is still keeping within the general time frame; so, again, his information to Sergeant White is not necessarily flawed, just void of details. This also situates better with PC Smith's timing, but it does fail to recognize the people leaving from the club when the discussion ended, as well as Marshall's initial sighting at around 11:45. Not only is Packer's shift in time important, but so is his description of Elizabeth. Additionally, it should be noted that the couple was first at the Board School, after buying the grapes, and then they came back and stood near the club.

Batchelor and Le Grand's enthusiasm regarding Packer and the grape stalk has been viewed as more to justify their own pay than any real attempt to uncover significant information. The integrity of the duo's report in the *Evening News* is also in question because of Le Grand's criminal record. Le Grand served seven years in prison, from 1877 to 1884, for larceny. (Seven months after the double-event, he was charged with and ultimately convicted of conspiring to defraud and injure for sending threatening letters of extortion to various women of means, using the name of an innocent surgeon.) This might be one reason why the newspaper sent its "special commissioner" to interview Packer the following evening on Wednesday, October 3rd.

By now, press interviews with neighbors like Mrs. Mortimer, club members like Morris Eagle, and the body's discoverer, Diemschütz had been in print for at least a day. Additionally, the inquest had already seen three sessions, and it may be remembered that Packer reportedly saw Eddowes's body on Tuesday and had not yet visited the St. George's mortuary.

> Some time between half past eleven and twelve a man and woman came up Berner street from the direction of Ellen street, and stopped outside my window...
>
> The man was about thirty to thirty five years of age, medium height, and with rather a dark complexion. He wore a black coat and a black, soft felt hat. He looked ... like a clerk or something of that sort ... certain he wasn't ... a working man...
>
> She was dressed in dark clothes, looked a middle aged woman, and carried a white flower in her hand ... I am sure I should know the woman again. I was taken today to the see the dead body of a woman lying in Golden land mortuary, but I can swear that wasn't the woman that stood at my shop window on Saturday night...
>
> He spoke like an educated man, but he had a loud, sharp sort of voice, and a quick commanding way with him.
>
> INTERVIEWER: But did he speak like an Englishman or more in this style? [Imitating "Yankee twang"]
>
> Yes, now you mention it, there was a sound of that sort about it...
>
> First of all, they stood near the gateway leading into the club for a minute or two, and then they crossed the road and stood right opposite... More than half an hour ... me and my missus left 'em standing there when we went to bed ... it must have been past midnight a little bit, for the public houses was shut up.

The salient point is that Packer adjusts his time for when he first sees the couple, from "about 11.45" to "sometime between" 11:30 and 12:00. It would be possible to be exceptionally harsh on this, but most people might do the same thing; although many people would probably have said 'about 11:45' in the later interview as a way of simplifying the time for when they saw the couple. However, there is no mention of the club members who left for home after that night's discussion. And that occurred between 11:30 and 11:45, which could indicate that Packer closed up after the street was relatively deserted again. So there is a certain amount of compatibility between his first several statements, even though they are out of sync with Marshall's sighting, which could be explained. For the first time, Packer offers a direction from which Elizabeth and the grape-buyer came. (This might afford some compatibility with Marshall, assuming he saw Elizabeth first.) After buying the grapes, the couple now switches its actions from what Packer had previously said — the couple stood in front of the club and then crossed over to the Board School. This is not overly surprising, but it should be mentioned, because he does maintain a certain amount of consistency that the couple stood near the club and near the school, before he closed shop. Packer unwaveringly stated how long he watched the couple, "more than half an hour."

The differences in the description he gave for the young man are almost negligible: from "middle aged, perhaps 35 years" to "about thirty to thirty five years." "About five feet seven" became "medium height." These can be viewed as being fairly similar, as were his description of the man's clothes: "wide awake hat and dark clothes," simplified to "black coat and a black, soft felt hat." In both of these last two interviews, Packer was consistently consistent (in contrast to how he is typically viewed, as being consistently inconsistent), as to what the man probably was — "a clerk," although between the two reports, the man is "stout, square built" with a "rather dark complexion." This latter comment about skin pigment almost seems to come out of the blue. Such a description has tended to imply a foreigner. One such example is Elizabeth Long's description of the man she saw in Hanbury Street with Annie Chapman, he "looked like a foreigner" and she "noticed that he was dark," which leads to the high point of this interview.

When the interviewer tried to imitate the American accent or "twang" as he called it, Packer's reply was an almost reflexive acceptance. "Yes, now you mention it, there was a sound of that sort about it." Since there was no previous mention of or hint at a foreign accent, this prompting is suspicious, and readily suggests that the *Evening News* was using Packer as a means to advance its own agenda. (After Annie Chapman's murder, commentaries and letters-to-the-editor said that no Englishman could have perpetrated such a horrible crime.) This explains why the interviewer tried to imitate an American accent, instead of any other accent, or what would have been more appropriate, simply ask if there was any accent at all. (And it might further explain why the paper sent a separate interviewer after having Batchelor and Le Grand's report. To be fair, however, the *Daily Telegraph* would pull a similar stunt several days later. Nevertheless, the attempt at Americanizing Elizabeth's young man would have an impact beyond this particular interview, by staying within Packer's psyche. (One humorous example is that toward the middle of November, Packer claimed that a man who bought some rabbits stated that his cousin in America was the killer.)

A final comment about this interview deals with Packer's unfair ranting about the police. No doubt the fruiterer was pandering to himself, in the sense that the police were not making as much of a fuss over him as the media was. But based on Packer's position in society and the rancor against the police typically published by the radical press, his statements are more disgruntled sentiments than reality, and such comments tend to be popularized by the media, even today.

Because of the *Evening News* articles, Sergeant White was sent to reinterview Matthew Packer. That Thursday, however, the fruit shop owner was once again engaged with the two detectives, Batchelor and Le Grand. This time, they paraded him in front of Elizabeth's body at the mortuary. During their return to Berner Street, Sergeant White caught up with them. The exchange was brief and seemed to solicit very little: "Viewed the body at St. George's mortuary. Believe she was at the shop about 12 o'clock, Saturday."

From the evening of October 3 to when Sergeant White first saw Packer on October 4, Packer shifted the time in the opposite direction, from sometime "between 11:30 and 12:00" to "about 12 o'clock." This does put Packer in a better position, time wise, with respect to PC Smith and the club members, but it still ignores Marshall's information, unless, again, it is accepted that Marshall saw Elizabeth first. Yet the laborer was outside his house before 11:45, when he eventually saw the couple for about ten minutes, when the couple walked past, heading south toward Ellen Street. He did not go back inside until midnight. For a couple to have left Marshall's and arrived at Packer's, moving at the pace they were, they would have to have turned onto Everard Street, then headed north up Back Church Lane, which might be possible if they quickened their pace, since Marshall never observed which street they actually turned onto. Packer's temporally challenged statements, among everything else, would cause most to wonder if the fruit-seller could remember what he said or only what someone might have said for him or led him to say, especially since he told his story several times. Giving Packer some benefit of the doubt, his comment to Sergeant White, while not exactly made in passing, was not a formal statement either.

Later that afternoon, the two private inquiry men again coaxed Packer away from Sergeant White. What passed between the sergeant and the fruit-seller is unreported, but what is known is that Packer did give evidence at Scotland Yard.

> On Sat. night [29 September] about 11 P.M., a young man from 25–30, about 5 [feet] 7 [inches], with long black coat buttoned up, soft felt hat, kind of Yankee hat, rather broad shoulders, rather quick in speaking, rough voice. I sold him ½ pound black grapes, 3d. A woman came up with him from Back Church end (the lower end of street). She was dressed in black frock & jacket, fur round bottom of jacket, a black crepe bonnet, she was playing with a flower like a geranium white outside & red inside. I identify the woman at the St. George's Mortuary as the one I saw that night.
> They passed by as though they were going up [to] Commercial Road, but instead of going up they crossed to the other side of the road to the Board School, & were there for about ½ an hour till I should say 11.30, talking to one another. I then shut up my shutters. Before they passed over opposite to my shop, they went near to the club for a few minutes apparently listening to the music. I saw no more of them after I shut my shutters.

The residual effect of Packer's previous press interview can be seen with the enigmatic description of a "kind of Yankee hat," and it would not be surprising if Batchelor and Le Grand had coached Packer prior their arrival at Scotland Yard. There is no proof of this, but if it had occurred, neither the two detectives nor Packer should be overly criticized for it. Lawyers do it all the time with their witnesses, especially a key witness, and Packer was indeed viewed as an important eyewitness by the newspaper. Yet he still maintained the "soft felt hat" that he described the day before. This would be an indicator of Packer actually recalling what he saw, instead of trying to remember what someone else had said.

In a seemingly odd move, however, Packer completely shifted his time by a half an hour, from 11:30–12:00 to 11:00–11:30. Unfortunately, the conversation was not recorded, so the actual questions that Packer might have answered are unknown. However, Packer's new time frame is in better keeping with other known events, such as PC Smith's patrol down Berner Street, the end of the club's discussion, and Marshall's sighting.

The statement of the grape-buyer stays about the same except the black coat becomes a "long black coat." Notably absent is any reference to the man's skin pigmentation as is any reference to the man's possible occupation of clerk; and the man becomes younger, going from early thirties to 25–30. (This change in age is curious, since it now neatly spans the estimated age given by PC Smith.) Elizabeth's description pretty much stays the same, except there is more detail about her clothes, which might have resulted from the trip to the mortuary, and the adjustment in the flower, which has been previously discussed.

One final aspect about this particular piece of information comes from the research and personal experiences of Stewart P. Evans. Inspector Abberline, through Superintendent Arnold, submitted Sergeant White's report of his dealings with Packer (ref MEPO 3/140, f.212–214). The initialed comments within the margins have typically been viewed as coming from Sir Charles; however, these annotations are almost certainly from Assistant Commissioner Bruce, who read the report the following day. Sergeant White's report and the involvement of the assistant commissioner were a direct result of Packer's claims of neglect in duty as reported in the newspaper.

Packer's last known recorded interview took place after the inquest's fourth session on October 5. This time, it was the *Daily Telegraph* who sought out the fruit-seller:

> He has also identified the body of Elizabeth Stride as that of the woman who accompanied the man who came to his shop, not long before midnight on Saturday...
>
> These [sketch portraits] were submitted to Packer, who unhesitatingly selected one of these here reproduced — the portrait of the man without the moustache, and wearing the soft felt or American hat ... the man's age was not more than thirty ... supported by the police-constable, who guessed him to be twenty-eight... A man like the one without the moustache, and wearing the soft black felt deerstalker hat, as drawn...
>
> On Saturday night about half-past eleven o'clock, this man and the woman he [Packer] has identified as the deceased came to the fruiterer's shop ... the woman, who wore a dark jacket and a bonnet with some crepe stuff in it, was playing with a white flower which she carried. The man was square-built, about 5ft. 7in. in height, thirty years of age, full in the face, dark complexioned, without moustache, and alert-looking. His hair was black. He wore a long black coat and soft felt hat. It seemed ... he was a clerk, and not a working man. He spoke in a quick, sharp manner ... purchased half a pound of black grapes... The couple then stood near the gateway of the club for a minute or so, and afterwards crossed the road and remained talking by the Board School for some time. They were still there when Packer had had supper and when he went to bed...

Starting with the hat, it is necessary to give some background information. In modern terms, the hat pictured in the sketch could be considered a type of floppy fedora, and would be a soft felt type of hat possibly viewed as "American" (Similar to the type of hat Indiana Jones wears.) But the true fedora was not invented until around 1915, although the hat's name does come from the title of an 1882 play, in which the female lead wore a similar type of hat. However, the fedora is similar to the trilby hat in England. This hat's name came from a play based on the 1894 novel, Trilby. Similarly, the porkpie, or pork pie hat, was in use in the mid-nineteenth century, is similar to the trilby and fedora, and was a "staple of the British man-about-town style for many years." (For comparison, the wide-awake was a round, soft felt, low-crowned, wide brimmed hat.)

What makes the hat the more fascinating aspect of this interview is the fact that interviewer, J. Hall Richardson, gave it several descriptions, "soft felt," "American," and "deerstalker." While "soft felt" applies to more than one style of hat (including the wide-awake hat described days earlier), a deerstalker is not American in origin. Nor was it ever widely used within the U.S., to even consider classifying it as American. (In fact the deerstalker's claim to fame in America only comes from a theatrical portrayal of Sherlock Holmes, which would have been after 1891; and, traditionally, a deerstalker was checked twill for camouflage purposes, and should not have been a solid color.) The use of the term "American" was most likely Richardson's take on what the *Evening News* had previously published. Additionally, Richardson wrote "deerstalker hat, as drawn." This is incorrect. What was "drawn" in the two sketches was a narrow brim, high crowned, soft felt hat for one and a bowler in the other. A deerstalker was never portrayed in the two sketches. While this might have been an editorial error, it was most likely added because PC Smith mentioned a deerstalker at the inquest. In other words, the *Daily Telegraph* was hedging its bets.

The description of the man himself stays pretty much the same, but we see again a reference to the dark complexion, which probably reappeared to help support the media's take (if not the popular desire), that the killer had to be a foreigner. The man is given the firm age of "thirty," which was probably an attempt to split the difference between the age given by PC Smith and that previously given by Packer, and we have the added description of black hair and no moustache. This is the first time that such a facial feature is mentioned, and it is important to recall Marshall's comment, "I cannot say [if he had any whiskers]. I do not think he had." Because Richardson would have been aware of this statement, the added description of "no moustache" is suspect, and is reminiscent of the added "deerstalker" hat. While Elizabeth was given a minimal description, Packer remained fairly consistent about her, indicating that he was working from memory.

The other notable aspect is the time of "11:30." In the Scotland Yard statement, the couple appeared around 11 o'clock, and for *Daily Telegraph*, Packer said they showed up a half an hour later. This timeframe might be possible depending on what "remained ... for some time" actually meant, but even a fairly conservative definition runs into the complication of the club members leaving, as well as Marshall's sighting.

After Packer's last interview, there were fourteen days before the final session of the inquest. Even though he presented his information at Scotland Yard, the police viewed the greengrocer as tainted, if not completely unreliable. This is somewhat unfortunate, since Packer's final thoughts on the matter might have laid to rest several questions regarding his participation in the whole affair. Yet if Packer had testified at the inquest, there is little doubt that Coroner Baxter would have closely questioned him with Inspector Reid cautioning him, probably in more than the usual way. What ultimately would have remained are the basic points upon which he was fairly consistent, once the grape-buyer was brought to light. The man stood about 5'-7", was about thirty years of age, wore dark clothes and a hat, had a quick way of talking, and appeared to be a clerk. Elizabeth's description might have been just as brief, if not more so (which would have been in keeping with some of the other generally vague descriptions that were given of her). And his time for seeing the couple would most likely have been comparable to what was in his statement at Scotland Yard. But even that would not necessarily explain some of the spots of detail that appear throughout all the clutter. Having looked at each statement separately, it is important to examine them together and see how the final tally specifically relates to other known information.

There are three main areas to consider: time, who was in the street, and the rain. Packer's first interview could be viewed as his most accurate, since Sergeant White asked no leading questions. Packer gave a time of 12:30 for closing up. He also commented that he did so "in consequence of the rain," adding that he saw no one standing about. The official weather recordings (at Camden Square) cited that the rain lasted till after midnight. However that information is not 100 percent accurate for Whitechapel, due to difference between locations. And while Best stated that it was "raining very fast" at shortly before 11, the rain did not last much longer after that, according to several other eyewitnesses.

Witness	Timing	Rain
PC Smith	On patrol since ten o'clock	"It rained very little after eleven o'clock."
William Marshall	Outside his door between 11:30 and midnight.	"While I was standing at my door ... there was no rain at all."
James Brown	Around 12:45 A.M.	Testified to no rain.
Dr. Blackwell	At the murder scene, 1:16 A.M.	Elizabeth's "clothes were not wet with rain."

This clearly shows that the weather front was moving inland and that Camden Square continued to see rain for a further thirty minutes to over an hour, even though Whitechapel did not. So the rain had pretty much subsided after

Elizabeth and her young man left the Bricklayer's Arms. But because it did not completely stop until around 11:30, Packer may have viewed the sprinkles or spots of rain as "still raining," as he stated to Sergeant White, and as he reportedly exclaimed to his wife. (I ran into a similar situation myself while living in the state of Indiana. It was barely sprinkling, and an elderly woman called it "raining.") However this interpretation does prevent Packer from having closed up shop at 12:30 that morning.

Moving backwards on the clock, the next time that Packer gave for closing up shop is 12 midnight, after watching the couple for about thirty minutes while it rained. Again we have the rain issue, but more importantly, we have Marshall's statement. The laborer saw Elizabeth and a young man around 11:45, where they stood three doors north for about ten minutes (around 11:55), loitering and kissing. Afterwards, they slowly made their way past Marshall heading in the direction of Ellen Street. It would have been impossible for Packer to have seen them for about a half an hour while Marshall (who was farther south down the street), watched them for more than ten minutes. This also negates any possibility of Packer having seen the couple, initially, at midnight (as he briefly commented to Sergeant White on October 4). It would have taken more than five minutes for a slow moving couple to come into Packer's view, even if they had turned onto Boyd Street. True, Packer did use the qualifying adjective, "about." But Elizabeth's and the young man's pace, as witnessed by Marshall, makes it unlikely that they would have sped up enough to fit within that timeframe, especially when past Marshall's was the George IV pub at the northern corner of Berner and Boyd, which was still open for at least a few more minutes. Across Boyd at the southern corner was Louis Friedman's baker shop, at 70 Berner Street, and two doors farther south from there at 74 Berner Street was Jacob Lubin's greengrocer shop. In other words, they were not in a hurry to get to Packer's place of business for any particular reason.

Continuing backwards, the next time range we are given is "sometime between" 11:30–12:00 (or "about 11:45") with Packer either interacting with and/or observing them for "more than half an hour," eventually losing sight of them sometime after midnight. Again, we have the impossible situation of the couple being sighted in two locations at the same time. Packer could not have seen Elizabeth at the same time as Marshall. Again, it was not raining at that time, making Marshall's time for his sighting more realistic. Additionally, neither Packer nor PC Smith referenced each other. Packer never stated he saw a constable passing through at that time and PC Smith never indicated that the greengrocer shop was still open. The significance of the latter is that Scotland Yard would not have waited until learning of Packer's interview in the newspaper to speak with him again. If PC Smith had given any indication to his superiors that a nearby shop was possibly open after his 12:30–12:35 patrol through the neighborhood, the police would have been knocking on Packer's door, and he probably would have been at the inquest. Additionally, there is a significant event absent from every one of Packer's stories — the ending of that Saturday's discussion at the club.

According to Morris Eagle, about seventy or so people left the club through the front door. This was between 11:30 and 11:45, and Eagle should know, since he chaired the discussion that night, and left at the same time to walk his girlfriend home. A greengrocer who was still open and hoping to sell his wares would not have missed hearing, let alone seeing that many people in the street especially since he had had a slow day with his barrow. He would have been very eager to sell what he could to those passing by on their way home. Yet Packer mentions none of this. It is very doubtful that he would have either ignored it or forgotten about it, once he started remembering what he saw, during the various interviews. Simply put, Packer never mentioned it, because he never saw it. But Packer did mention something else, somewhat consistently, in relation to when he closed up shop — the pubs being closed. Now it has already been established that Packer could not have interacted with or seen Elizabeth and her young man around the time the pubs closed, midnight. So what was Packer referring to when he mentioned this? In his last interview, Packer claimed he went off to have his supper; afterwards he went to bed. No doubt he closed up shop beforehand with knowledge of only Elizabeth and her young man having been in the area. Heading off for bed, he would have to have heard the sounds of the numerous club members exiting after that night's discussion. Discerning the hour from an event that commonly occurred (pubs closing at midnight), Packer incorrectly assumed that that was what took place. This accounts for the relative ease (or willingness, some might suggest) with which he shifted his times for seeing the couple for each successive interview. After winding through this maze, what results is that the more accurate of the five reports of what Packer saw that night is from his Scotland Yard interview on the late afternoon of October 4.[2]

What He Saw

But even though his more timely statement might have been his initial interview with Sergeant White, and his most accurate with Scotland Yard, they do not necessarily give a complete picture of what Packer saw that night, considering the other various interviews that took place. The last leg of this journey specifically involves Elizabeth and her young man. Shortly after 11 o'clock, they left the pub in Settles Street. Unfortunately Best and Gardner did not watch long enough to know which direction the couple took, except to say they "went off like a shot" towards Commercial Road. To reach Packer's shop, they had two basic routes, straight on to Christian Street then right onto Fairclough, or right onto Commercial Road, where they could have wandered down Batty Street, Back Church Lane, or even Berner Street itself. Each is generally possible and perhaps could be accomplished within the time that elapsed, depending on how fast the couple walked. But only one actually occurred.

When Packer described the couple's movement, he consistently claimed that they came from the lower end of the street, which has been otherwise described as "from Back Church end" and as "from the direction of Ellen street." But Packer is not situated on the corner of Berner and Fairclough streets. He is on the western side of the street and one door north of the junction. His shop front has been described as "a half window in front, and most of his dealings are carried on through the lower part of the window case, in which his fruit is exposed for sale." In other words, he had a limited view. From this vantage, however, Packer could have easily seen the couple coming west down Fairclough Street from the direction of Christian or Batty Street, but he did not see this. Nor did he state that they came down southerly through Berner Street, which would also negate the idea of them cutting through Sander Street. Because of the timing with Packer, Elizabeth and her young man could not have stopped somewhere nor meandered along some other bye-street. The only remaining option involves Back Church Lane.

If Elizabeth and her young man passed Fairclough as they walked down Back Church Lane, then they had several choices: Boyd Street, Everard Street or farther south, Ellen Street. Anything beyond Ellen Street would readily put the couple out of sync with other witnesses, like Marshall and the club members. Beginning with the farthest away, Ellen Street, it would have taken the couple approximately fifteen minutes to reach Ellen (walking at an average pace, which is gauged at traveling 500 yards in 8 to 9 minutes), turn east, and then head north up Berner Street. (Going by this route, the Bricklayer's Arms pub is approximately 828 yards to Packer's greengrocer shop.) It would have been about 11:20, at the earliest, by the time they reached Packer's shop. I say, at the earliest because they were taking their time, as noted by Marshall and by Packer. There, they would have had no more than ten minutes to buy the grapes, stand in front of the club, stand in front of the Board School, and leave by the time Packer closed up shop. This sounds reasonable except for one thing — Packer having said that they stood about for half an hour. Obviously Packer could not have watched Elizabeth and her young man for a full thirty minutes. But even being generous, ten minutes or less would not fall within the basic timeframe of half an hour. Additionally, it seems unlikely that they would have spent their time crisscrossing Berner Street.

Moving north, the next possible street would be Boyd (Everard Street is intentionally ignored because is it just south of Boyd and would have a slightly greater timing). If they traveled down Back Church Lane and turned east onto Boyd Street, before walking toward the junction of Berner and Fairclough Streets, they would have arrived shortly after 11:15. (From the Bricklayer's Arms pub to Packer's greengrocer shop via this route is approximately 710 yards.) This is better with respect to what information we have, and it could *feel* like half an hour to someone not paying close attention to the time. When someone is busy, a half-hour can easily slip by and only seem like five minutes. However, if they turned onto Fairclough Street from Back Church Lane, the couple could be at Packer's before 11:15, because the distance from pub to shop in this instance is approximately 577 yards. This would make more sense and place Elizabeth and her young man more within the *spirit* of half-an-hour, if not the actual timeframe.

Packer was fairly consistent in what the couple did after they bought the grapes. They stood in front of the club and walked across the street. Loitering by the Board School, they stood there talking and "eating" grapes. Relying on Packer's first two interviews as being accurate in the sense of seeing no one about when he closed up shop, the couple had moved on by no later than 11:30. At that point, Packer trotted off for supper and then to bed. Since no club member reportedly saw any couple in the vicinity when exiting the club that night, then Elizabeth and her young man had moved on toward Fairclough Street before the club's discussion let out. So the couple either interacted with or was observed by the greengrocer from sometime before 11:15 to no later than 11:30.

Packer was also fairly consistent about his description of Elizabeth, and the added details about her clothes are readily explained by his visit to the mortuary, as indicated earlier. However, Batchelor and Le Grand took Packer to the Golden Lane mortuary first, in a layman's attempt to be tricky. It can be assumed that Packer had no clue where he was being taken, just as it can be readily deduced that Packer was not as slow as the newspapers had thought and realized that a corpse removed from Berner Street would have been taken to the mortuary in St. George's. However, the striking bit of information comes from a detail about Batchelor and Le Grand's report, which was published on October 4. They first interviewed him two days before, and it was not until then that they accompanied the greengrocer to St. George's. Because Packer could not identify Catherine Eddowes and was able to describe Elizabeth consistently, there is little if any doubt that Packer actually saw her. Some may be quick to point out Packer's scant description of Elizabeth. But his information has no more nor less detail than that provided by those who testified at the inquest (reference PC Smith's description, in particular).

In describing the grape-buyer, Packer was fairly consistent, except on the following points: age, skin pigmentation, and hat. The hat has been sufficiently discussed, already, but a brief re-cap is worthwhile. The hat's first description is "wide awake." It then simplifies to "black, soft felt," and then later is described as a "soft felt kind of Yankee hat" and then as "soft felt or American," and "deerstalker." The influence from the *Evening News* and the *Daily Telegraph* reporters, as well as PC Smith's description can be readily seen, as previously described. What is left is wide-awake and black soft felt. A wide-awake hat was typically a dark, soft felt hat. Because press interviews with Best and Gardner were already out in print by the time Batchelor and Le Grand spoke with Packer, it is possible they might have led him to say "wide awake," just as the *Evening News* reporter led Packer to think "Yankee." Unfortunately, the specific questions that were put to Packer by the two private detectives were not published, as they had been for the special commissioner, but "soft felt hat" remained ever present throughout all the descriptions. At worst, the grape-buyer wore, simply, a dark, soft felt hat. At best, the hat was a wide-awake, in light of it being specifically mentioned first, without any known influence.

Reference to the skin pigmentation of Elizabeth's young man was never mentioned until the *Evening News* reporter called on Packer. During the interview, it was obvious the journalist wanted to indicate a foreigner, more specifically a non–Englishman. Yet skin color disappeared when Packer spoke to Scotland Yard. The reason it was not present is because Packer never said it. (For an example of such a description in a police statement, refer to George Hutchinson's description of the man he saw with Kelly; MEPO 3/140, f227–229, 230–232.) And it was not seen again until J. Hall Richardson, a correspondent for a competitive newspaper, arrived at 44 Berner Street. From Richardson's various descriptions, he apparently tried to ride the fence, between what the *Evening News* published, what Packer told him, and what was presented at the inquest. Bottom line — the grape-buyer did not have a dark complexion.

In deciphering the age of Elizabeth's grape-buyer, it has been noted that the man grew younger, then older again. In the first two interviews, he was said to be middle-aged, "perhaps 35," or more specifically, 30–35 years old.

While it is uncertain if Richardson was fully aware of what Packer stated at Scotland Yard, it is known that the reporter knew of PC Smith's inquest testimony, during which the constable stated "he was twenty-eight years of age." And it is doubtful that Richardson ignored what PC Smith stated. Instead, he seemingly tried to account for '28' and '30–35,' by simply writing "thirty years of age," probably figuring, give or take a couple of years and 30 hits the mark for either side of the scale. (Similarly, this probably explains why Scotland Yard stated 25–30, spanning PC Smith's description of 28.) Based on the ages reportedly given by Packer, there seems little doubt that the fruiterer saw the young man as 32–33, give or take a couple of years.

The remaining aspects of the man's appearance were either consistently presented or merely further details, which added to the grape-buyer's description. In the end, what presents itself is a composite of the man whom Packer saw that night. He was about five-foot-seven, about 32 to 33 years old (plus or minus two years), stout, square built with broad shoulders, full in the face with black or dark hair. He wore a long black coat (buttoned up) and a wide-awake hat (dark/black). He had a rough voice, and a quick sharp way of talking. He was alert looking, and had the appearance of a clerk.[3]

Grapes and the Bloody Stalk

One of the more legendary aspects of the Berner Street case is the grape stalk that was seen and yet not seen near Elizabeth's body. Once the grape-buyer was mentioned (starting with the second interview), Packer consistently stated that the man bought one-half pound of black grapes for three pence, leaving little room for doubt that the fruit was actually sold to the couple. According to Dr. Phillips, Elizabeth did not actually swallow any grape skin or grape seed while she and her young man ate grapes, as observed by Packer. If she had, the autopsy would have readily revealed grape or partially digested grape within her stomach. If Elizabeth chewed on some, she eventually spat them out. Unfortunately, Batchelor and Le Grand seemed to be too concerned about the grape stalk, instead of trying to locate any partially consumed grapes near Dutfield's or near the school. But even that might have come to nothing considering the number of people who eventually filled Berner Street that Sunday morning. Dr. Phillips did opine that Elizabeth's handkerchief had fruit stains on it, but it can only be assumed that those stains came from her eating the grapes, which seems reasonable. Grapes are not dry fruit. However, Dr. Phillips did not describe the discoloration of the stains. Nor would he have been able to tell if the stains appeared that night/morning, or days earlier.

From those who viewed the body in situ, there are several contradictory reports. Diemschütz told a news reporter that when the doctor opened Elizabeth's hands, one held grapes and the other held sweetmeats. Mrs. Mortimer claimed to have seen something similar: "in her hand were found a bunch of grapes and some sweets." However, Spooner, who knelt down to inspect the body, noticed only "that she had a piece of paper doubled up in her right hand." PC Lamb "did not notice anything" in her hand. And Kozebrodski claimed that "she had some grapes in her right hand and some sweets in her left." Yet the doctors who performed a more detailed examination said the exact opposite. Dr. Phillips stated, "Neither on the hands nor about the body of the deceased did I find grapes, or connection with them," adding that "the left arm was extended from elbow, and a packet of cachous was in the hand. Similar ones were in the gutter," which Dr. Blackwell accidentally spilled. Dr. Blackwell concurred with Dr. Phillips. "The packet [of cachous wrapped in tissue paper] was lodged between the thumb and the first finger [of the left hand], and was partially hidden from view." He also did not see any grapes near the body nor did he hear anyone say that they had seen grapes. Additionally, the right hand was open and across the chest, while the left hand was on the ground and partially closed.

Because the doctors had better lighting from the constable's lantern and spent more time with the body, there should be no doubt that Mortimer, Diemschütz, and Kozebrodski did in fact err when they stated that Elizabeth had a grape stalk (or grapes) in her hand. There were over fifteen civilian bystanders in the yard, preventing a good view of the body. Additionally, the stalk definitely could not have been in her left hand, since that contained the cachous wrapped in tissue. On this point, Spooner was incorrect (but he only had a lit match for light), and depending on his kneeling position with respect to the body, it might have appeared as though the tissue paper was in the right hand. No doubt Mortimer and the others were not influenced by Batchelor and Le Grand's story, because the two detectives did not appear on the scene until two days later, with their findings not being published until two days after that. The most likely root-cause for the few onlookers to think that Elizabeth held a grape stalk or grapes comes from the bystanders themselves. From Mortimer's description, "...and in her hand were found a bunch of grapes and some sweets," it almost sounds like she was repeating conversation, instead of giving an actual eyewitness account. The civilians in the yard did talk amongst themselves, as indicated by the discussion that Diemschütz and Heahbury had. So while the doctors might not have heard what was being said, innocent murmuring about a grape stalk began. As an interesting side note to this, Diemschütz did not repeat his alleged sighting of the grapes at the inquest.

Within Batchelor and Le Grand's published report, they claimed to have "amidst a heap of heterogeneous filth, discovered a grape stalk." The odd part of this is that they did not describe the "discovered" grape stalk as being bloodied, caked with blood, nor stained with blood. Their published report, however, does mention Rosenfield claiming to see a bloodstained grape stalk that Sunday morning. But that is the only connection given between blood and stalk. It is reasonable to think that Packer sold more grapes between 5:30 Sunday morning and the time the two detectives showed up that Tuesday. Hence their discovery has no real significance, as indicated by the *Evening News*: "...so that the finding of this fragment of grape stalk ... was scarcely necessary to establish the fact that the victim had been eating the fruit immediately before her death." Yet the newspaper ignored the fact that Drs. Blackwell and Phillips only referenced the cachous, and that no mention of grapes entered the inquest until the day after this article went public. And while it is possible for Elizabeth and her young man to have crossed the street again, eventually tossing the stalk into the yard, it seems unlikely that they remained in that area for that long. More than likely, they finished the grapes and tossed the empty stalk aside as they walked down Berner Street. Marshall provides some reasonable support for this in how long the couple stood near his house and that he did not readily notice anything in either of their hands. Chances are, the couple's grape stalk (and the bag that held the grapes) was left behind on Berner Street between the Board School and No.58.[4]

~12~

The Secrets of Berner Street

Artisans, laborers, shopkeepers, and homebodies, poor or comfortably well off, commonly went about their business as they lived and worked along a stretch of road situated within the St. George's area of London's East End. And while they had many stories to tell about their own lives, some residents had a great deal to say about the life of someone who was neither a neighbor nor a friend. From passing moments, the various inhabitants of this quiet neighborhood described the last hour and a half of Elizabeth's life, as she strolled along Berner Street with her young man.

But not everyone who saw something that morning testified at the inquest. And even then the press occasionally gave different views of the evidence that was presented, which might be due to reporters mishearing things such as names, their attempts to summarize, or possibly their efforts to better record what was said. It is therefore important to discuss what might be called the "mini-mysteries" within this murder case. This is not as grand as it might sound. Unlike some of the other Whitechapel murders, Elizabeth's death does not involve alleged coins, absent organs, or chalked messages. The mystery lay with the events themselves, as observed by the various witnesses, as presented in the papers. As with any murder mystery, not everything or everyone has a direct bearing on who killed the victim. Yet ambiguous statements, conflicting actions, and mysterious people still exist, and having a good feel for what the witnesses really saw does have a direct impact on what happened. In order to gain a better perspective for when things occurred, we pick up where we left off, after Elizabeth and the grape-buyer left the fruiterer, Matthew Packer.

William Marshall

At 11:45 P.M., Saturday, Marshall was standing outside his dwelling, No.64 Berner Street, which sat on the western side of the road. Three doors north of him, Elizabeth and her young man were loitering and kissing. There is no doubt about whom Marshall saw and when, but there is a discrepancy as to where the couple was. The *Times* reported Marshall saying, "I recognize it as that of a woman I saw on Saturday evening about three doors off from where I am living in Berner-street.... She was on the pavement opposite No. 63, and between Christian-street and Boyd-street."

This was misreported by the *Times*, because 63 Berner Street was across the road and one door south from Marshall (the odd street numbers were on the eastern side while the even numbers were on the western side of the road). If the couple had actually stood by No.63, then they never would have passed Marshall when they continued south down Berner. Additionally, Christian Street was about three blocks to the west of Marshall's location. It would have been impossible for someone to stand in Berner Street and still be between Christian and Boyd, which never intersect.

Fortunately, the *Daily Telegraph* clarified this with its version of Marshall's comment: "She was on the pavement, opposite No. 58, between Fairclough-street and Boyd-street." Location-wise, was 58 Berner Street is not only on the same side of road as Marshall, but it was three doors north of him; so when the couple walked south, they did indeed pass by, directly in front of him, as he described. During his testimony, he also stated that they stood "opposite No. 58." By this he meant *in front of* 58, not across the road from it, which would be dwellings 53 and 55.[1]

Morris Eagle and Joseph Lave

According to the papers, around 12:30, Lave exited the club to remove himself from the oppressive smoke and returned indoors around 12:40: "I was in the yard of the club this morning about twenty minutes to one. At half-past twelve I had come out into the street to get a breath of fresh air."

Despite his certainty, he seems to be off on his time. Between 12:30 and 12:35, PC Smith's patrol brought him back onto Berner Street, traveling south from Commercial Road. At the Board School opposite Dutfield's Yard, the constable saw Elizabeth and a young man. If Lave had been in the yard (with the gates open) and stood out at the street during this time, he should not have missed seeing a patrolman plodding along and could not have missed the couple across the road, especially since about five minutes after his reentering the club, Elizabeth was standing where Lave had been, and he never noticed a woman walking or standing around. Apparently Lave was outside for his fresh air before Constable Smith came by.

There is a similar problem with Morris Eagle, who claimed to have returned to club at 12:40, first trying the front door, and then going through the yard. If he had, it also seems unlikely that he would have missed seeing a woman standing or walking about within the vicinity of the club. And the discovery of the murder surely would have jogged his memory, and he never expressed anything of the sort to reporters or at the inquest. Eagle must have returned prior to PC Smith's appearance.[2]

Charles Letchford

At around 12:30 Sunday morning, Letchford walked through Berner Street on his way home to No. 30, where he lived since he was at least fifteen. When he spoke to reporters, most notably from the *Daily News* and the *Evening News*, he made a comment that has since puzzled researchers genealogically . "My sister was standing at the door at 10 minutes to one, but did not see anyone pass by." Based on other accounts, his "sister" seems to be Mrs. Fanny Mortimer, who is the only person known to have been standing outside her door at that hour. Mrs. Mortimer and her husband, William, lived only three doors south from the Letchfords' residence, on the same side of the street. An odd coincidence is that the Mortimers' had a son named Charles, who was around the same age as Letchford, approximately 21–22 years old. And Charles Letchford had an older sister, Florence, who would have been 28 at the time of the murder. Obviously 28-year-old Florence Letchford could not be mistaken for the 48-year-old Fanny Mortimer, nor would Letchford mistakenly say "sister" if he meant *mother* (which would be impossible for Letchford since his mother's name was Susannah). Even though Letchford had several other younger sisters, none of them are known to have spoken to reporters. Mortimer saw only the young couple by the Board School and Leon Goldstein, who walked down the street. There are two possibilities to answer the question "who was Charles Letchford's *sister*?"

At approximately ten minutes to one, Mortimer was outside and saw a young couple at the corner. Sadly, she never mentioned the name of the young woman or that of her beau, but Mortimer obviously knew the young woman, because they talked after the body's discovery: "They [young couple] told me [Mortimer] they did not hear a sound." The possibility here is that this young woman was Letchford's sister. For what could be a number of reasons, Letchford thought, was asked to say or was told by his sister that she was outside their residence at the time, instead of by the Board School with her boyfriend. And Mortimer supported this by not giving any names, thus helping Letchford's sister avoid any possible problems with the family or possibly avoid excessive media coverage, as ultimately happened with Packer.

The other possibility is simpler, but just as uncertain. While not a modern practice, it was common to refer to a half-sister or sister-in-law, as "sister." Whereas today, one would say "my sister-in-law" when referring to your spouse's brother's wife. It is an indirect family relation by marriage. Since Fanny Mortimer's maiden name is Skipp, this suggests the possibility that Charles Letchford might have married Mortimer's husband's sister, but present genealogical research neither confirms nor rules out this idea.

However, one aspect of Letchford's statement seems to negate either suggestion: "[She] did not see anyone pass by." She could not have been Mortimer, who did state that she saw a man pass by. This man later turned out to be Leon Goldstein, and he did indeed walk down Berner Street and then east onto Fairclough Street at the time Mortimer and the couple were outside. So Mortimer would not have told her neighbors that she did not see anyone, when she readily informed reporters that she did. This brings us back to the above notion that the young woman by the Board School was one of Letchford's actual sisters. For possibly personal reasons, she indicated to or asked her brother Charles to say that she was outside their door, and she might have asked the *Evening News* reporter to not use her name. This would also explain the seemingly relative ease with which the news reporter tracked down the unnamed young woman seen by Mortimer.[3]

Israel Schwartz

On the evening of Sunday, September 30, Schwartz presented himself to the Leman Street Police Station. With the aide of a translator, the Hungarian gave his statement concerning the incident he witnessed in front of Dutfield's Yard. Afterwards, he was taken to the mortuary, where he viewed and identified the body as that of the woman he saw being accosted. The authorities took Schwartz's statement seriously: "If Schwartz is to be believed, and the police report of his statement casts no doubt upon it...." This is also corroborated by the fact that Schwartz's description of the man who accosted Elizabeth was viewed as an official description and published in the *Police Gazette* on October 19: "At 12.45 A.M., 30th, with same woman, in Berner-street — A MAN, age about 30, height 5 ft. 5 in., complexion fair, hair dark, small brown moustache, full face, broad shoulders; dress, dark jacket and trousers, black cap with peak."

Yet even an important piece of evidence like Schwartz's can be confusing.

The original report no longer exists. What is known comes from Inspector Swanson's summary, also dated 19 October 1888. What is potentially misleading about the statement comes from the narrative style that was used. Inspector Swanson wrote it in the third person, as expected; yet he wrote it from Schwartz's point of view. Even though Schwartz's statement was presented earlier in this book, it is given again to provide a better overall view.

> 12.45 A.M. 30^ [next to statement]
> Israel Schwartz of 22 Helen Street, Backchurch Lane stated that at that hour, turning into Berner Street from Commercial Road, and having gotten as far as the gateway where the murder was committed, he saw a man stop and speak to a woman, who was standing in the gateway. He tried to pull the woman into the street, but he turned her round and threw her down on the footway and the woman screamed three times, but not very loudly. On crossing to the opposite side of the street, he saw a second man lighting his pipe. The man who threw the woman down called out, apparently to the man on the opposite side of the road, "Lipski," and then Schwartz walked away, but finding that he was followed by the second man, he ran as far as the railway arch, but the man did not follow so far. Schwartz cannot say whether the two men were together or known to each other. Upon being taken to the mortuary Schwartz identified the body as that of the woman he had seen.
> Schwartz described the first man as about 30 years old, standing 5ft-5in tall, fair complexion, dark hair with a small brown moustache. He had a full face with broad shoulders. He had nothing in his hands, but wore a dark jacket and trousers and a black cap with a peak.
> Schwartz then described the second man as 35 years old, standing 5ft-11in tall, fresh complexion with light brown hair. He wore a dark overcoat and an old black hard felt hat with a wide brim. This man had a clay pipe in his hand.

The somewhat ambiguous section is: "On crossing to the opposite side of the street, he [Schwartz] saw a second man lighting his pipe. The man who threw the woman down called out, apparently to the man on the opposite side of the road, 'Lipski'...." In the first sentence, it is Schwartz who crossed to the opposite or eastern side of the street (toward the Board School). When Schwartz eventually saw the "man on the opposite side of the road," this man, who lit his pipe, was on the opposite or western side of the street (same side as Dutfield's Yard) from Schwartz. This is corroborated by the only other known version of Schwartz's statement, which was printed in the *Star* on October 1: "...just as he [Schwartz] stepped from the kerb a second man came out of the doorway of the public-house a few doors off...." This pub was the beer house, The Nelson, which sat at the northwest corner of Berner and Fairclough Streets and was on the same side of the street as and only three doors away from Dutfield's. The *Star*'s article does not fully agree with the official version, however, and it is also given in full for a better side-by-side comparison to the official report.

INFORMATION WHICH MAY BE IMPORTANT

was given to the Leman-street police late yesterday afternoon by an Hungarian concerning this murder. This foreigner [Schwartz] was well dressed, and had the appearance of being in the theatrical line. He could not speak a word of English, but came to the police-station accompanied by a friend, who acted as an interpreter. He gave his name and address, but the police have not disclosed them. A *Star* man, however, got wind of his call, and ran him to earth in Backchurch-lane. The reporter's Hungarian was quite as imperfect as the foreigner's English, but an interpreter was at hand, and the man's story was retold just as he had given it to the police. It is, in fact, to the effect that he

SAW THE WHOLE THING.

It seems that he had gone out for the day, and his wife had expected to move, during his absence, from their lodgings in Berner-street to others in Backchurch-lane. When he came homewards about a quarter before one he first walked down Berner-street to see if his wife had moved. As he turned the corner from Commercial-road he noticed some distance in front of him a man walking as if partially intoxicated. He walked on behind him, and presently he noticed a woman standing in the entrance to the alley way where the body was afterwards found. The half-tipsy man halted and spoke to her. The Hungarian saw him put his hand on her shoulder and push her back into the passage, but, feeling rather timid of getting mixed up in quarrels, he crossed to the other side of the street. Before he had gone many yards, however, he heard the sound of a quarrel, and turned back to learn what was the matter, but just as he stepped from the kerb

A SECOND MAN CAME OUT

of the doorway of the public-house a few doors off, and shouting out some sort of warning to the man who was with the woman, rushed forward as if to attack the intruder. The Hungarian states positively that he saw a knife in this second man's hand, but he waited to see no more. He fled incontinently, to his new lodgings. He described

THE MAN WITH THE WOMAN

as about 30 years of age, rather stoutly built, and wearing a brown moustache. He was dressed respectably in dark clothes and felt hat. The man who came at him with a knife he also describes, but not in detail. He says he was taller than the other, but not so stout, and that his moustaches were red. Both men seem to belong to the same grade of society. The police have arrested one man answering the description the Hungarian furnishes. This prisoner has not been charged, but is held for inquiries to be made. The truth of the man's statement is not wholly accepted.

To begin with, the *Star* claimed that the second man had a knife in his hand, instead of lighting a pipe. Obviously wielding a weapon instead of casually smoking is more exciting for the readers. But it worked out nicely as a lead-in for another discrepancy. According to the *Star*, it was the knife-carrying man, who "shouted some sort of warning" to the first man and then he supposedly "rushed forward" at this first man. In both instances, there is no reason to accept the *Star*'s variation. Had the second man flashed a blade instead of lit a pipe, the police would have been *all over it*, as the saying goes, and it probably would have been his description that was published, not the first man's. Plus the police attached no suspicion to this second man. "The Police apparently do not suspect the 2nd man whom Schwartz saw on the other side of the Street & who followed Schwartz." Additionally, if the second man was acting as rescuer, he did a lousy job of it, since he and Schwartz left the area.

Despite some embellishment from the *Star*'s reporter, their account does provide additional detail that otherwise would not be known, such as why Schwartz was walking down Berner Street in the first place. But more importantly, it offers a further description of the two men. "The 'half-tipsy man' [Schwartz's first man] is also described as 'rather stoutly built... He was dressed respectably...'" The "second man" [Schwartz's second man or pipe man] is also described as "taller than the other [first man], but not so stout, and ... his moustaches were red. Both men seem to belong to the same grade of society."

Interestingly enough, the article does not give the second man's height. Because of the apparent propensity of the *Star*'s reporter for sensationalizing (knife instead of clay pipe), one would think that a five-foot-eleven person, as written in the official view, would be a more threatening knife-wielder than someone who was merely taller than five-foot-five. So it seems Schwartz might have taken a moment to reflect on this and had doubts about how tall this second man actually was. (This is not necessarily uncommon. Many police detectives experience this when dealing with eyewitnesses.) And while "same grade of society" says little about either man, when combined with "dressed respectably," it could indicate some profession that requires more than a basic education, so it is doubtful that either man was a laborer.

The *Star*'s final comments present a puzzling modern perspective: "The police have arrested one man answering the description the Hungarian furnishes. This prisoner has not been charged, but is held for inquiries to be made. The truth of the man's statement is not wholly accepted." Typically, the last sentence is commonly accepted as referring to Schwartz, even though the newspaper gives no indication of disbelieving him. "Prisoner" obviously does not refer to Schwartz. And actually, neither does the final sentence. The "man" whose truth is being questioned is the one arrested by the police. Unfortunately, the *Star* does not offer the prisoner's name.

One question that has been brought up in modern times is, "Did Schwartz actually hear 'Lipski' or did he mishear the name, 'Lizzy?'" They can sound similar. But there is a guttural distinction between the sounds "psk" and "zz," especially since the word was "called out" (or yelled as some writings put it), and not merely spoken. Even though Schwartz spoke Hungarian and virtually no English, many European languages on the continent make extensive use of multiple consonants that are very difficult to properly enunciate or audibly recognize by those who only speak English — Russian in particular is a good example of this. There is little doubt that Schwartz would have been able to recognize the difference. Plus there is no information to suggest that Elizabeth was seeing several "respectably" dressed men, beyond the one individual seen by Gardner, Marshall, et al., let alone that she knew Schwartz's first man at all. Additionally, the police had no doubt that the word spoken was "Lipski." This term is an anti–Semitic remark, stemming from the death of Miriam Angle. She died the year before at the hands of her fellow lodger and Jew, Israel Lipski, just one block over in Batty Street. Nevertheless, there was some disagreement among the authorities as to the recipient of the slur. According to the assistant commissioner for the Metropolitan Police, Dr. Anderson, "The opinion arrived at in this office upon the evidence given by Schwartz at the inquest of Eliz Stride's case is that the name Lipski ... used by a man whom he saw assaulting the woman in Berner S' on the night of the murder, was not addressed to the supposed accomplice but to Schwartz himself."

Dr. Anderson accepted this probably because it had been said that Schwartz had a "Jewish" appearance. Nevertheless, Schwartz was already crossing the road, trying to avoid the situation and the first man was involved with Elizabeth when the second man appeared. Based on the two known accounts, the first man was looking more toward Elizabeth and not at Schwartz. Upon noticing the second man, probably when he lit his pipe, the first man called out "Lipski" to this second man. Why the slur Lipski? Given the location, next door to a Jewish Socialist club, the first man probably thought this new guy on the scene was Jewish. The insult was a subtle warning, but one given to the second man to stay away, which according to Schwartz, both he and the second man had taken by leaving the area.

Dr. Anderson's above comment said something else, though, about "evidence given by Schwartz at the inquest...." This memo was dated approximately three weeks after the end of the Stride inquest. The official inquest records no longer exist, but no known news account of the inquest places Schwartz inside the Coroner's Court, let alone testifying there. Schwartz would have been a sterling witness, and given Coroner Baxter's pursuit of the truth, he would not have let such evidence slip through his hands, had he known about it. Yet it is certain that the police would not have withheld such information from the coroner. More than likely, Dr. Anderson was correct, except that Schwartz probably presented his evidence behind closed doors, away from the public and the media.

It could be suggested that Schwartz might have been off his time, like some other witnesses, but based on the wording used by Inspector Swanson, the police had no doubt that Schwartz saw the incident in front of Dutfield's Yard, at fifteen minutes to one: "At that hour [12:45 A.M.], turning into Berner Street from Commercial Road, and having gotten as far as the gateway...." It is unknown whether or not Schwartz had a watch, as Dr. Blackwell had, and the average civilian might not even stop to think about looking at his watch under such circumstances. Chances are Schwartz knew the time as Diemschütz did — from the baker's clock near the corner of Berner Street and Commercial Road. An earlier chapter gave Schwartz's approximate time for turning onto Berner as about ten minutes after PC Smith saw Elizabeth and her young man. This has been estimated from an average of walking 500 yards in 8–9 minutes, covering the approximate 132 yards, with respect to his reported 12:45 A.M. sighting at the gateway. (Martin Fido worked out the average walking time.)

As mentioned, the *Star* is the only newspaper known to have carried Schwartz's statement of the incident he witnessed. However, another paper might have referenced Schwartz. According to the *Evening News*, "What they [Batchelor and Le Grand] go to establish is that the perpetrator of the Berner street crime was seen and spoken to whilst in the company of his victim, within forty minutes of the commission of the crime and only passed from the sight of a witness ten minutes before the murder and within ten yards of the scene of the awful deed." It might be suggested that this referred to Mrs. Mortimer, but there is nothing in her statement or how the press reacted to it that would lead to such a conclusion. This particular statement was published in the *Evening News* three days after the *Star* published its article on Schwartz. Because he is the last known person to have seen Elizabeth alive, *approximately* "ten minutes" before her body was discovered, then this unnamed "witness" is apparently an obscure reference to Schwartz.[4]

Fanny Mortimer

Mrs. Mortimer comes across almost like a favorite aunt, but she is nearly as enigmatic with her timing as Packer was. According to the *Times*,

I [Mortimer] was standing at the door of my house nearly the whole time between half-past 12 and 1 o'clock on Sunday morning, and did not notice anything unusual. I had just gone indoors and was preparing to go to bed when I heard a commotion outside, and immediately ran out, thinking that there was a row at the Socialists' club close by. I went to see what was the matter, and was informed that another dreadful murder had been committed in the yard adjoining the club-house... A man Spooner: touched her face and said it was quite warm, so that the deed must have been done while I was standing at the door of my house. There was certainly no noise made, and I did not observe any one enter the gates. It was just after 1 o'clock when I went out [after hearing the commotion], and the only man I had seen pass through the street previously was a young man [Goldstein] carrying a black, shiny bag, who walked very fast down the street from the Commercial-road. He looked up at the club and then went round the corner by the Board school.

The *Evening News* corroborates the *Times*'s version, but added, "A young man and his sweetheart were standing at the corner of the street, about twenty yards away, before and after the time the woman must have been murdered, but they told me they did not hear a sound." Yet more important is what the *Evening News* published in the same edition, immediately after the statement made by the young man's "sweetheart."

A woman [Mortimer] who lives two doors from the club has made an important statement. It appears that shortly before a quarter to one o'clock she heard the measured, heavy tramp of a policeman passing the house on his beat. Immediately afterwards she went to the street-door, with the intention of shooting the bolts, though she remained standing there ten minutes before she did so. During the ten minutes she saw no one enter or leave the neighbouring yard, and she feels sure that had any one done so she could not have overlooked the fact. The quiet and deserted character of the street appears even to have struck her at the time. Locking the door, she prepared to retire to bed, in the front room on the ground floor, and it so happened that in about four minutes' time she heard Diemschitz's [sic] pony cart pass the house, and remarked upon the circumstance to her husband.

In these two statements, Mortimer placed herself outside her residence "nearly the whole time" between 12:30 and 1 o'clock *and* for only ten minutes, "shortly before" 12:45. To some, this contradiction might make her seem unreliable, yet she was outside her house before Diemschütz returned home, as corroborated by Goldstein and the young couple by the Board School. After she returned inside to prepare for bed, roughly four minutes had passed when she heard Diemschütz drive by.

After reviewing the actions of the other known witnesses, Mortimer was obviously not outside the entire time between 12:30 and 1:00. If she had been, she missed several people, such as PC Smith coming back into Berner Street at 12:30–12:35 and Elizabeth and her young man standing by the Board School (and they were obviously not the young couple seen by Mortimer). And Mortimer missed the entire incident witnessed by Schwartz (as did the young couple). Other potential witnesses also were in the street apparently before

PC Smith, such as Eagle returning to the club, who first tried the front door before entering via Dutfield's Yard, and Lave, who was in the yard but also "strolled into the street." Neither Lave nor Eagle noticed a couple by the Board School or a woman standing only three doors away. Obviously Mortimer missed a great deal if she had been outside her door for half an hour.

It is possible for Mortimer to have been outside for approximately ten minutes, though, because she saw the young couple who moved in from Fairclough Street, saw Goldstein, and shortly after going back inside, heard Diemschütz. But this ten minutes could not have been just before 12:45, or she would have seen Schwartz and the others. Mortimer's timing, as with Packer's estimated times for closing up shop, was based on one event. For Packer it was the club members leaving the IWEC, which he mistook for the pubs closing. In Mortimer's case, it was her having heard the "measured heavy tramp." Now Mortimer never claimed to have seen this person, but it was assumed to be a policeman. Living in a neighborhood which has regular patrol beats, one might discern the hour from the patrolman's rounds. This is precisely what Mortimer did, except the heavy tramp she heard outside her house was not PC Smith. Mortimer was outside her house, standing on the sidewalk in front of her door. She just happened to be there after the Schwartz incident.[5]

The Young Couple

As previously mentioned, the young couple that spoke with and was seen by Mortimer could not have been near the corner of Berner and Fairclough streets, standing by the Board School for twenty minutes, as indicated by the press: "It also transpired that shortly before the man with the pony trap raised the alarm that a woman had been murdered. A young girl had been standing in a bisecting thoroughfare not fifty yards from the spot where the body was found. She had, she said, been standing there for about twenty minutes, talking with her sweetheart, but neither of them heard any unusual noises." As presented, the young couple left prior Diemschütz's arrival, yet standing in that vicinity for twenty minutes would place them at the corner around 12:40, and as the young woman said, "neither of them heard any unusual noises." Hence the couple was obviously not there prior the Schwartz incident, and it is doubtful that they would have missed another couple standing only yards away, if Elizabeth and the young man moved from where PC Smith saw them. In addition, PC Smith never claimed to have seen a second couple by the Board School. But the young couple was there when Mortimer went outside.

This leaves the couple having walked towards the area while the Schwartz incident occurred, arrived at the Board School, as witnessed by Mortimer (which was after Schwartz and the second man left), and then departed before Diemschütz arrived, as the young woman stated.[6]

Leon Goldstein

Before Mortimer returned indoors and before the young couple left the area, Goldstein walked down Berner Street and then headed east onto Fairclough. In spite of rumors, Goldstein's appearance on the scene was innocent, which was why he voluntarily went to the Leman Street Police Station to give a statement. Yet beyond establishing who was where and when, Goldstein has no bearing on the case, except for one thing. Jack the Ripper is commonly portrayed with a black bag. Chances are it was because of the press accounts from Mortimer, who saw Goldstein carrying such a bag, a common type of bag typically referred to as a gladstone bag, after Prime Minister Gladstone, even though the original model was developed in France.[7]

James Brown

Brown is commonly viewed as being uncertain, particularly because he was "almost certain" that the woman he saw in the mortuary was the same as the one he saw by the Board School, but also because his descriptions of the couple were just as uncertain. But Brown might be considered a pivot point, because he either saw Elizabeth and her young man, Mortimer's couple, or a previously unknown third couple. So it is prudent to review when he saw this couple and how it relates to other events, in order to determine whom he might have seen.

On Friday, October 5, Brown testified at the inquest. He stated that he originally came home (probably from work) at ten minutes after midnight. Some time later, he left to fetch some supper from Henry Norris's chandler shop at the southwest corner of Berner and Fairclough. From Brown's residence to the cook shop, it is approximately 110 yards and he could have walked that distance in about two minutes. Even though he never noticed the time while at Norris's, he estimated that he was there for three, maybe four minutes. Another trek back to his digs, and he had been home for about fifteen minutes, nearly having finished his supper, when he heard screams of "murder" and "police." Like most of the eyewitnesses who testified, Brown seemed pretty confident in his times, and an approximation for when he was in the Berner and Fairclough intersection can be determined.

The cries heard by Brown came from Diemschütz and Jacobs as they ran down Fairclough Street. Since the club steward arrived home at one o'clock, it was most likely five minutes past when Brown heard the vocal alarms. By this point Brown had already returned to his lodgings, with supper in hand, around ten minutes to midnight. About two minutes before that, he left the chandler shop, where he stayed for less than five minutes. While such timing cannot be exact it does correspond with his 12:45 sighting. However, he passed through the intersection before and after the Schwartz incident. This is further evidenced by the fact that Brown never noticed anything related to the incident such as Elizabeth being pushed onto the footway, the first man calling out "Lipski," or Schwartz and the second man leaving the scene heading south, at which point they traveled through the intersection.

It can be accepted that Brown was fairly close as to *when* he claimed to be passing through the intersection, but whom did he see and in what direction was he walking when he saw them? The latter might seem like a silly question, but it is not. On Saturday, October 6, the *Times* and the *Daily Telegraph*, along with others, published their account of the previous day's inquest session. Essentially, they agree except for one major difference. According to the *Times*:

> I [Brown] live at 35, Fairclough-street. I saw the deceased about a quarter to 1 on Sunday morning. At that time I was going from my house to get some supper from a chandler's shop at the corner of Berner-street and Fairclough-street. As I was going across the road I saw a man and woman standing by the Board School in Fairclough-street. They were standing against the wall. As I passed them I heard the woman say, "No, not to-night, some other night." That made me turn round, and I looked at them.

Yet, according to the *Daily Telegraph*:

> I [Brown] live in Fairclough-street, and am a dock labourer. I have seen the body in the mortuary. I did not know deceased, but I saw her about a quarter to one on Sunday morning last.
> THE CORONER: Where were you?—I was going from my house to the chandler's shop at the corner of the Berner-street and Fairclough-street, to get some supper. I stayed there three or four minutes, and then went back home, when I saw a man and woman standing at the corner of the Board School. I was in the road just by the kerb, and they were near the wall.

Situations like this make a researcher wish Coroner Baxter had a modern-day stenographer. Brown either saw the couple on the way to Norris's or after he left Norris's. While either might seem possible, the difference is important.

When PC Smith came through Berner Street, he saw Elizabeth and her young man standing by the Board School. The couple was on the Berner side of the school and not moving from where they stood. They gave no indication that they might intend to walk a mere few yards away, down to the corner, only to lean against the building they were already next to. Though doubtful, it could be suggested that they did just that. There was, after all, enough time between PC Smith and Brown. Combining the aforementioned interpretation with the *Times* version, then Brown would have seen Elizabeth and her young man on the Fairclough side of the school while he went to get his supper, before the Schwartz incident. There is a problem with this, however. Referring back to Mortimer and her young couple, if the *Times* was correct, then Brown would have seen this young couple, also, while on his way back home from the chandler shop. And Brown never stated that he saw two couples — only one.

With Elizabeth and her young man on the Berner side, where PC Smith saw them, Brown would not have noticed them while he walked to Norris's. Leaving the chandler shop sooner than estimated (before Schwartz) has a potential problem as well. Schwartz never saw anyone moving about in the distance as he walked down Berner. And Elizabeth was already standing in front of Dutfield's Yard. Like PC Smith, Brown gave no indication that the couple he saw on the Fairclough side of the school was anxious to move. In all probability, The *Daily Telegraph*'s version is correct — Brown saw a couple while on his way back to his lodgings with his supper. More importantly, however, Brown's return home would have been after the Schwartz incident, but before Mortimer. This is further supported by the fact that Mortimer never saw anyone walk through or across the intersection while she stood outside. This and the darkened area where the couple stood would explain why Brown was uncertain about his identification of the body.[8]

The residents and neighbors of Berner Street — average people suddenly turned witness in a murder investigation. No doubt they would have preferred to simply be about their business, whether working near the bustling corridor of Commercial Road or living quietly on one of the side streets. Yet they told their tales as best they could, presenting what they saw or heard. True, what they offered, at times, could be likened to a play within a play, and some might prefer a more straightforward account, but that is part of the mystery, if not mystique, of the Whitechapel murders.

$\sim$13$\sim$

A Killer in Whitechapel

E lizabeth Stride died in the early hours on Sunday, September 30, 1888, between 12:45 when Schwartz saw her being accosted and 1 o'clock when Diemschütz discovered her body. Historically, her death is attributed to Jack the Ripper, as the first victim of the double-event. As such, she is recognized as the third canonical victim. The concept of what is called the double-event has been around ever since October 1, 1888. With news of two deaths within a half-mile of each other and discovered not even an hour apart, the press readily presented its thoughts on the subject:

> Two more murders must now be added to the black list of similar crimes of which the East-end of London has very lately been the scene. The circumstances of both of them bear a close resemblance to those of the former atrocities. The victim in both has been a woman. In neither can robbery have been the motive, nor can the deed be set down as the outcome of an ordinary street brawl. Both have unquestionably been murders deliberately planned, and carried out by the hand of some one who has been no novice to the work.

No doubt the media added Elizabeth's death to Nichols, Chapman, and Eddowes, but they also included Smith and Tabram in this tally when they published sketched maps of the "Locality of the Six Murders," thus placing Elizabeth as victim five. Some papers went so far as to eventually reference a non-existent murder at Christmas 1887, which ultimately resulted in the fictitious victim "Fairy Fay." Based on Emma Smith's own statements to her friend and at the hospital, she was attacked by a group of young men, who robbed her then brutally assaulted her with a blunt instrument; she died in the hospital on April 4. By all accounts, Smith was not a victim of a serial killing, while some acknowledge Martha Tabram as the start of Jack's escalating rampage. But does Elizabeth belong in the death toll? To better answer the ultimate mystery within the Berner Street case, the wounds received by the victims should be reviewed.[1]

The Injuries

Even though Tabram is not a canonical victim, because of her manner of death and the nearness of her death to that of Mary Ann Nichols, it is prudent to include her. She is the *quintessential* grey area — a victim who is not firmly accepted, nor wholly dismissed by present-day investigators. Mary Kelly will not be referenced since her murder followed Elizabeth's by almost six weeks. (Kelly has not been mentioned in this book because her death occurred after the end of the Stride inquest.) The listed injuries are those that have been described as occurring during the times of the murders and do not include descriptions of old bruises, stomach contents, etc.

Martha Tabram: Found lying on her back; possibly killed first; stabbed 39 times. She had at least 22 stab wounds to the trunk: 17 in the breast (which included five stabs wounds to the left lung, two stabs to the right lung) and the heart was stabbed once. The liver was stabbed five times. The spleen was stabbed twice. The stomach was stabbed six times. The lower portion of the body had one stab wound, 3 inches long and 1 inch deep, but it was not mutilated. There were nine stab wounds to the throat, yet it was not cut, and there was no evidence that the carotid arteries had been severed.

Tabram's death certificate simply records the cause of death as "violent wilful murder."

Mary Ann Nichols: Found lying on her back; killed first; slashed and cut post-mortem. There was a bruise on the lower part of her right jaw and a circular bruise on the left side of her face. On the left side of her neck, 1 inch below the jaw, there was a 4 inch incision starting immediately below the left ear. A second throat incision starting 1 inch below and 1 inch in front of the first, ran 8 inches in a circular direction around the throat and stopped 3 inches below the right ear, completely severing all tissues down to the spine, including the large vessels of the neck on both sides. On the lower part of the abdomen, 2–3 inches from the left side, ran a very deep, jagged wound, cutting the tissues through. Several incisions ran across the abdomen. Three or four similar cuts ran down the right side of the abdomen.

Nichols's death certificate states cause of death as "syncope due to loss of blood from wounds to neck and abdomen inflicted by some sharp instrument."

Annie Chapman: Found lying on her back; killed first; mutilated post-mortem. Three scratches were below the lower left jaw, 1½–2 inches below the left ear lobe, going in the opposite direction of the throat wounds, and a bruise corresponded with these scratches. She had a bruise on her right cheek and an abrasion on the head of the proximal phalanx of the ring finger. The upper eyelid was bruised. A bruise was on the middle part of the bone of the right hand. The shortest throat incision ran from the front of the throat and terminated on the right side between the lower jaw and the breastbone. The longest throat incision completely encircled the throat, running along the line of the jaw. The incisions ran from her left to right, two clean and distinct cuts on the left side of the spine, which were parallel to each other and were ½ inch apart. The small intestines and other portions were attached but lying on the ground above her right shoulder. Missing were the womb, the upper part of the vagina, the greater part of the bladder, and part of the belly wall that included the navel. Chapman's death certificate states her cause of death as "violent injuries to throat and abdomen by a sharp instrument."

Elizabeth Stride: Found lying on her left side; slash to the throat; no post-mortem injuries. Over both shoulders, especially the right, from the front aspect under the collarbones and in front of chest there was a bluish discoloration. On the neck, from the victim's left to her right, there was a clean-cut incision that was six inches in length. This single incision started two and a half inches in a straight line below the angle of the left jaw. The wound ran three-quarters of an inch over undivided muscle, then became deeper, about an inch in depth, dividing the sheath and the vessels, ascending a little, and then grazed the muscle outside the cartilage on the left side of the neck. The left carotid artery, along with the other vessels contained in the sheath, was cut through, except for the posterior portion of the artery, to a line about ¹⁄₁₂ inch in extent, which prevented the separation of the upper and lower portion of the artery. The cut through the tissues on the right side of the cartilage was more superficial, and tailed off to about two inches below the right angle of the jaw. It was evident that the hemorrhage, which produced death, was caused through the partial severance of the left carotid artery. Except for the neck, there was no recent external injury.

Stride's death certificate states the cause of death as "violent haemorrhage from severance of blood vessels in the neck by a sharp instrument."

Catherine Eddowes: Found lying on her back; killed first; mutilated post-mortem. There was a recent bruise, the size of a sixpence, on her left hand between the thumb and first finger. The left eyelid was cut. She had a cut on her right cheek. and a deep cut on the bridge of her nose. The tip of the nose was detached. She had two abrasions on her left cheek under the left ear. Her throat was cut nearly ear-to-ear, dividing all tissues down to the bone. The frontal abdominal walls were cut open from the pubic area to the breastbone. The liver was stabbed, as was the area left of the groin. There were cuts made between the thighs and labium on both sides. The pancreas was cut. One section of intestines was placed on the ground above her right shoulder and the other section placed between her body and left arm. The left kidney was removed. The uterus lining was cut. The womb was cut through leaving a three-quarter-inch stump; the womb was removed.

Eddowes's death certificate states the cause of death as "hemorrhage from the left carotid artery by being cut by a sharp instrument."

A direct comparison of the injuries readily shows that Elizabeth did not receive a second throat wound nor any post-mortem injuries. And her throat wound did not run deep enough to nick a vertebra. Although Tabram could be an exception, unless the stab wound to her heart came first, which would have caused instant death. Like the other victims, Elizabeth was killed where she was found. Yet she was left alive and bled to death. It is common knowledge that Elizabeth received the fewest injuries — a sliced throat, instead of slashes, stabbing, and/or mutilation. The differences in injuries alone do not necessarily preclude her from having been a "Riper" victim. A look at the weapon is also important.[2]

The Knife

Unlike victims Nichols through Eddowes, Tabram was brutalized with two weapons: the one producing the heart wound was a long, strong instrument, possibly a dagger-like knife similar to a stiletto, while a penknife inflicted her other injuries. The knife that caused all of Nichols's injuries was long bladed and moderately sharp. The knife that killed Chapman was a sharp, probably thin, narrow blade that was at least six to eight inches in length, perhaps longer. A sharp pointed knife that was at least six inches long caused the injuries inflicted on Eddowes. However, the doctors agreed that a different type of knife was used to kill Elizabeth. A long knife, like the one found by Coram, was viewed as an unlikely weapon because of its length. Instead, Drs. Blackwell and Phillips believed a short, well-ground knife had been used. They likened it to a shoemaker's knife, which is not the same as a penknife.

Granted the same doctors did not cover all five deaths, but Dr. Phillips is the only one who was involved with the bodies in situ and in post-mortems for both the Hanbury and Berner Street murders. So he would have had a better opportunity to distinguish between the types of knives used in making the injuries. It has been suggested, however, that Jack might have carried two knives, thus explaining the difference in Elizabeth's case. While two weapons were clearly used on Tabram, Elizabeth's death would actually suggest a total of four knives used by the killer: penknife, a shoemaker's-type of knife, a dagger-like knife, and what has been viewed as a post-mortem kind of knife. The killer apparently had no preference or weapon of choice. Alternately, the killer learned from Tabram and decided to carry a different set: the long, thin bladed knife and the short knife. Changing to a more preferred weapon is not unknown; Son of Sam is a good example of that. At first he used a knife, but he was basically too squeamish and reverted to a gun for distance. Yet there is something missing from this idea. If the killer wanted to inflict an injury initially with the short knife, as might be suggested from Elizabeth's wound, then he did not do so in any of the other murders. In either victim before and after Elizabeth, there is no indication that he used multiple weapons or changed methods. And given his prior successes, he had no reason to; in fact, he would have been more emboldened to continue as he had. And how was this short knife used?[3]

Manner of Death

There is no doubt that the other victims were lying on their backs when the attacks occurred, and they were rendered unconscious first. On this point there is some disagreement with respect to Elizabeth. As Coroner Baxter stated in his summation, "the throat was not cut until after she was actually on her back." It could be suggested that she was knocked out like the others, and various methods for doing so have been suggested. But that is not possible in Elizabeth's situation. The mud on her jacket clearly shows that she was lying on her left side, which was how she was found, and there were no signs of a struggle or cries for help. Even if she were unconscious, it is impossible to imagine Elizabeth lying on her left side with the killer bending or kneeling over her, possibly from behind, to slice her throat. And doing so from in front would have been even more difficult and awkward. In addition, he would have had his back towards the wall with little maneuvering room. And the wound would have been much different, for it would have started towards the middle of the neck by the windpipe, and would not have nearly severed the left carotid artery. The injury actually started on her left and trailed off on her right. It *was not* superficial on the left, running deeper at the windpipe and then tapering off again. Elizabeth's injury could only have been produced with a knife being drawn across her throat, which would place the killer behind her, using his right hand. This means they were both standing up and Elizabeth was conscious when it happened. Based on their injuries, the other canonical victims were killed by the knife being plunged into the left side of throat, with the primary incision encircling the neck. Death was instant. This is a significant inconsistency. But what about blood spatter?[4]

Blood Spatter

Unlike at Annie Chapman's murder scene, there were no discernable spatters of blood near Elizabeth or on her clothes, although instant severance of the carotid artery should have produced a spray of blood. Several pieces of evidence could account for its absence. In the process of causing the injury, the killer cut Elizabeth's scarf, which means the wound coincided with the bottom border of the neckerchief. The scarf was pulled tight to the left, indicating that the killer held the scarf by its tails. This would have interfered with any squirting blood, albeit slightly. Elizabeth herself caused the greatest interference, however. The only explanation for the back of her right hand being smeared in blood is that she put her hand to her throat after she was cut in a very natural reaction. But it is reasonable to expect a certain amount of arterial spray between when the injury was inflicted and when Elizabeth reacted to the pain; yet the wall was free of blood. When Elizabeth was found, she was lying on her left side facing the wall. This would indicate that Elizabeth faced the wall when she was cut. Any initial spray from the left carotid artery would have sprayed more towards her left than towards the wall. As she went down, the descending traces of blood fell with her. Once Elizabeth hit the ground, the blood that flowed from her neck down to the club's kitchen door probably overtook the majority of droplets. Afterwards, between the activity of the authorities and bystanders in the yard, the removal of the body, and the washing away of the blood, there would have been no real trace of arterial spray for Inspector Reid to find upon his return to Dutfield's Yard that morning. It is further explained if Elizabeth did not squarely face the wall. It also explains why there was no mud or blood on the front of her clothes — she did not simply fall to her knees or collapse and then fall onto her left side. People who faint fall forward. Elizabeth fell in the direction in which she laid, which was in the same direction as any spray of blood. The next question that should be answered is who did it?[5]

The Theories

To answer the question "who," it is necessary to look at the various possibilities. While the media and the public had no doubt that the infamous Whitechapel killer was responsible, reasons why he was not apprehended in the act surfaced as early as that Sunday.

Escaped. In her press interview, Mortimer suggested how the killer might have avoided detection. "He [Diemschütz] drove through the gates, and my opinion is that he interrupted the murderer, who must have made his escape immediately under cover of the cart." This is an interesting idea, but not very likely. The pony was more towards the left, because he shied away from something just inside the gates. The two-wheeled cart would have turned, at least slightly, in that direction. Diemschütz looked down to the right in the direction of the body. Even though he did not initially know what the mound was, he would have been able to tell if someone was moving about the body. Mortimer's scenario would be further complicated if the killer were positioned on Elizabeth's right side (facing her back), because Diemschütz would have looked right at him, yet he only saw the body. The club steward was close enough to touch the body with his whip. But Mortimer's thoughts give rise to another possibility.

Interrupted. Mortimer not only suggested how the killer managed to leave, but she also opined that he was interrupted, a sentiment expressed by Coroner Baxter during his summation. "If he [Diemschütz] had not actually disturbed the wretch in the very act, at least he must have been close on his heels; possibly the man was alarmed by the sound of the approaching cart." This is a more likely scenario than what Mortimer proposed. Hearing a cart, the killer would have gone further into the yard, and as expressed at the inquest by PC Lamb and Phillip Krantz, the killer had a better opportunity to leave after the commotion than before. This means hiding somewhere in the yard or the neighboring tenements for about four hours. This is not very likely either, because the area, buildings, neighbors, and bystanders were thoroughly searched while the body remained at the scene and again after its removal. Even Coroner Baxter alluded to the possibility that the club steward might have caught him "in the very act," which could make sense, because of the mere fifteen minutes between the last sighting and the discovery. However, this amount of time would have been sufficient for the killer to create more injuries, which he did not, nor were there any obvious indications that the killer attempted to do more. Yet this quarter-hour gave rise to another concept.

Multiple Attacks. Inspector Swanson's October 19 report considers the possibility of more than one assailant. "For only 15 minutes elapsed between 12.45 when Schwartz saw the man & 1.0 when the woman was found murdered on the same spot- That the suggestion is that Schwartz' man may have left her, she being; a prostitute then accosted or was accosted by another man, & there was time enough for this to take place & for this other man to Murder her before 1.0." While possible, it seems almost inconceivable that one person could have that much misfortune in such a short amount of time — be accosted by one man, leave the area, and come back with a new man, who then kills her. The odds must be astronomical. Mortimer and the young couple create problems for this theory. Between them, they were in Berner Street or at the corner by the Board School just before Diemschütz turned into the gateway. Neither saw Elizabeth, nor did they see a couple walk into the area. The club steward himself further complicates this notion, because he never saw anyone, let alone a couple, enter or leave the yard as he drove down the street towards the club. This also negates the two-man team concept, which usually involves both men seen by Schwartz, even though the second man, left the scene along with the Hungarian. However, others have looked to someone else.

The Clerk. Often enough, the question of Elizabeth's killer comes to the young man she was seen with. And the descriptions given by Best/Gardner, Packer, Marshall, and PC Smith are commonly compared. One reason is that a prostitute would not necessarily spend ninety minutes with the same client. At worst, however, Elizabeth can only really be described as a part-time prostitute. There is no evidence indicating that her sole livelihood was hooking, while there is information to suggest that she did so occasionally, as referenced by Thomas Bates, the night watchman who said, "When she could get no work she had to do the best she could for her living." (Refer also to the testimonies of Tanner, Lane, and Olsson.) These descriptions should be reviewed.

Witness	Timing	Description
J. Best & John Gardner	Shortly before 11:00. Soon after 11:00.	5ft-5in; weak eyes — sore eyes without any eyelashes (which has at times been taken to indicate a light blonde, sandy or other similar light color); black moustache; no beard; black morning suit; morning coat; collar and tie; billycock hat (aka wide-awake); respectably dressed Englishman.
Matthew Packer (previously derived composite)	c. 11:15 to c.11:30.	5ft-7in (about); 32–33 years (about); stout; square built; full in the face; black or dark hair; long black coat; dark wide-awake hat; appeared to be a clerk.
William Marshall	11:45 to c.11:55.	5ft-6in; middle-aged; rather stout; no apparent whiskers; black cut-away coat (aka morning coat); dark trousers; round cap with a small peak; appeared to be a clerk.
PC Smith	12:30–12:35 when he	5ft-7in (about); 28 years old; no

Witness	Timing	Description
	came back onto Berner Street.	whiskers; dark cutaway coat (aka morning coat); dark clothes; dark felt deerstalker; respectable appearance.

In general appearance, these witnesses could have observed the same man. The man was obviously English. This can be stated with certainty, not just from Best's statement, but because no accent, neither foreign nor other British (e.g., Irish, etc.), was detected or mentioned. Packer might seem to skew this, but the American accent was intentionally produced by the interviewer and did not come from the fruit-seller, as discussed in an earlier chapter. The man dressed respectably, seemed to be educated, and might have been a clerk or in a similar profession. The man's height might easily be viewed as five-foot-six give or take an inch, and his various ages are not necessarily that different, even though PC Smith placed him on the younger side. The constable admitted that he "did not notice him much," and people can underestimate age, as demonstrated by those in the yard during the exam. Some thought Elizabeth was in her late twenties when she was almost forty-five.

But there are differences. Reference to no whiskers might be taken as completely clean-shaven. However, the term refers to the beard. Marshall was uncertain about this, because the man's head was turned away, and PC Smith only caught a side and rear view as he passed by, because the man faced the Board School; hence, Marshall's and PC Smith's man might or might not have had a moustache. Best/Gardner and Packer were the only ones who did see or could have seen the man squarely on. Best had no doubt about the moustache without any mention of a beard, and Packer never mentioned a beard in any of his interviews. In all fairness, however, Packer never stated seeing a moustache either. In fact, the only reference to a moustache came out during Packer's last interview. Of the sketch portraits published by the *Daily Telegraph*, Packer chose the one whose hat more closely resembled what he saw. The face just happened to be sketched without a moustache, while the mustached portrait wore a bowler — a hat Packer would not have chosen. Based on the sighting times between Best/Gardner and Packer, the distance walked, and the couple's relatively slow pace, there is little doubt that they saw the same man.

The most notable difference is the most obvious one — the hat. Three different hats readily indicate three different people. After all, who walks around with one or more hats in his pocket? The bulk would have been noticed, which no one did. This would indicate a night of prostitution with Elizabeth having said goodnight to the first man and picking up a second man between Packer and Marshall. There would be enough time — fifteen minutes — but the puzzling thing is how slow Elizabeth and the young man were moving. Even at Packer's they were not in a hurry. They were already loitering and kissing when Marshall first saw them. How he never noticed the couple until they were only three doors away standing at the pavement is uncertain and leads one to question the laborer's powers of observation. For this scenario, Elizabeth and the grape-buyer would have parted company almost immediately after Packer closed up, at which point the couple was already walking towards Fairclough Street. The nearest spot for a new date would have been The Nelson, right next door, and then The Beehive, several blocks away. Or someone just happened to be walking along at the right time, and it is *very* doubtful that he was an exiting club member. After coming upon this second man who agreed to accompany her, Elizabeth and he resumed the stroll down Berner Street that she and grape-buyer started, stopping for talks and kisses, which is what caught Marshall's attention. Possible, but it seems dodgy. True, the couple did pass in front of Marshall, but it was a dark night. The moon was on its last quarter with an overcast sky and the nearest gas lamp was a further twenty feet away, possibly explaining a misperception.

The best opportunity for Elizabeth to pick up another date occurred after Marshall's sighting. There were approximately thirty-five to forty minutes between his sighting and that of PC Smiths. The parcel wrapped in newspaper could support this, as does the deerstalker hat. There should have been sufficient light from the gas lamps, and a patrolling constable is expected to be more observant than the average person. Yet PC Smith did not pay much attention to the man. And he had no reason to since the couple was not creating a disturbance. If Elizabeth had been with the same person for the past thirty-five to forty minutes then she and the man probably continued their stroll down Berner Street towards Ellen Street. With an occasional pause (like the one Marshall had noticed), they made their way over to Back Church Lane and up to Fairclough Street, but instead of walking on up to Commercial Road, they eventually decided to head back into Berner Street. But they had stopped somewhere along the way for more than hugs and kisses, possibly taking advantage of a chandler shop or some other business that still happened to be open. Which would also explain the parcel wrapped in newspaper.

Related to this is an aspect thus far overlooked — money. Earlier that Saturday, Elizabeth earned 6 pence for cleaning rooms at the lodging house, and she still had it when she left for the night. She did not pay for a bed, but she ate supper and possibly had some drinks, but seemed sober during her last hours, unlike Mary Ann Nichols. She was concerned about her appearance and her belongings, and seemed happy when she left. If she was worried about sleeping arrangements, she never showed it. And if she prostituted herself that night, as Annie Chapman had hoped to do, then she was not a very good streetwalker, for she had no money on her — not one farthing. That would be very odd if she had two or more clients within ninety minutes (and Packer's absent description of a moustache could be used to indicate a fourth man). Robbery might be considered but there is nothing from the scene or witnesses to suggest it. And as pointed out earlier, it is improbable that she was attacked twice, let alone three times, especially without the marks to show for it. Her demeanor at the gateway does not give any indication that she had been having a rough night; she seemed to be merely listening to the music coming from the club. For Elizabeth to have been mugged and have no money in her possession upon her body's discovery, she would have to have been accosted by Schwartz's first man, then robbed by another man, then killed by a third man, all within the span of fifteen minutes. (And those who simply mug do not typically kill.) But again, Mortimer, the young couple, and Diemschütz negate this idea. Had she been robbed during the ten minutes between PC Smith's sighting and that of Schwartz, it seems unlikely that she would have remained in an area where there were "few about in the bye streets" to secure a new client, if that was her purpose. So while it is possible for Elizabeth to have been with several men, because of the hats, it also seems just as plausible that at least one witness mistook what he saw, and Elizabeth spent the time with one man. If so, then her young man was most likely the one she claimed to be living with in Fashion Street. This is one of those instances where it has to be decided what to accept.[6]

The Same Man?

While most agree that Elizabeth probably spent her last moments with different men, Inspector Swanson raised the question of whether the man seen by PC Smith was the same as Schwartz's first man, especially considering that there are only ten minutes, approximately, separating them.

> *PC Smith's Man:* 28 years old; 5ft-7in (about); no whiskers; dark cut-away coat (aka morning coat); dark clothes; respectable appearance; dark felt deerstalker.
> *Schwartz's First Man:* About 30 years old, 5ft-5in tall, fair complexion, dark hair; small brown moustache; full face; broad shoulders; rather stoutly built; dark jacket and trousers; dressed respectably; black cap with a peak.

There are similarities in general appearance, but there are also differences, as pointed out by Inspector Swanson:

"There are serious differences in the description of dress;- thus the P.C. describes the dress of the man whom he saw as black diagonal coat, hard felt hat, while Schwartz describes the dress of the man he saw as dark jacket black cap with peak, so that at least it is rendered doubtful whether they are describing the same man."

However, it is unknown what type of coat Schwartz saw and he might have mistaken a deerstalker for a peaked cap. Yet there is a potential problem with Schwartz and PC Smith having seen the same man — the amount of time between the two sightings. Even ten minutes might not easily permit someone to walk congenially up to Commercial Road, go several blocks to one of the beer retailers, drink enough to feel put out and be seen as "half-tipsy," then return to Berner in time to be simply walking in front of Schwartz. Especially since Schwartz never noticed the man heading directly for Elizabeth. Nor did he notice anyone turning onto Berner Street; the man was already walking down the street when Schwartz turned onto Berner. Inspector Swanson's conclusion is more than likely correct — they each saw a different man.

An obvious follow-up question is, was Schwartz's second man seen earlier that night?

> *Schwartz's Second Man*: 35 years old; taller than 5ft-5in (initially given as 5ft-11in at the police station); fresh complexion; light brown hair; red moustache; dark overcoat; old black hard felt hat with a wide brim; a grade of society that is respectably dressed.

Again, there are similarities, but in this case, with respect to the man seen by Best/Gardner and Packer, especially the hat, which seems to be a description of a wide-awake. But which height to accept? It is possible for Schwartz to have reconsidered this when he spoke to the reporter; just as it is preferable to accept the official version, in which case the man was too tall — by about four inches. Would it matter if Schwartz's second man had been seen with Elizabeth? Not really, since he left the area with Schwartz, whose valor is questionable, in either case, since he did not help her.[7]

When?

One of the biggest questions surrounding Elizabeth's death is when did she die? Some simply place this as *about 1 o'clock*, based on when Diemschütz discovered the body. According to Dr. Blackwell, however, Elizabeth died twenty to thirty minutes before he arrived upon the scene. Entering the yard, he checked his watch. He noted the time of 1:16. This places Elizabeth's death somewhere between 12:46 and 12:56, which is further supported by Dr. Phillips. He arrived at the yard twenty to thirty minutes after Dr. Blackwell.

That puts Dr. Phillips at the scene between 1:36 and 1:46. Based on his exams of the body, Dr. Phillips believed that Elizabeth died about an hour prior his arrival, which would be sometime between 12:36 and 12:46. This does correlate with her relatively warm body but colder extremities, especially since she slowly bled to death with no real exposure in night air that was no cooler than 53–55 degrees.

After 12:45, Schwartz and his second man left the area, Mortimer went outside, and the young couple moved in by the Board School, along Fairclough. Mortimer returned indoors after she saw Goldstein pass by, and the young couple left a little later, probably as Diemschütz came onto or traveled down Berner. After the Schwartz incident, those outside did not see Elizabeth nor did they notice anyone going in or out of the gateway. Elizabeth had not been dead long enough for rigor to set in. She had only one injury and bled to death relatively slowly. There is no record that the doctors took liver or rectal temperature at the scene; yet their estimated time of death coincides with the information from the eyewitnesses. There is only one possibility — Schwartz's first man. And after slicing Elizabeth's throat, he moved north along Berner Street, which explains the footsteps heard by Mortimer.[8]

In recounting the story of Elizabeth's life, the moments leading up to her death and those after show that Schwartz's first man was her killer. But was he Jack the Ripper? From Berner Street to Mitre Square is no worse than a fifteen-minute walk. By the time Spooner arrived at Dutfield's Yard, Eddowes had already been released from jail. She and the killer could have met — assuming that this man went towards Aldgate in the first place. And yet, the above discussions reveal many differences from the Stride slaying, including:

- No evidence that the other victims were publicly molested prior to their being killed.
- No attempt to incapacitate Elizabeth first. She received her injury standing up, while the evidence points to the other victims being knocked out then laid out.
- A different type of knife was used, a short knife, instead of an unwieldy long-bladed knife. There is no indication from the other victims that they were initially killed with a short knife, then mutilated with a long knife.
- The knife was used in a different manner. The blade was drawn across part of her throat, instead of being plunged in and dragged across the entire neck.
- There was only one throat wound. The injury did not completely sever

the left carotid artery, let alone nick a vertebra. It was not an attempted decapitation.

- Elizabeth bled to death, instead of being killed on the spot.
- Elizabeth was found on her left side (in the fetal position), while the others were on their backs.
- The killer was not interrupted. He had plenty of time to at least attempt mutilation or stabbing or cutting, but did none of this. He quit after slicing her throat. Hence, he was not frustrated at being thwarted.
- A different description than that of the man who killed Eddowes: "Age 30, height 5 ft. 7 or 8 in., complexion fair, moustache fair, medium build; dress, pepper-and-salt colour loose jacket, grey cloth cap with peak of same material, reddish neckerchief tied in knot; appearance of a sailor."[9] While there are similarities (although 30, five-foot-seven-and-a half with a moustache could apply to thousands of people), Schwartz's first man was shorter, broad-shouldered with a brown moustache, and wore a different jacket without a neckerchief. If carrying around multiple hats is unrealistic, then carrying multiple coats is even more so. Additionally, Schwartz gives no indication of a sailor; the additional description by the *Star* suggests the opposite.

Each difference on its own might be explainable; together however, they clearly show that Jack the Ripper did not kill Elizabeth Stride. And if the *Star*'s description of Schwartz's first man as being "half-tipsy" is *somewhat* reliable, then she died at the hands of someone who reacted out of a sudden alcohol-induced anger, which is what Schwartz described.

Elizabeth's death was not one in a series, but simply one among thousands who die from an assault turned ugly. It was just a happenstance that she died during that terrible autumn. Had she been killed, say, two and a half months earlier, in mid–July, we might never have known that Elizabeth Stride even existed.

Epilogue

After more than a century, the Autumn of Terror remains an intriguing murder mystery. And I dare suggest that even though Jack the Ripper was not the most prolific serial killer in history, his actions have possibly been the most studied, compared to his present-day counterparts, possibly because he has been classified as the "first modern serial killer" and some want to understand why he took to murder. Some have worked to identify the infamous assailant; in the process, much has been learned about scarcely known characters. Others have dug deep into the history of the various aspects surrounding the murders. Some people evaluate the witnesses to see what might have been their motivation for doing what they did (or in some cases, for not doing what they probably should have), while others have looked at the crimes themselves in an attempt to have a better understanding of what might have actually happened.

Within these pages, I have presented Elizabeth's life: her early years in Sweden, migration to London, marriage to John Stride, her relationship with Michael Kidney, the subsequent downfall, as some might classify it, and the Victorian history through which she lived and worked. Her untimely death, which propelled her to the world stage. The public reaction to her murder and the activities related to apprehending her assailant. But there is more to the story. Puzzling aspects that I have attempted to answer — the mini-mysteries, or more theatrically, plays within a play, such as Elizabeth's interesting claims to friends and associates that have fascinated researchers. The more colorful one is her claim of involvement with the *Princess Alice* disaster, which is demonstrably a fabrication. Perhaps the more notable claims surround her early British life, the address given on the marriage certificate, and the Chrisp Street coffee shop location. Even the eyewitnesses have added depth to the story by providing puzzling details, like Charles Letchford's "sister" or Matthew Packer's timing, the grape stalk in the hand, or the various observations of differing hats.

But invariably discussions of Jack the Ripper ultimately turn to the question of who did it? Once the papers hit the streets on Monday October 1, 1888, Elizabeth Stride became world renowned as a victim of Jack the Ripper. Since that time, however, some have questioned whether she really was a true victim in what has been dubbed the double-event. And although Elizabeth will probably continue to be viewed as the third canonical victim, my evaluation of the biggest mystery in the Berner Street case presents the idea that Schwartz's first man was her murderer and not the notorious serial killer. Some may disagree with this conclusion while others might be disappointed that I have not offered a name to an otherwise faceless person among a crowd of more than five million. In fact, between 1831 and 1925, London was the world's largest city. It can boast being one of the first cities to reach a population of one million and the first to hit five million people. However, this book is not about Elizabeth's killer, but about the Swedish farm girl, herself, Elisabeth Gustafsdotter.

I have often thought that the police might have questioned the killer, as they did hundreds if not thousands of his fellow Londoners. Such was the case with the Yorkshire Ripper who was questioned by police and let go before he was finally caught. Elizabeth's killer might have spoken with a detective or constable during a house-to-house search and given a good account of himself at the time. Somewhere in a policeman's notepad could be the recorded comments of a brief discussion. A scrawling which revealed a name. But no known notebook exists, and yet there is a spark of hope.

Years ago, there was a television series, *Secrets of the Unknown*, hosted by Edward Mulhare. One of its episodes discussed the mystery of Jack the Ripper. It also featured the well-respected researcher, Donald Rumbelow. During those thirty minutes, many aspects were discussed, but there was one thing in particular that I have always remembered, a sentiment expressed by Mr. Rumbelow. *We are still near enough to the crimes.* And he is right. That show aired in 1989, a year after the centennial of the horrendous murders. Since that somber 100-year mark, researchers, investigators, and others have looked deeper into what really happened, instead of solely relying on the stories that might have been handed down. Since that time, there has been a concerted effort to seek out and understand first-hand accounts.

From these efforts, it has been shown that while the case might be cold, it is not dead, for new information has indeed surfaced, such as Stephen Gouriet Ryan uncovering a tell-tale report about the Mary Kelly case. The Masonic outfit used by George Lusk was found. New photographs of Annie Chapman and her family have surfaced. A new reference to the Schwartz incident has been recently identified and a news article describing a secondhand account of a chase scene is being evaluated. Also new are the significant genealogical history of Elizabeth Stride unearthed by Daniel Olsson, previously unknown 1909 photographs of Berner Street and an enlightening interior sketch of the gateway of Dutfield's Yard. Gerry Nixon has exposed part of Le Grand's colorful history. A revealing sketch of 29 Hanbury Street's backyard gives support to an eyewitness account. Other, similar murders and their culprits are being investigated to determine if a connection exists. And in a fairly recent *Discovery Times* special, a behavioral analyst from Scotland Yard employed the modern techniques of victimology and geographic profiling. Archives that once seemed out of reach to many are now readily available thanks to the Internet and the excellent works published by the dedicated. And the information that is discussed, perhaps with a different perspective, will aid those who take up this subject of mutual interest, a topic that might be called the mystery of all mysteries. While I might not have a name to suggest as the man who killed Elizabeth Stride, I have no doubt that some present or future investigator will run him to earth. One day, one of these researchers will bring to ground the man himself—Jack the Ripper.

Glossary of
Names, Things and Terms

This appendix is offered as a quick reference to the various individuals, slang, etc. mentioned throughout this book with respect to the Elizabeth Stride case. This is basic information that might not appear in the main text. It is not an encyclopedic coverage, as such books are already available.

Because the press often misspelled people's names, two abbreviations will be used extensively:

aka = *also known as*; an alias or common nickname, e.g., aka Long Liz.

ala = *also listed as*; a misspelling or misprint, e.g., ala Sergeant Thicke.

All references used for this appendix are consolidated into a single source listing; however, specific page numbers and/or web pages will be absent, due to the extensive number of items.

People — Individuals and Groups

Abberline, Detective-Inspector (First Class) Frederick George: Warrant No. 43519. Scotland Yard Central Office. Born 1843; Died 1929. In charge of the White-chapel case on the ground.

Anderson, Dr. (later Sir) Robert: Assistant Commissioner Metropolitan Police CID. Born 1841; Died 1918.

Arnold, Superintendent Thomas: Head of H Division (Whitechapel). Born 1835.

Arundell, John: Alleged resident at the 32 Flower and Dean Street lodging house. Never testified at the Stride inquest, but viewed the body and was mentioned by the press.

Barnardo, Dr. Thomas J.: East End street preacher who commonly visited doss houses to speak to prostitutes. Resided at 18 to 26, Stepney-causeway. Born 1845; Died 1905. Never testified at the Stride inquest, but allegedly viewed the body and wrote a letter to the editor.

Batchelor, J. H.: Private detective.

Bates, Thomas: Night watchman for the 32 Flower and Dean Street lodging house. Never testified at the inquest but spoke to the press.

Baxter, Coroner Wynne Edwin: Coroner for East London and Tower Hamlets (ala

South-Eastern Division of London, East Middlesex). Born 1844; Died 1920. Presided over the Stride inquest.

Best, J.: Laborer. Resided at 82 Lower Chapman Street. Never testified at the Stride inquest, but viewed the body and spoke to the press.

Blackwell, Dr. William P. (ala Mr. Frederick William Blackwell): Physician and surgeon. Resided at 100 Commercial Road. Born 1851; Died 1900. Testified at the Stride inquest on session two, Tuesday, October 2, and on session four, Friday, October 5.

Brown, Dr. Frederick Gordon: Surgeon, City of London Police. Resided at 17 Finsbury Circus. Born 1843; Died 1928. Attended at St. George's-in-the-East mortuary with Drs. Blackwell and Phillips, probably on Thursday, October 4, 1888.

Brown, James: Dock laborer. Resided at 35 Fairclough Street. Testified at the Stride inquest on session four, Friday, October 5.

Bruce, Assistant Commissioner Alexander Carmichael. Assistant Commissioner, Metropolitan Police. Born 1850; Died 1926.

Christmas, Mr.: Owned a laundry. 253 Whitechapel Road. Never testified at the Stride inquest, but his laundry was mentioned during the inquest.

Collins, Reserve Police Constable Albert: Warrant no. 56929, 12HR, H Division Reserve (Whitechapel), Metropolitan Police. Born 1847.

Constable: 357H, H Division (Whitechapel), Metropolitan Police.

Constable: 426H (ala 436H), H Division (Whitechapel), Metropolitan Police.

Coram, Thomas: Worked for a coconut dealer. Resided at 67 Plummer's Road. Testified at the Stride inquest on session three, Wednesday, October 3.

Diemschütz, Louis (ala Lewis and Diemschitz, Diemshitz, or Dienishitz. The correct spelling is probably "Diemshitz"): Russian Jew. Traveling jewelry salesman (costume jewelry). IWEC steward (ala secretary). Resided at the IWEC along with his wife, who was stewardess. Testified at the Stride inquest on session one, Monday, October 1.

Diemschütz, Mrs.: Russian Jewess. IWEC stewardess. Resided at the IWEC along with her husband, who was steward. Never testified at the Stride inquest, but spoke to reporters.

Drage, Police Constable Joseph William: Warrant No.63548, 282H, H Division (Whitechapel). Born 1836. Testified at the Stride inquest on session three, Wednesday, October 3.

Eagle, Morris: Russian Jew. Traveling jewelry salesman. Resided at 4 New Road, Commercial Road. IWEC member. Testified at the Stride inquest on session one, Monday, October 1.

Gardner, John: Laborer. Resided at 11 Chapman Street. Never testified at the Stride inquest, but viewed the body and spoke to the press.

Gilleman (ala Gidleman): IWEC member. Never testified at the Stride inquest, but was mentioned by the press.

Goldstein, Leon: Resided at 22 Christian Street, Commercial Road. Never testified at the Stride inquest, but gave a statement to police.

Harstein, Miss Eva: Resided at 14 Berner Street. Never testified at the Stride inquest but spoke to private detectives.

Heahbury, Abraham (ala Heshburg, Hoshburg. Possibly Ashbrigh). Resided at 28 Berner Street. Never testified at the Stride inquest, but spoke to the press.

Jacobs: IWEC member. Never testified at the Stride inquest, but was mentioned by the press.

Johnston, Edward (ala Johnson): Assistant to Drs. Blackwell and Kaye. Resided at 100 Commercial Road. Testified at the Stride inquest on session three, Wednesday, October 3.

Kentorrich, Barnett. Resided at 38 Berner Street. Never testified at the Stride inquest, but spoke to the press.

Kidney, Michael: Waterside laborer and former Army reservist. Lived at 38 Dorset Street by the time of the Stride inquest. Born 1852. Testified at the Stride inquest on session three, Wednesday, October 3, and on session four, Friday, October 5.

Kozebrodski, Isaac M. (aka Isaacs): Young Russian Pole born in Warsaw. IWEC member. Never testified at the Stride inquest, but was mentioned by the press.

Krantz, Philip (ala M. Rombrow): Russian Jew. Born Jacob Rombro; prior coming to London, he changed his name based on advice that he was given in France. Editor of *Der Arbeter Fraint*. Resided at the IWEC. Testified at the Stride inquest on session four, Friday, October 5. Born 1859; died 1922.

Lamb, Police Constable Henry: 252H (ala 262H), H Division (Whitechapel), Metropolitan Police. Testified at the Stride inquest on session two, Tuesday, October 2.

Lane, Catherine: Charwoman. Resided at the 32 Flower and Dean Street lodging house. Married to Patrick Lane, a dock laborer. Testified at the Stride inquest on session three, Wednesday, October 3.

Lave, Joseph (ala Love): Russian Jew recently emigrated from America. IWEC member. Never testified at the Stride inquest, but spoke to the press.

Le Grand (ala Grand; aka Christian Nelson, Charles Grandy, Charles Grant; his actual surname is Briscony): Private detective. 283 The Strand.

Letchford, Charles: A steam sawyer's assistant. Resided at 30 Berner Street (his parents' house in 1881). Born c.1866. Father Edward Letchford, born c.1838. Mother Susannah Letchford, born c.1838. Brothers and sisters: Mary A., born c.1877; Ada, born c.1873; Henry, born c.1870; Elizabeth, born c.1868; Martha, born c.1862; Florence, born c.1860. Never testified at the Stride inquest, but spoke to the press.

Lipski, Israel (formerly Israel Lobulsk): Resided at 16 Batty Street. Convicted of and hung for the poisoning death of a fellow lodger and Jew, Miriam Angel. As a result, "Lipski" would ultimately become an anti–Semitic insult; the slur called out during the Schwartz incident.

Malcolm, Mrs. Mary (ala "sister from Holborn."): A trousermaker. Resided at 50 Eagle Street, Red Lion Square. Married to Andrew Malcolm, a tailor. Testified at the Stride inquest on session two, Tuesday, October 2.

Maria (ala Mrs. Wijsner, Wejsner, Wenzel): Born Inga Maria Hansdotter; May 23, 1845. Married to Carl Wenzel Wiesners, a German musician who worked in Gothenburg's Grand Theatre and later joined the West Goetha Regiment; Born 27 April 1826. The couple had a total of five children.

Marshall, William: Laborer at an indigo (ink) warehouse. Resided at 64 Berner Street. Testified at the Stride inquest on session four, Friday, October 5.

Mill, Mrs. Ann: Bedmaker. Resided at the 32 Flower and Dean Street lodging house. Never testified at the Stride inquest but was mentioned by the press.

Moore, Chief Inspector Henry: Warrant No. 51712. Born 1848; Died 1918. Possible liaison between Inspector Swanson and Inspector Abberline.

Mortimer, Mrs. Fanny. Wife and mother. Resided at 36 Berner Street. Born c.1840. Married to William Mortimer, carman, born c.1839. They had five children: Samuel, born 1881 [?]; Rose, born c.1877; Edward, born c.1873; Charles, born c.1867; Minnie, born c.1866. Never testified at the Stride inquest, but spoke to the press.

Norris, Henry: Owner of a chandler shop. 48 Berner Street. Located on the southwest corner of Berner Street and Fairclough Street.

Olofsson, Lars-Fredrik (ala Lars Frederick Olofson): A månadskarl (ala workman). Born April 21, 1828. Married to Johanna Carlsdotter Nilsson, domestic servant; born April 21, 1828; died August 9, 1872 from Bright's disease. They ultimately had six children, Johanna Elisabeth, 1853 (died 1860); Carl-Otto, 1856; Johan Fredrik, 1857; Anders Gustaf, 1863; Augusta Theresa, 1865; and Hjalmar, 1867.

Olsson, Sven (ala Sven Ollsen): Clerk for the Swedish Church. Lived at 23, Prince's-square, St. George's-in-the-East. Testified at the Stride inquest on session four, Friday, October 5.

"One-armed Liz": Alleged friend of Elizabeth Stride's. Never testified at the Stride inquest, but viewed the body and spoke to the press.

Packer, Matthew: Greengrocer/fruiterer. Resided at 44 Berner Street with his wife, Harry Douglas, and Sarah Harrison. Born 1830, Middlesex; died June 1907. Previously a costermonger at 25 Fairclough Street. Married September 1867 to Rose, born c.1832, Maidstone, Kent. Never testified at the Stride inquest, but gave numerous interviews, including one at Scotland Yard.

Phillips, Dr. George Bagster (ala Dr. George Baxter Phillips): H Division Police Surgeon. Resided at 2 Spital Square, Spitalfields. Born 1834; died 1897. Testified at the Stride inquest on third session, Wednesday, October 3, and session four, October 5.

Pinhorn, Inspector Charles: Warrant No. 51109. Leman Street Police Station. Born 1849.

Powell, Rev. Will: Minster who married Elizabeth and John Stride in 1869. This may be Reverend William Powell, son of Reverend Thomas Baden Powell and Sarah Louisa Cotton, rector in 1868, Newick, Sussex. Born January 25, 1817; died January 28, 1885.

Preston, Charles: Barber. Resided at the 32 Flower and Dean Street lodging house. Testified at the Stride inquest on session three, Wednesday, October 3.

Reid, Detective Inspector Edmund John James (ala Detective Inspector E. Reid): Warrant No. 56100. Head of the local CID. Born 1846. Either testified at or observed (on behalf of the police) each day of the Stride inquest.

Reigate, Dr.: Attended part of the Stride's post-mortem on Monday, October 1.

Richardson, Joseph Hall: *Daily Telegraph* journalist. Born c.1857.

Ronis, Mary A. (ala Rogers): A thirty-one-year-old, unmarried "Fancy reporitory," who was apparently with the Strides on the night of the 1871 census. However, there is a discrepancy between the online census listing and the photocopy of the original record. According to the actual record, Mary A. Rogers is listed with 176 Poplar High Street, as compared to the online record of Mary A. Ronis, who is listed with the Strides at 178. It is presently unknown which name or address is correct, since the actual record has a double-hash mark before and after her name. (This marking was used to help separate or differentiate the group of names that belonged to a particular address.)

Rosenfield, Mrs.: Resided at 14 Berner Street. Never testified at the Stride inquest but spoke to private detectives.

Schwartz, Israel: Hungarian immigrant. Resided at 22 Ellen Street, Back Church Lane. Did not testify at the Stride inquest, at least not publicly, but gave a statement to the police and the *Star*.

Smith, Mrs.: Next-door neighbor to Elizabeth Stride and Michael Kidney. Resided in Devonshire Street. Never testified at the Stride inquest, but was mentioned during the inquest.

Smith, Police Constable William: 452H, H Division (Whitechapel), Metropolitan Police. Born 1862; retired 1910. Testified at the Stride inquest on session four, Friday, October 5.

Spooner, Edward: Horse-keeper with Messrs. Meredith, biscuit bakers. Resided at 26, Fairclough Street. Testified at the Stride inquest on session two, Tuesday, October 2.

Stanley, Louis (ala Stansley): IWEC member. Never testified at the Stride inquest but was mentioned by the press.

Stokes, Elizabeth. Resided at 5 Charles Street, Tottenham. Married to Joseph Stokes, a brickmaker. Her first husband was Mr. Watts, a wine merchant of Bath. Sister of Mrs. Malcolm. Testified at the Stride inquest on session five, Tuesday, October 23.

Stride, Elizabeth (aka Long Liz; ala Elizabeth Gustifson): Born Elisabeth Gustafsdotter at the family farm in/near Stora Tumlehed, Torslanda, Sweden. Recognized as the third canonical victim of Jack the Ripper. The only canonical victim born outside of Great Britain. Long Liz was her common nickname ("Long" was a typical reference for someone with the last name of Stride. It does not refer to Elizabeth's height, five-foot-two); might have used the aliases of "Annie Morris," "Wally Warden," or "Annie Fitzgerald," but this is uncertain. Had one child, a daughter, stillborn, April 21, 1865, given the last name of "Gustafsson." English census records incorrectly cite her birth year as c.1844 or c.1847 and her birth city as Stockholm. Born November 27, 1843; died September 30, 1888; buried October 6, 1888; grave site, East London Cemetery Co. Ltd., Plaistow, London, E13. Grave 15509, square 37. Married John Thomas Stride, St. Giles in the Fields Church on March 7, 1869; separated late 1881. Father, Gustaf Ericsson born September 5, 1811, Alingsås Parish, northeast of Gothenburg; died 1879; married October 27, 1839, Church of Torslanda, to Beata Carlsdotter, daughter of Carl Larsson and his wife; domestic servant; born July 4, 1810; died August 25, 1864 of chest disease. Elizabeth's parents had four known children: Anna Christina Gustafsdotter, born October 15, 1840; Elisabeth Gustafsdotter, born November 27, 1843; Carl-Bernhard Gustafsson, born January 4, 1848; and Svante Gustafsson, born July 22, 1851. Of the children, it is only known, presently, that Anna and Elisabeth married.

Stride, John Thomas (ala John Thomas William Stride): Husband to Elizabeth Stride. A carpenter and later a coffee shop owner. Married Elizabeth at St. Giles in the Fields Church on March 7, 1869; separated late 1881. One newspaper incorrectly reported his date of death as October 4, 1884. The census records incorrectly cite his birth year as 1827. Born February 8, 1821, Sheerness, Kent; died October 24, 1884, Poplar Sick Asylum of heart failure. Father, William Stride, a shipwright; son of James Stride and Elizabeth; born November 7, 1784, Plymouth, Devon; died September 6, 1873, 8 Stride's Row, Sheerness, Kent; married June 14, 1817, Chatham, Kent, to Eleanor Elizabeth Monk, daughter of John Monk and Susannah. Born March 25, 1794, Sheerness, Kent; died c.1853, Sheerness, Kent.

Stride, Police Constable Walter Frederick: Warrant No. 62349. John Stride's nephew. Born 1858; Retired 1902. Testified at the Stride inquest on session five, Tuesday October 23.

Swanson, Chief Inspector Donald Sutherland: CID in the Commissioner's Office. Born 1848; Died 1924. In charge of the actual investigation of the murders for the Metropolitan Police.

Tanner, Elizabeth: Widow and lodging house deputy at 32 Flower and Dean Street. Testified at the Stride inquest on session three, Wednesday October 3.

Thew, Charles: A fifteen-year-old boy, born in Portsmouth, Hampshire.

Thick, Sergeant William (ala Thicke): Warrant No. 49889. H Division (Whitechapel). Born 1845; Died 1930.

Warren, General Sir Charles: Metropolitan Police Commissioner, 1886–1888. Born February 7, 1840; died January 21, 1927. Due to differences with the Home Office in how the office of commissioner should be run, Sir Charles tendered his second resignation on November 8, 1888, which was accepted.

West, Chief Inspector John: Metropolitan Police. Born 1842. Acting superintendent for H Division during Superintendent Arnold's absence.

Wess, William (ala West): IWEC secretary and printer (ala Overseer) for *Der Arbeter Fraint*. Resided at 2 William Street, Cannon Street Road. Testified at the Stride inquest on session one, Monday, October 1.

White, Detective Sergeant Stephen: Warrant No. 59442, H Division (CID). Born 1854; Died 1919.

Whitechapel Vigilance Committee: One of several such "committees" established early– to mid–September as a result of the murders.

Things — Items and Terms

Ambulance: A wheeled, covered stretcher.

Annuitant: A beneficiary of an annuity.

Billycock Hat: See Wide-awake Hat.

"Bloody Sunday": Descriptive phrase used by the radical press after the police cleared Trafalgar Square of squatters and protestors in November 1887. This phrase has since been used in connection with at least one modern-day clash between people and authorities in Dublin, Ireland, on January 30, 1972.

Bright's disease: Cause of death of Johanna Nilsson, wife of Lars Olofsson. A term describing inflammation of the kidneys.

Canonical: This term is specifically used to reference the murder victims Nichols, Chapman, Stride, Eddowes, and Kelly, based on the views of Chief Constable Macnaughten. By dictionary definition it refers to forming a canon (i.e., canonization) or conforming to a general rule. Some of its synonyms are "sanctioned," "approved," and "authorized."

Carman: A cart driver.

Cachous (aka Sweetmeats, Sweets): Used to freshen breath. Despite its pronunciation, it is not to be confused with the nut, cashew.

Census Records: Taken every ten years. In England they are taken at the beginning of each new decade: 1861, 1871, 1881, etc. In the U.S., by comparison, they are taken at the end of each decade: 1860, 1870, 1880, etc.

Chandler shop: Small grocery store and/or cook shop.

Charring: Cleaning (e.g., charwoman, one who cleans for a living).

Chipped: Teased.

CID: Criminal Investigation Department.

Chest disease: Cause of death of Elizabeth Stride's mother. A contemporary term, describing either pneumonia or tuberculosis.

Costermonger: A hawker of fruit or vegetables.

Cutaway Coat: See morning coat.

Der Arbeter Fraint ("The Workers' Friend"): A local, yet internationally recognized, Yiddish publication for socialist Jews. Owned by the IWEC.

Doss: A lodging house (aka doss house). Dossers were people whose residence was typically a lodging house. Doss money paid for the bed (e.g., money for a night's doss). Not every lodging house permitted men and women to sleep together, and strangers might share a multi-person bed.

"Farinaceous Edibles": Flour-based foods.

"Funny": Queer, odd, etc.

Fortnight: Two weeks.

"Gay Life": Prostitution.

Ground Floor: In America this is typically the *first floor* in most buildings. In Britain, the *first floor* is the second story, and so forth. (Throughout the text, I have endeavored to keep this straight for all readers by listing the building's "story," rather than "floor.")

Ha'penny: One-half penny.

"Inst.": Abbreviation for "this month."

Månadskarl: Swedish for a workman who sells his labor to various employers, for one month at a time.

Morning Coat (aka Cutaway Coat): Single-breasted coat with a button in the middle and curving away to tails in the back. A casual form of "half dress."

Princess Alice: Thames passenger ship that collided with the *Byewell Castle* and sank in September 1878.

Swedish Crown (aka Krona): The Krona (SEK) has been the primary Swedish currency since about 1873. In 1865, Elizabeth Stride received an inheritance of 65 Swedish Crowns, because of her mother's death in 1864. The exchange rate on January 30, 2006 was £1.00 = 13.52 SEK.

"Unfortunate": Common reference to a prostitute.

"Ult.": Abbreviation for "last month."

Water closet: Contemporarily, an outhouse commonly situated in the backyard.

Wide-awake Hat (ala Wideawake; aka Billycock Hat, Quaker Hat): A soft felt, round, low-crowned hat with a wide brim. It received its name because it "never had a *nap* and never wants one."

Appendix: Conversion Rates

The table below provides the equivalent purchasing power based on the Retail Price Index, using the January 30, 2006, exchange rate of £1 = $1.7688 (£0.565355 = $1.00).

1888	Modern UK	Modern US
1 pound (£)		
(£1 = 20s)	£76.58	$135.45
1 shilling (s)		
(1s = 12d)	£3.83	$ 6.77
1 penny (d)	32 pence	$ .57

Recommended Reading

All of these excellent books are highly recommended for their insightful and valuable information. They are also recommended for aspects specifically pertaining to the Elizabeth Stride case, as indicated.

The Jack the Ripper: A–Z, by Paul Begg, Martin Fido, and Keith Skinner, Headline, 1996 (3rd ed.). A highly recommended encyclopedic guide on Jack the Ripper.

Jack the Ripper: The Definitive History, by Paul Begg, Longman, 2003. In addition to being an excellent historical source, I recommend this particularly for more detailed information on Philip Krantz, *Der Arbeter Fraint*, and the IWEC.

Jack the Ripper: Scotland Yard Investigates, by Stewart P. Evans and Donald Rumbelow, Sutton Publishing, 2006. Recommended as an excellent source for the internal workings of the police during the murders.

The Man Who Hunted Jack the Ripper: Edmund Reid and the Police Perspective, by Nick Connell and Stewart P. Evans, Rupert Books, 2000. A great source on Inspector Reid, one of the main policemen involved in the investigations.

The News from Whitechapel: Jack the Ripper in the Daily Telegraph, by Alex Chisholm, Christopher-Michael DiGrazia, and Dave Yost, foreword by Paul Begg, McFarland, 2002. Provides a detailed coverage of the contemporary press accounts and the public's reaction during the time of the murders.

Ripperology: The Best of Ripperologist Magazine, Jack the Ripper and the Victorian East End, edited by Paul Begg, Barnes & Noble, 2007. An excellent collection of well thought out discussions, covering the Jack the Ripper gamut. I recommend this also especially for more information on the private detective, Le Grand in Gerry Nixon's "Le Grand of the Strand"; Elizabeth Stride's immediate family and her Swedish employers in Daniel Olsson's "Elisabeth's Story"; as well as for its valuable exposés on Victorian life in the East End.

The Ultimate Jack the Ripper Companion, by Keith Skinner and Stewart P. Evans, Carroll & Graf Publishers, 2000. An excellent and detailed encyclopedic work on the numerous case files related to Jack the Ripper.

Web site: *Casebook: Jack the Ripper*, www.casebook.org, created and operated by Stephen P. Ryder and John Piper. In addition to being the largest internationally recognized Web site on Jack the Ripper, it also has transcriptions of the census recordings for Berner and Fairclough Streets, 1881 and 1891, and the largest known transcribed collection of contemporary press reports.

Chapter Notes

Chapter 1

1. JTRTO; MQ; NYPLDR, 11, 13; RBRM, 44–46; SCGD; TF; TG.
2. JTRTO; RBRM, 46–48.
3. PI/JB; RBRM, 47–48. (J.B. is a medical doctor. At the time I wrote asking about venereal disease treatment in the 1800s he was working for the Allegheny Neurological Associates, Pittsburgh.)
4. DT, 06 October 1888, 3; JTRDH, 168; RBRM, 48, 50; MSEE, Prostitution; Wikipedia, Prostitution in Sweden.
5. PI/SPE; RBRM, 50 51; WLE.
6. DT 04 October 1888, 5 and 06 October 1888, 3; GBA, 1888; JTRCC, 77; JTRDH, 168; NYPLDR, 11, 13; RBRM, 51, 52; SCL.
7. JTRDH, 74; MSEE, Fenians; Wikipedia, Fenians, List of London Bombings.
8. ARU; CC; CRO81; CUK; DT, 04 October 1888, 5 and 06 October 1888, 3; HO 144/221/a49301c, f31; MQ; SF; SGFC; TPC, 6346.
9. A–Z, 434, 438; BLPM; CC; GBPA, 1888; THHOL, articles; VLM.
10. A–Z, 434, 438; CC; CR, 1871; DT 24 October 1888, 3; GBA, 1888; T, 24 October 1888; VLM.
11. A–Z, 434, 438; CC; CRO71; DT, 13 Nov 1888, 5 and 20 October 1888, 3; GBA, 1888; MWOD. (Refer also to CRO81).
12. A–Z, 434; ARU; DT, 06 October 1888, 3; GB, 1888; KD, 1875; OSM, 1894; RUKI, Workhouses; Wikipedia, Workhouses; WW, Workhouse Locations.
13. Wikipedia, Princess Alice.
14. BLPM; DT, 04 October 1888, 5 and 06 October 1888, 3; MG, 06 and 08, 1888; T, 24 October 1888.
15. CRO81; BLPM; GB, 1881; RBRM, 45, 49; VLM.
16. A–Z, 434; BLPM; CBJTR, Stride; DT, 04 September 1888, 2; GBA, 1888; JTRDH, 170; RUKI, Workhouses; WW, Workhouse Locations.
17. A–Z, 434, 438; CBJTR, Stride; DT, 24 October 1888, 3; HLS, Fenian Movement; JTRDH, 74; MPU, History; MSEE, Thomas Burke; T, 24 October 1888; GBA, 1888; VLM; WW, Workhouse Locations.

Chapter 2

1. DT, 04 October 1888, 5; JTRDH, 170; PI/AM; Ripperologist, No. 22, 37; Wikipedia, list of London bombings.
2. BLPM; DT, 21 September 1888, 3, 04 October 1888, 5, and 06 October 1888, 3; FSOL; GBA, 1888; JFW, Dorset Street; JPVE; OSM, 1894; PI/AMP.
3. A Z, 434; DT, 06 October 1888, 3; JFW, General Time Line; JTRDH, 132 136.
4. A–Z, 223, 435; BLPM; CHJTR, 195; GBA, 1888; JTRDH, 170; PI/SY; T, 01 October 1888.
5. A–Z, 33, 469; JFW, General Time Line; JTRDH, 142 143; TRF, 929; Wikipedia, Bloody Sunday, Social Democratic Federation.
6. A–Z, 32, 33.
7. A–Z, 222, 223, 434, 435; DT, 04 October 1888, 5 and 06 October 1888, 5; GBA, 1888; Ripperologist, No. 22, 37.
8. BLPM; GBA, 1888; GFP, 1888; MOA; PI/AMP; S, 7 Aug 1888, 2; T, 10 Aug 1888.
9. CBJTR, Stride; GBA, 1888; MG, 11 Aug 1888; PI/AMP.
10. DT, 24 Aug 1888, 6.
11. A–Z, 93–94, 136, 163, 342, 444; CHJTR, 38; GBA, 1888; MOA; MEPO 3/140, f239; T, 03 September 1888, 12.

12. CBJTR, Nichols; DC/MAN; HO 144/220//A49301.B.

13. A–Z, 37, 254; DT, 03 September 1888, 3; T, 03 September 1888, 12.

14. DT, 04 September 1888, 2; S, 05 September 1888, 3. (Refer also to A–Z, 371, 372, 2nd ed.)

15. BLPM; CHJTR, 61, 62, 82, 84; DT, 11 September 1888, 3 and 07 October 1888, 5; JTRCC, 47; MOA; Ripperana, No. 14, 15; T, 10 September 1888.

16. A–Z, 32, 77, 449, CHJTR, 85, 86, 143; DT, 11 September 1888, 2 and 11 September 1888, 3; JTRCC, 49, 234, 236; JTRUF, 63, 81, 82; NFW, 79; S, 08 September 1888, 3; T, 11 September 1888. (For further police views of the Nichols and Chapman murders, refer to MEPO 3/140, f9 11.)

17. A–Z, 163, 239, 415; DT, 13 September 1888, 3; HO 144/221/A49301C (8c) f, 184–194; MG, 10 September 1888; S, 05 September 1888, 3.

18. DT, 14 September 1888, 3; VLM.

19. CBJTR, Stride; CHJTR, 103 104; DT, 15 September 1888, 3; Ripperana, No. 14, 15.

20. A–Z, 259, 464 465; JTRDH, 163.

21. DT, 18 September 1888, 2 and 20 September 1888, 2.

22. CBJTR, Stride; DT, 18 September 1888, 2 and 24 September 1888, 3; JTRUF, 63; GBA, 1888.

23. A–Z, 38, 56; DT, 27 September 1888, 2, 04 October 1888, 5, and 06 October 1888, 3; T, 06 October 1888; Wikipedia, Asphyxia.

Chapter 3

1. DT, 04 October 1888, 5 and 06 October 1888, 3; MOA; Ripperologist No. 22, 37; S, 01 October 1888, 3.

2. DT, 01 October 1888, 5 and 02 October 1888, 3; GFP, 1888; JFW, Berner Street; JTRDH, 171 174; PDY; SDY.

3. DT, 04 October 1888, 5; GFP, 1888; MEPO 3/140, f212 213; MOA; PI/AJ; Ripperologist, No. 22, 37; T, 06 October 1888; PDY.

4. BLPM; DT, 03 October 1888, 3; EN, 04 October 1888; GBA, 1888; GFP, 1888; JTRDH, 171; MG, 6 October 1888; OSM, 1894. (Refer also to JTRCC; DN, 01 October 1888; RBRM, 239, 240.)

5. EN, 01 October 1888; GBA, 1888; MOA; PI/AMP; Ripperologist No. 23, 42; VLM.

6. DT, 01 October 1888, 5 and 02 October 1888, 3; EN, 04 October 1888; MEPO 3/140, f212 213; MOA. This is the first description Packer gives of Elizabeth and her young man. The *Evening News* was not the first to interview Packer, but its report of events is the first time he mentioned the couple.

7. DT, 04 October 1888, 5, 03 October 1888, 3, and 06 October 1888, 3; EN, 04 October 1888; GBA, 1888; MEPO 3/140, f214; MOA; Ripperologist, No. 22, 36. (Refer also to testimonies of Morris Eagle, William Wess, William Marshall, and Dr. Blackwell regarding the weather.)

8. DT, 01 October 1888, 5 and 02 October 1888, 3; JTRUF, 97.

9. DT, 06 October 1888, 3.

10. DT, 02 October 1888, 3 and 06 October 1888, 3; PI/TW; T, 02 October 1888.

11. CRO81; DN, 01 October 1888; EN, 01 October 1888, 3; MA, 01 October 1888.

12. DN, 01 October 1888; DT, 02 October 1888, 3, 03 October 1888, 3, and 06 October 1888, 3.

13. HO/144/221/A49301C 8a; S, 01 October 1888, 2.

14. DN, 01 October 1888; DT, 02 October 1888, 3, 03 October 1888, 3, 04 October 1888, 5, and 06 October 1888, 3; EN, 01 October 1888.

15. DT, 06 October 1888, 3; T, 06 October 1888.

16. DN, 01 October 1888; DT, 06 October 1888, 3; EN, 01 October 1888; GBA, 1888; JTRUF, 100; OSM, 1894.

Chapter 4

1. EN, 01 October 1888; DN, 01 October 1888; HO 144/221/A49301C 8a.

2. EN, 01 October 1888; DN, 01 October 1888; DT, 02 October 1888, 3; JTRDH, 174; MQ; T, 01 October 1888 and 02 October 1888; Wikipedia, Crystal Palace.

3. DN, 01 October 1888; DT, 02 October 1888, 3; EMA, 01 October 1888; EN, 01 October 1888; T, 01 October 1888 and 02 October 1888.

4. DN, 01 October 1888; DT, 02 October 1888, 3 and 06 October 1888, 3; EN, 01 October 1888; MG, 1 OCT 1888; T, 01 October 1888 and 02 October 1888.

5. DN, 01 October 1888; DT, 06 October 1888, 3 and 03 October 1888, 3; EMA, 01 October 1888; PI/AMP; Ripperologist, No. 22, 37.

6. DN, 01 October 1888; DT, 02 October 1888, 3 and 06 October 1888, 3.

7. DN, 01 October 1888; DT, 03 October 1888, 3; EN, 01 October 1888.

8. DN, 01 October 1888; DT, 02 October 1888, 3 and 03 October 1888, 3.

9. DN, 01 October 1888; DT, 02 October 1888, 3, 03 October 1888, 3, and 06 October 1888, 3.

10. DT, 03 October 1888, 3 and 04 October 1888, 5; VLM.

11. DT, 04 October 1888, 5 and 06 October 1888, 3.

12. DN, 01 October 1888; DT, 03 October 1888, 3 and 04 October 1888, 5.

13. DN, 01 October 1888; DT, 03 October 1888, 3 and 06 October 1888, 3.

14. DT, 03 October 1888, 3, 04 October 1888, 5; and 06 October 1888, 3; NFW, 102.

15. DT, 03 October 1888, 3 and 04 October 1888, 5; JTRUF, 110; T, 01 October 1888.

16. EIR.

17. DT, 03 October 1888, 3 and 06 October 1888, 3.

18. DN, 01 October 1888; DT, 04 October 1888, 5 and 06 October 1888, 3.

19. DT, 01 October 1888, 3; S, 01 October 1888; T, 01 October 1888.

20. DN, 01 October 1888; DT, 06 October 1888, 3; EMA, 01 October 1888; GBA, 1888; JTRCC, 64; MOA; OSM, 1894; PI/AMP; T, 01 October 1888 and 03 October 1888; VLM.

21. CHJTR, 189; DT, 06 October 1888, 3; T, 06 October 1888.

22. DT, 06 October 1888, 3; MEPO 3/140, f212 213. (Sergeant White's questions to Packer are based off White's descriptions of the interview.)

23. DT, 06 October 1888, 3; PI/AMP; T, 01 October 1888.

24. DN, 01 October 1888; EN, 01 October 1888; T, 01 October 1888.

25. EN, 01 October 1888.

26. DN, 01 October 1888; EMA, 01 October 1888.

27. EN, 01 October 1888; S, 01 October 1888; T, 01 October 1888.

28. MA, 01 October 1888.

29. JTRDH, 170; S, 01 October 1888.

30. DT, 04 October 1888, 5; EN, 01 October 1888; IDS; S, 01 October 1888.

31. EN, 01 October 1888. (The news reporter's questions to Best and Gardner are projected from the reported comments.)

32. HO/144/221/A49301C 8a.

33. A–Z, 327; CHJTR, 191; DT, 03 October 1888, 3; MA, 01 October 1888; S, 01 October 1888.

Chapter 5

1. DT, 04 October 1888, 5 and 06 October 1888, 3.

2. EN, 01 October 1888.

3. DN, 01 October 1888.

4. S, 01 October 1888, 1.

5. S, 01 October 1888.

6. DT, 01 October 1888, 5.

7. EN, 01 October 1888; DT, 02 October 1888, 3; IDS; PI/TW; T, 01 October 1888 and 02, October 1888.

8. T, 02 October 1888.

9. A–Z, 41 42; DBL, DN, 01 October 1888, DT, 01 October 1888, 3; JTRDH, 217 219; SJPC.

10. CHJTR, 190, 191, 204 205; JTRCC, 78; HO 144/221/A49301C 8a.

11. DT, 01 October 1888, 3 and 04 October 1888, 5; EFS, 616 620; HO 144/221/A49301C 8a.

12. A–Z, 438; DT, 04 October 1888, 5; NFW, 112; T, 24 October 1888.

Chapter 6

1. A–Z, 37, 148 149; HO 144/221/A49301C (8a), f148 159; MEPO 3/140, f214. (Refer also to DT, 10 September 1888, 3 and 12 September 1888, 3 for examples of police willingness to pursue any/every lead.)

2. EN, 04 October 1888.

3. EN, 04 October 1888.

4. DT, 02 October 1888, 3 and 03 October 1888, 3; T, 03 October 1888.

5. DT, 04 October 1888, 5.

Chapter 7

1. DT, 03 October 1888, 3 and 04 October 1888, 5; T, 04 October 1888.

2. EN, 04 October 1888; LWN, 09 September 1888, 1.

3. MEPO 3/140, f213 214. (Sergeant White's questions to Matthew Packer are hypothesized based on his report of the interview.)

4. DT, 05 October 1888, 3; EIR.

5. DC/ES; MEPO 3/140, f 214 216.

6. DT, 06 October 1888, 3.

Chapter 8

1. DT, 04 October 1888, 5 and 06 October 1888, 3; T, 06 October 1888.

2. DT, 06 October 1888, 3; PG, 19 October 1888.

Chapter 9

1. A–Z, 437; DC/ES; Ripperana, No. 14, 16; S, 01 October 1888.
2. A–Z, 126; DT, 08 October 1888, 3 and 09 October 1888, 3; EIR; Ripperana, No. 14, 15.
3. T, 09 October 1888.
4. DT, 12 October 1888, 2; EIR.
5. DT, 19 October 1888, 3.
6. HO 144/221/A49301C (8a), fl48 159.
7. PG, 19 October 1888.
8. DT, 06 October 1888, 3; T, 24 October 1888.

Chapter 10

1. RBRM, 44, 45–46, 47, 48–49, 51, 52.
2. DT, 04 October 1888, 5 and 06 October 1888, 3; JTRTO; MSEE, Sweden; RBRM, 51–52; T, 04 October 1888; VLM.
3. RBRM, 48; WLE.
4. A–Z, 434; BLPM; CBJTR, Stride; DT, 06 October 1888, 3.
5. A–Z, 434; CC; PI/AMP. (Refer also to DT 24 October 1888, 3; T, 24 October 1888.)
6. ARU; CC; CRO71.
7. CRO81; DT, 04 October 1888, 5 and 06 October 1888, 3; JTRDH, 169; MG, 08 October 1888; VLM.
8. DT, 04 October 1888, 5 and 06 October 1888, 3; S, 01 October 1888; T, 09 October 1888 and 24 October 1888. (Refer also to JTRDH, 184–185.)
9. DN, 01 October 1888; DT, 02 October 1888, 3, 03 October 1888, 3, 04 October 1888, 5 and 06 October 1888, 3; EMA, 01 October 1888; EN, 01 October 1888 and 04 October 1888; JTRO; MEPO 3/140, f215 216; T, 01 October 1888 and 06 October 1888.
10. DT, 03 October 1888, 3 and 04 October 1888, 5.
11. DT, 04 October 1888, 5 and 06 October 1888, 3.
12. DN, 01 October 1888; DT, 03 October 1888, 3 and 06, October 1888, 3; EMA, 01 October 1888; EN, 01 October 1888 and 04 October 1888; MEPO 3/140, f215 216; T, 01 October 1888.

Chapter 11

1. DT, 04 October 1888, 5; HO 144/221/A49301C 8a, fl48 159; T, 20 September 1888.
2. A–Z, 338; DT, 20 September 1888, 2, 02 October 1888, 3, 03 October 1888, 3, and 06 October 1888, 3; EN, 04 October 1888; GBA, 1888; HITM, Men's Costumes and Men's Hats; LWN, 09 September 1888, 1; MEPO 3/140, f212 214, 215 216; MOA; MWOD, Cutaway and Wideawake; PI/AMP; PI/SPE; PI/TW; RBRM, 110 112; VLM; Wikipedia, Fedora, Pork pie hat, Sherlock Holmes, and Trilby. (Refer to KIR for witnesses being cautioned.)
3. DT, 06 October 1888, 3; EN 01 October 1888 and 04 October 1888; GBA, 1888; MEPO 3/140, f215 216; MOA; VLM.
4. DN, 01 October 1888; DT, 02 October 1888, 3 03 October 1888, 3, 04 October 1888, 5, and 06 October 1888, 3; EN, 01 October 1888 and 04 October 1888; S, 01 October 1888; T, 01 October 1888.

Chapter 12

1. DT, 06 October 1888, 3; T, 06 October 1888.
2. DT, 02 October 1888, 3 and 06 October 1888, 3; EN 01 October 1888; MA, 01 October 1888.
3. CRO 81; DN, 01 October 1888; EN, 01 October 1888; HO 144/221/A49301C 8a.
4. EN, 04 October 1888; HO/144/221/A49301C 8a; MEPO 3/140, f207; PG, 19 October 1888; PI/MF; S, 01 October 1888, 2; VLM.
5. DT, 02 October 1888, 3 and 06 October 1888, 3; EN, 01 October 1888; HO 144/221/A49301C 8a; MA, 01 October 1888; T, 01 October 1888.
6. DN, 01 October 1888; DT, 06 October 1888, 3; HO 144/221/A49301C 8a.
7. EN, 01 October 1888; HO 144/221/A49301C 8a; Wikipedia, Gladstone Bag.
8. DN, 01 October 1888; DT, 02 October 1888, 3 and 06 October 1888, 3; EN, 01 October 1888; HO 144/221/A49301C 8a; MA, 01 October 1888; Ripperologist, No. 22, 37; T 06 October 1888; VLM.

Chapter 13

1. DC/EES; DT, 01 October 1888, 3, 02 October 1888, 3, and 06 October 1888, 3; HO/144/221/A49301C 8a; LWN, 08 Apr

1888; NFW, 37; NYPLDR, 11, 13; RBRM, 36
43; T, 01 October 1888; S, 01 October 1888.

2. DC/AC; DC/CE; DC/ES; DC/MAN;
DC/MT; DT, 03 September 1888, 3; 14 September 1888, 3; 01 October 1888, 3, 04 October 1888, 5, and 06 October 1888, 3; EIR, 14 20; MG, 11 August 1888; T, 10 August 1888; T, 03 September 1888.

3. DT, 03 September 1888, 3, 14 September 1888, 3, and 06 October 1888, 3; EIR, 14 20; MG, 11 August 1888; T, 10 August 1888 and 03 September 1888.

4. DT, 04 October 1888, 5 and 06 October 1888, 3; T, 24 October 1888. (Refer also to previously cited inquest testimonies within these sources.)

5. DT, 14 September 1888, 3, 02 October 1888, 3, 03 October 1888, 3, 04 October 1888, 5, and 06 October 1888, 3.

6. DN, 01 October 1888; DT, 04 September 1888, 2; 11 September 1888, 3; 02 October 1888, 3, 03 October 1888, 3; 04 October 1888, 5, and 06 October 1888, 3; EMA, 01 October 1888; EN, 01 October 1888 and 04 October 1888; HO/144/221/A49301C 8a; MEPO 3/140, f215 216; MOA; MWOD; Ripperologist, No. 22, 37; S, 01 October

1888; T, 01 October 1888, 06 October 1888, and 24 October 1888; Wikipedia, Whiskers. (Refer also to DT, 20 September 1888, 2 and 05 October 1888, 3.)

7. DT, 06 October 1888, 3; HO/144/221/A49301C 8a; Ripperologist, No. 22, 37; S, 01 October 1888.

8. DN 01 October 1888; DT, 01 October 1888, 3, 04 October 1888, 5, and 06 October 1888, 3; EN 01 October 1888; HO/144/221/A49301C 8a; MOA.

9. EIR; PG, 19 October 1888.

Appendix I

A–Z; ARU; BLPM; CBJTR; CRO 71; CRO 81; CUK; *Daily News*; *Daily Telegraph*; EIR; EHN; *Evening News*; FSOL; GBA, 1888; GFP, 1888; HITM; HO files; JPVE; JTRCC; JTRDH; JTRUF; MOL; MQ; MSEE; MWOD; NFW; OSM, 1894; PI/AJ; PI/AMP; PI/SPE; PI/TW; RBRM; *Ripperana*, No.14; *Ripperologist*, No. 22 and No. 23; RUKI, SCL; SF; SGFC; *Times*; TPC; VLM; VLW; Wikipedia; WW; XRW.

Bibliography

Abbreviations

For cited sources throughout the book, the following abbreviations are used:

A–Z = *The Jack the Ripper A to Z* (Begg, Fido, Skinner).
AO = Allegheny Observatory.
ARU = *Ancestry Records, UK.*
BLPM = *Booth's London Poverty Map*, Web site.
CBJTR = *Casebook: Jack the Ripper*, Web site (Ryder).
CC = "Jack the Ripper and 'The Coffee Connection'" (Phypers, *Ripper Notes*).
CHJTR = *The Complete History of Jack the Ripper* (Sudgen).
CR, yyyy = Census Records, <year>.
CRO71 = *1871 Census Records "on line,"* Web site.
CRO81 = *1881 Census Records "on line,"* Web site.
CSE = *Causes of Swedish Emigration*, Web site.
CUK = *Census UK*, Web site.
DBL = "Dear Boss" Letter.
DC/xx = *Death Certificate/<initials>* (referencing a specific person).
DN = *The Daily News.*
DT = *The Daily Telegraph.*
E = *The Echo.*
EFS = *The Encyclopedia of Forensic Science.*
EHN = *EH.Net*, Web site.
EIR = Eddowes inquest records.
EMA = *East Morning Advertiser.*
EN = *The Evening News.*
FSOL = *Fathom: The Source for Online Learning*, Web site.
GBA, yyyy = G. Bacon's Atlas, <year>.
GFP, yyyy = Goad's Fire Plan, <year>.
HITM = *History in the Making*, Web site.
HLS = *History Learning Site*, Web site.
HO = *Home Office files.*
IDS = "*The Identification of Liz Stride*" (Yost with Evans, *Ripper Notes*).
JFW = *The J-Files*, Web site (Yost).
JPVE = *Jewish Population of Victorian England*, Web page.

JTRCC = *Jack the Ripper: The Complete Casebook*, U.S. ed. (Rumbelow).
JTRDH = *Jack the Ripper: The Definitive History* (Begg).
JTRTO = *Jack the Rippers Tredje Offer* (Leufstadius)
JTRUF = *Jack the Ripper: The Uncensored Facts* (Begg).
KD, yyyy = Kelly's Directory, <year>.
KIR = Kelly inquest records.
LWN = *Lloyd's Weekly News.*
MA = *Morning Advertiser.*
MEPO = Scotland Yard files.
MG = *The Manchester Guardian.*
MOA = Meteorological Office & Archives.
MOL = Maps of London, 1806–1877 (as referenced below).
MPU = *Metropolitan Police, UK*, Web site.
MQ = *Mapquest*, Web site.
MSEE = MS Encarta Encyclopedia.
MWOD = *Merriam-Webster Online Dictionary*, Web site.
NFW = *The News from Whitechapel* (Chisholm, DiGrazia, Yost).
NYPLDR = *The New York Public Library Desk Reference.*
OFA = *Old Farmers Almanac.*
OSM, yyyy = Ordnance Survey Map, <year>.
PDY = Photo of Dutfield's Yard (exterior shot from the southeast corner of Berner and Fairclough), 1909.
PG = *Police Gazette.*
PI/abc = Private Information / <initials>.
RBRM = *Ripperology: The Best of Ripperologist Magazine* (edited by Paul Begg)
RUKI = *Rossbret UK Institutions*, Web site.
S = *The Star.*
SCGD = *Swedish Churches — Gothenburg Diocese*, Web site.
SCL = *Swedish Church in London*, Web site.
SDY = Sketch of Dutfield's Yard (interior view with gates closed and man door open; *The People*, 14 Oct 88).
SF = *Stepney Folk*, Web site.
SGFC = *St. Giles in the Fields Church*, Web site.
SJPC = Saucy Jack Post Card.
T = *The Times.*
TF = *Torslanda församling*, Web site.
TG = *Torslanda-Gothenburg*, Web site.
THHOL = *Tower Hamlets History On Line*, Web site.
TPC = *The Peerage.com*, Web site.
TRF = *The Royal Family*, Web site.
USNO = *U.S. Naval Observatory*, Web site.
VLM = Visitor's London Map.
VLW = *The Victorian Literature Website — Everything Victorian.*
WDBS = *"The Whitechapel Dossier No. 2: Berner Street"* (DiGrazia, *Ripper Notes*).
Wikipedia = *Wikipedia*, Web site.
WLE = Wijsner's letter of employment.
WW = *Workhouses*, Web site.
XRW = *X-Rates*, Web site.

Files

Census Records, 1871, 1881.
"Dear Boss" letter.
Death certificate of Annie Chapman, Registrar General, London.
Death certificate of Elizabeth Stride, Registrar General, London.
Death certificate of Emma Smith, Registrar General, London.
Death certificate of Martha Tabram, Registrar General, London.
Death certificate of Mary Ann Nichols, Registrar General, London.
Eddowes inquest records, Corporation of London Public Records Office.
Home Office 144/221/A49301C.
Kelly inquest records, London Metropolitan Archives.
Kelly's London Post Office Directory, 1869, 1870, 1875.
MEPO 1/55.
MEPO 3/140.
MEPO 3/3153.
Meteorological Office & Archives, London.
Photos and Sketches
"Saucy Jack" Post Card.
Wijsner's Letter of Employment for Elizabeth Gustufsson.
Note: The official coroner's inquest records for Elizabeth Stride no longer exist.

Maps

Charles Booth's London Poverty Map, 1889.
Goad's Fire Plan, 1888.
The London's Visitor Map, Sampson Souvenirs, Ltd, 1987.
Map of London, 1806, Bowles's.
Map of London, 1813, Laurie & Whittle's.
Map of London, 1815, Edward Mogg's.
Map of London, 1818, John Cary's.
Map of London, 1827, Christopher & John Greenwood's.
Map of London, 1830, Christopher & John Greenwood's.
Map of London, 1846, G.F. Cruchley's.
Map of London, 1859, James Reynold's.
Map of London, 1861, Cross's.
Map of London, 1862, Edward Stanford's.
Map of London, 1865, Josiah Whitbread's.
Map of London, c.1871, Josiah Whitbread's.
Map of London, c.1872, Edward Stanford's.
Map of London, 1877, Edward Standford's
New Large-Scale Ordnance Atlas (G. Bacon), 1888.
Ordnance Survey Maps (Godfrey ed.), 1873, 1893, 1894.

Newspapers

Copartnership Herald
Daily News
Daily Telegraph

East London Observer
East Morning Advertiser
Evening News
Illustrated Police News
Lloyd's Weekly News
Manchester Guardian
Morning Advertiser
Pall Mall Gazette
Penny Illustrated Paper and Illustrated Times
Police Gazette
The Star
Star of the East
The Times

Books

Begg, Paul. *Jack the Ripper: The Definitive History*. London: Longman, 2003.
Begg, Paul. *Jack the Ripper: The Uncensored Facts*. London: Robson Books, 1988.
Begg, Paul, Martin Fido, and Keith Skinner. *The Jack the Ripper A–Z*. 3rd ed. London: Headline, 1996.
Begg, Paul, ed., *Ripperology: The Best of Ripperologist Magazine, Jack the Ripper and The Victorian East End*. New York: Barnes & Noble, 2007.
Chisholm, Alex, Christopher-Michael DiGrazia, and Dave Yost. *The News from Whitechapel: Jack the Ripper in* The Daily Telegraph. Jefferson, N.C.: McFarland, 2002.
Connell, Nick and Stewart Evans. *The Man Who Hunted Jack the Ripper: Edmund Reid and the Police Perspective*. Cambridge: Rupert Books, 2000.
Lane, Brian. *The Encyclopedia of Forensic Science*. London: Headline, 1992.
Leufstadius, Birgitta. *Jack the Rippers Tredje Offer*. Partille, Sweden: Warne, 1994, as excerpted at http://mindthegap.se/KRIM JTR.html. Trans. by Dave Yost.
Rumbelow, Donald. *Jack the Ripper: The Complete Casebook*. New York: Berkley Publishing Group, 1988.
Sugden, Philip. *The Complete History of Jack the Ripper*. London: Robinson Publishing, 1994.

Journals/Magazines

Ripper Notes, editor Dan Norder, 2 N. Lincoln Ridge Dr. #521, Madison, WI 53719, USA (http://www.rippernotes.com)
Ripperana, editor N.P. Warren, 16 Copperfield Way, Pinner, Middlesex, HA5 5RY, England (http://mysite.wanadoo-members.co.uk/ripperana/index.html)
Ripperologist, editor-in-chief Paul Begg, P.O. Box 735, Maidstone Kent, ME17 1JF, England (http://www.ripperologist.info)

Dissertations/Essays

DiGrazia, Christopher-Michael. "The Whitechapel Dossier No. 2: Berner Street." *Ripper Notes*, January 2002.
Phypers, Adrian. "Jack the Ripper and 'The Coffee Connection.'" *Ripper Notes*, July 2002.

Yost, Dave with Stewart P. Evans. "The Identification of Liz Stride." *Ripper Notes*, March 2000.

Internet

1871 Census Records (http://www.1871-census.co.uk)
1881 Census Records (http://www.1881-census.co.uk)
The American Dahlia Society (http://www.dahlia.org)
Ancestry Records, UK (http://www.ancestry.co.uk)
Booth's 1889 London Poverty Map (http://www.umich.edu/~risotto)
Casebook: Jack the Ripper (http://www.casebook.org)
Causes of Swedish Emigration (http://library.thinkquest.org/26786/en/articles/list.
    php3)
Census UK (http://www.censusuk.co.uk/stride.htm)
EH.Net (http://eh.net/hmit)
Exchange Rates (http://www.x-rates.com)
Fathom: The Source for Online Learning (http://www.fathom.com/feature/122537/
    index.html)
Free Dictionary (http://www.freedict.com)
Greenwood's Map of London 1827 (http://users.bathspa.ac.uk/greenwood/)
History in the Making (http://www.historyinthemaking.org/catalog/menhat.htm)
History Learning Site (http://www.historylearningsite.co.uk/fenian_movement.htm)
The History of Fingerprints (http://onin.com/fp/fphistory.html)
The J-Files (http://jfiles00.tripod.com)
Jewish Population of Victorian England (http://www.clas.ufl.edu/users/agunn/teach
    ing/enl3251_spring2005/omf/MAR.htm)
John Snow's London (http://www.ph.ucla.edu/epi/snow/1859map/)
Lexicon — Swedish-English Dictionary (http://lexin.nada.kth.se/swe-eng.html)
London Old Maps (http://freepages.genealogy.rootsweb.com/%7Egenmaps/)
Mapco: Map And Plan Collection Online (http://archivemaps.com/mapco/)
MapQuest (http://www.mapquest.com)
Merriam-Webster's on-line dictionary (http://www.m-w.com)
Metropolitan Police, UK (http://www.met.police.uk)
Motco (http://www.motco.com/Map/81003/)
Old London Maps (http://www.oldlondonmaps.com/)
The Peerage.com (http://www.thepeerage.com)
The Proceedings of the Old Bailey (http://www.oldbaileyonline.org)
Rossbret UK Institutions (http://www.institutions.org.uk)
The Royal Family (http://www.royal.gov.uk)
Stepney Folk (http://website.lineone.net/~fight/Stepney/namess.htm)
St. Giles in the Fields Church (http://www.stgilesonline.org)
Swedish Churches — Gothenburg Diocese (http://www.svenskakyrkan.se/goteborgs
    stift)
Swedish Church in London (http://www.swedish-church.org.uk)
Torslanda församling (Torslanda Gathering) (http://www.svenskakyrkan.se/pastorat/
    torslanda)
Torslanda-Gothenburg (http://www.goteborg.se or http://www.torslanda.goteborg.se)
Tower Hamlets History On Line (http://www.mernick.co.uk/thhol)
The Victorian Web (http://www.victorianweb.org)

The Victorian Literature Website (http://victorian.fortunecity.com/whistler/23/money.html)
Whitbread's Map of London c.1871 (http://www.victorianlondon.org/1871map/r17.htm)
Wikipedia (http://en.wikipedia.org)
Workhouses (http://www.workhouses.org.uk)

Other Sources

Allegheny Observatory, Pittsburgh.
MS Encarta Encyclopedia. Redmond, Wash.: 1999.
The New York Public Library Desk Reference. 2nd. ed. New York : Prentice Hall General Reference, 1993.
The Old Farmers Almanac. 1888, USA.

Miscellaneous

The given times for sunrise and sunset are based on the following longitude and latitude for London: Longitude: E0.0 & Latitude: N51.0
The "Official" weather records come from the Meteorological Office at Camden Square.
The "Unofficial" weather records originate from the Royal Meteorological Society at St Luke's, Old Street (approximately 3 miles southeast of Camden Square).

Index

... don't buy a vehicle until you've read one of these!

Also from Veloce Publishing –

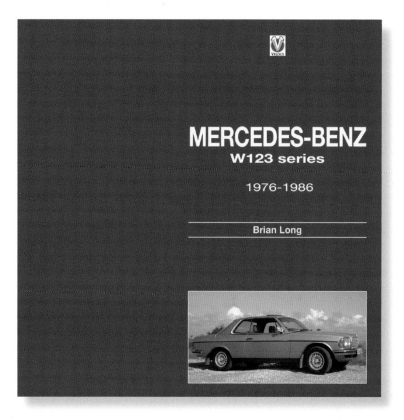

The definitive history of the entire Mercedes-Benz W123 series. From the saloons/
sedans, coupés, and estates/wagons, to LWB and chassis only vehicles, this book
contains an overview of all the models sold in each of the world's major markets.
Packed full of information and contemporary illustrations sourced from the factory.

ISBN: 978-1-845847-92-0
Hardback • 25x25cm • 192 pages • 321 colour pictures

For more information and price details, visit our website at www.veloce.co.uk
email: info@veloce.co.uk • Tel: +44(0)1305 260068

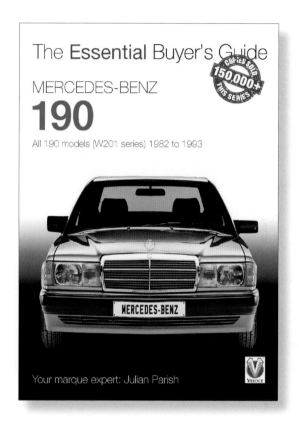

The **Essential** Buyer's Guide

MERCEDES-BENZ

190

All 190 models (W201 series) 1982 to 1993

150,000+ COPIES SOLD THIS SERIES

Your marque expert: Julian Parish

VELOCE

Looking for Mercedes' legendary build quality in a car you can use every day? The 190 (W201) range offers a unique blend of timeless styling and advanced engineering. But buying any car of this age demands care: follow the helpful guidance in this book to assess a promising car like a professional, and find the right car at the right price!

ISBN: 978-1-845849-27-6
Paperback • 19.5x13.9cm • 64 pages • 102 pictures

For more information and price details, visit our website at www.veloce.co.uk
email: info@veloce.co.uk • Tel: +44(0)1305 260068

Index